"The Map is Not the Territory"

Parallel Paths—Palestinians, Native Americans, Irish

"The Map is Not the Territory": Parallel Paths-Palestinians, Native Americans, Irish
A Touring Exhibition

© Jennifer Heath, 2015

Designed by Sweet Design
Boulder, Colorado USA

Cover image © Najib Joe Hakim, 2013
Cover design based on a poster created by Dagmar Painter, 2013

This publication is the definitive and only catalogue for "The Map is Not the Territory": Parallel Paths-Palestinians, Native Americans, Irish, and is distinct from all and any program brochures that may have accompanied its exhibition in any given venue.

No part of this book may be reproduced without permission of the publisher.

All rights reserved

Baksun Books & Arts
for social and environmental justice
1838 Pine Street
Boulder, Colorado 80302 USA
baksunarts@aol.com

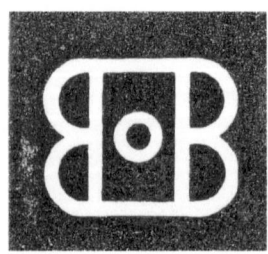

ISBN 1-887997-32-6

themapisnottheterritory-artshow.weebly.com

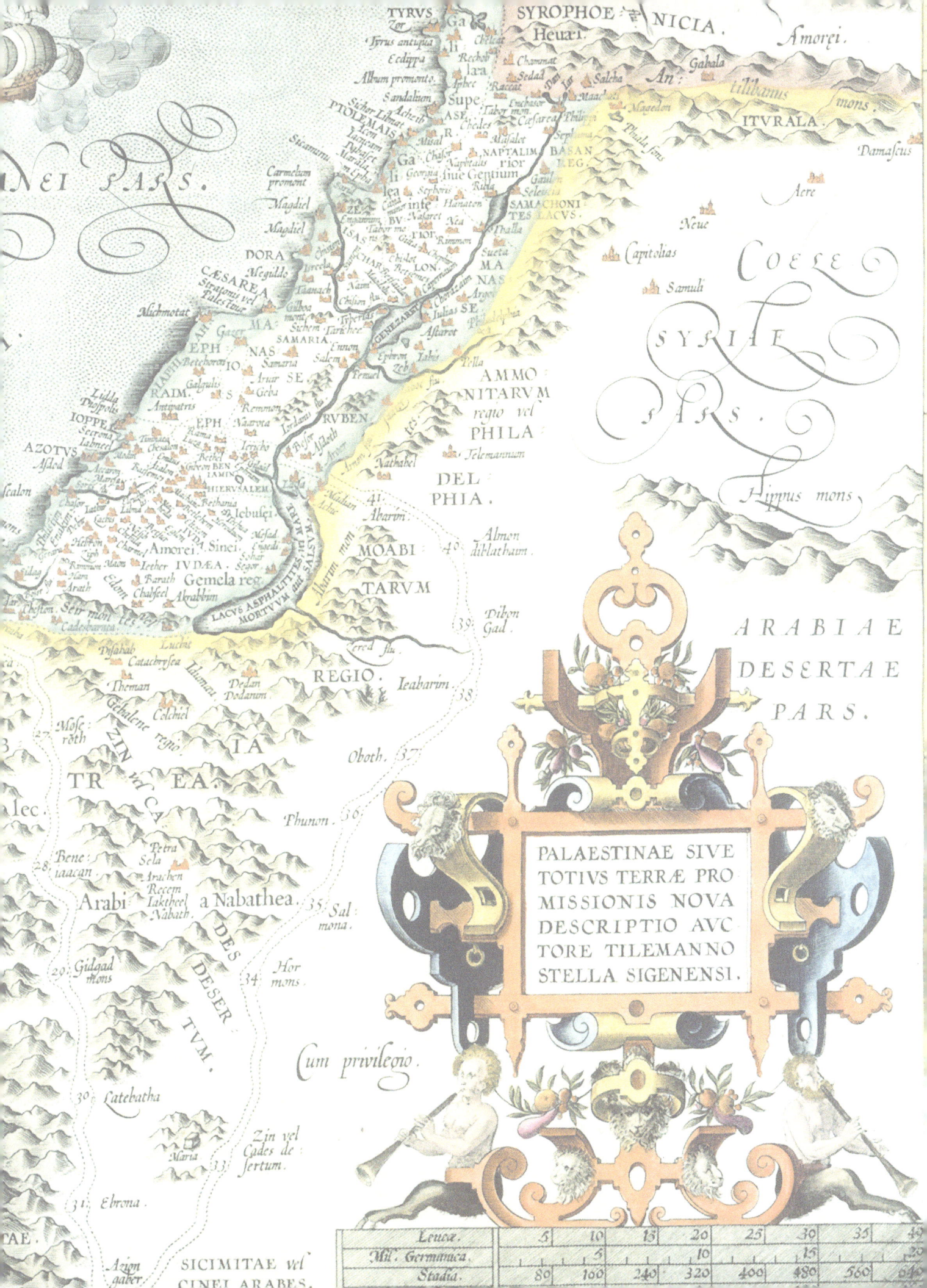

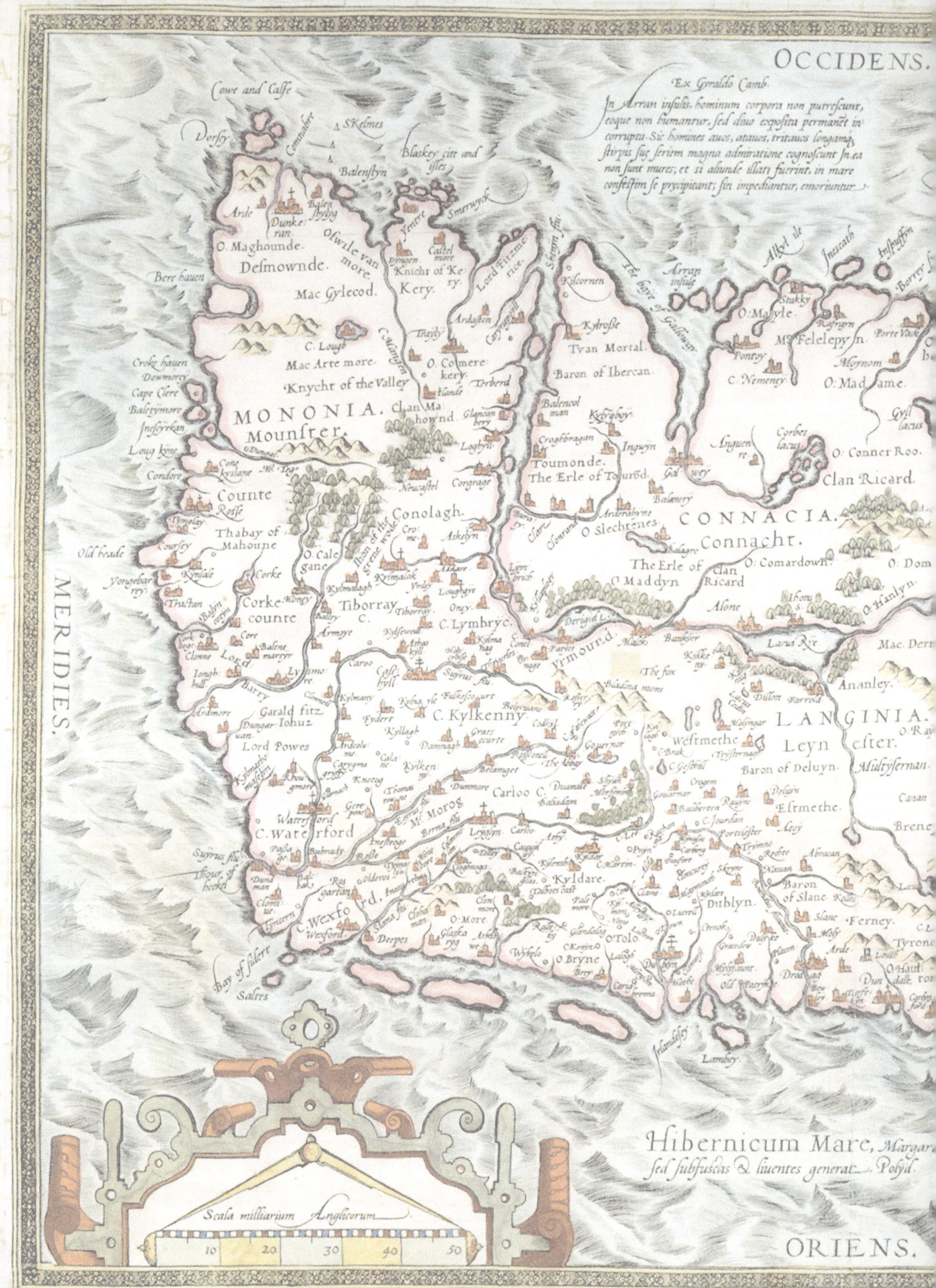

"The Map is Not the Territory"

Parallel Paths—Palestinians, Native Americans, Irish

A Touring Art Exhibition

Edited by Jennifer Heath

"The Map is Not the Territory"

wishes to thank:

The Jerusalem Fund Gallery Al-Quds
Contemporary Middle East and Arab American Art

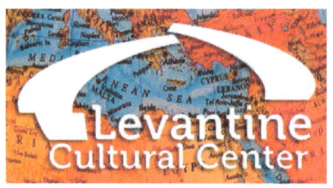
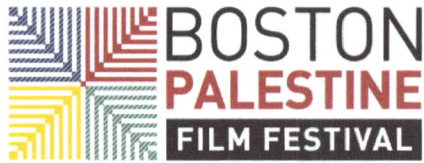
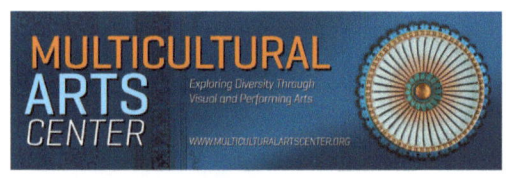

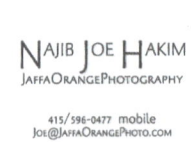
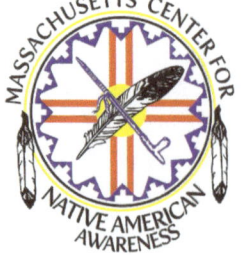
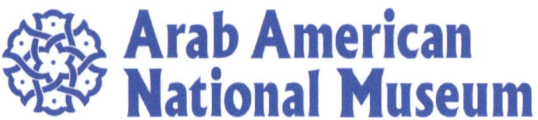

For the
Palestinian, Native American and Irish peoples

and for

all men and women worldwide whose lands, cultures and ecologies
are desecrated by invasion, occupation and colonization

"We can always pinpoint differences, it is the easiest of all scholarly tasks, since everything is always different in some ways from everything else across time and space. What is harder and takes priority is to discover similarities."

—Immanuel Wallerstein

Parallel Paths: Three Poems

Speech of the Red Indian (excerpt)

1.
So, we are who we are, as the Mississippi flows,
and what remains from yesterday is still ours--
but the color of the sky has changed,
the sea to the East has changed.
O white master, Lord of the horses,
what do you want from those making their way
to the night woods?
Our pastures are sacred, our spirits inspired,
the stars are luminous words where our fable
is legible from the beginning to end
if only you'll lift up your eyes:
born between water and fire,
reborn in clouds on an azure shore
after Judgement day...

Don't kill the grass any more,
it possesses a soul in us that could
shelter the soul of the earth.

Tamer of horses, teach your horse
to ask forgiveness of nature's soul
for the way you've treated our trees:
O Sister tree,
look how they've tortured you
the way they've tortured me;
never ask forgiveness
for the woodcutter whose axe felled
both your mother and mine...

...

We'll emerge from the flower of the grave.
We'll lean out of the poplar's leaves
of all that besieges you, O white man,
of all the dead who are still dying,
both those who live and those
who return to tell the tale.

Let's give the earth enough time to tell
the whole truth about you and us.

The whole truth about us.
The whole truth about you.

7
In rooms you build,
the dead are already asleep.

Over bridges you construct,
the dead are already passing.

There are dead who light up the night
of butterflies,
and the dead who come at dawn
to drink your tea
as peaceful as on the day your
guns mowed them down.

O you who are guests in this place,
leave a few chairs empty

for your hosts to read out
the conditions for peace
in a treaty with the dead.

—Mahmoud Darwish, 1992

Indian Singing in 20th Century America

We wake; we wake the day,
the light rising in us like sun—
our breath a prayer brushing against the feathers in our hands.
We stumble out into streets;
patterns of wires invented by strangers
are strung between eye and sky,
and we dance in two worlds,
inevitable as seasons in one,
exotic curiosities in the other
which rushes headlong down highways,
watches us from car windows, explains
us to its children in words
that no one could ever make
sense of. The images obscure
the vision, and we wonder
whether anyone will ever hear
our own names for the things we do. Light dances in the body,
surrounds all living things—
even the stones sing
although their songs are infinitely
slower than the ones we learn
from trees. No human voice lasts
long enough to make such music sound.
Earth breath eddies between factories
And office buildings, caresses the surface
of our skin; we go to jobs, the boss
always watching the clock to see
that we're on time. He tries to shut
out magic and hopes we'll make
mistakes or disappear. We work
fast and steady and remember
each breath alters the composition
of the air. Change moves relentless,
the pattern unfolding despite their planning—
we're always there—singing round dance
songs, remembering what supports
our life—impossible to ignore.

—Gail Tremblay, 1988

The Second Coming

Turning and turning in the widening gyre
The falcon cannot hear the falconer;
Things fall apart; the centre cannot hold;
Mere anarchy is loosed upon the world,
The blood-dimmed tide is loosed, and everywhere
The ceremony of innocence is drowned;
The best lack all conviction, while the worst
Are full of passionate intensity.

Surely some revelation is at hand;
Surely the Second Coming is at hand.
The Second Coming! Hardly are those words out
When a vast image out of Spiritus Mundi
Troubles my sight: somewhere in sands of the desert
A shape with lion body and the head of a man,
A gaze blank and pitiless as the sun,
Is moving its slow thighs, while all about it
Reel shadows of the indignant desert birds.
The darkness drops again; but now I know
That twenty centuries of stony sleep
Were vexed to nightmare by a rocking cradle,
And what rough beast, its hour come round at last,
Slouches towards Bethlehem to be born?

—William Butler Yeats, 1919

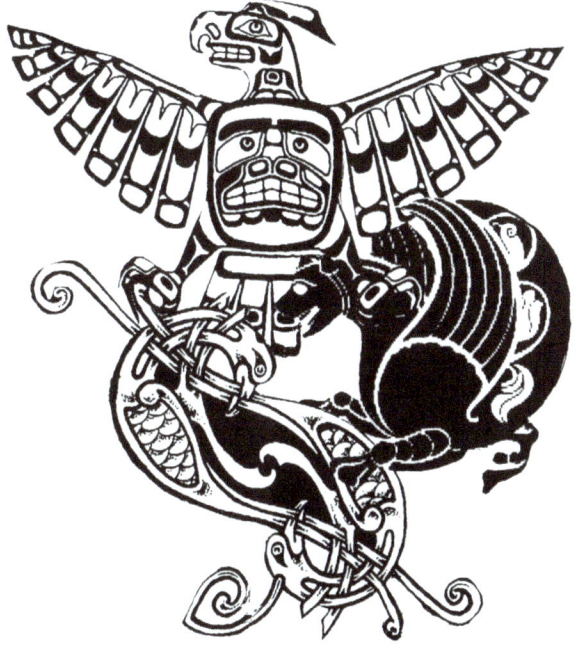

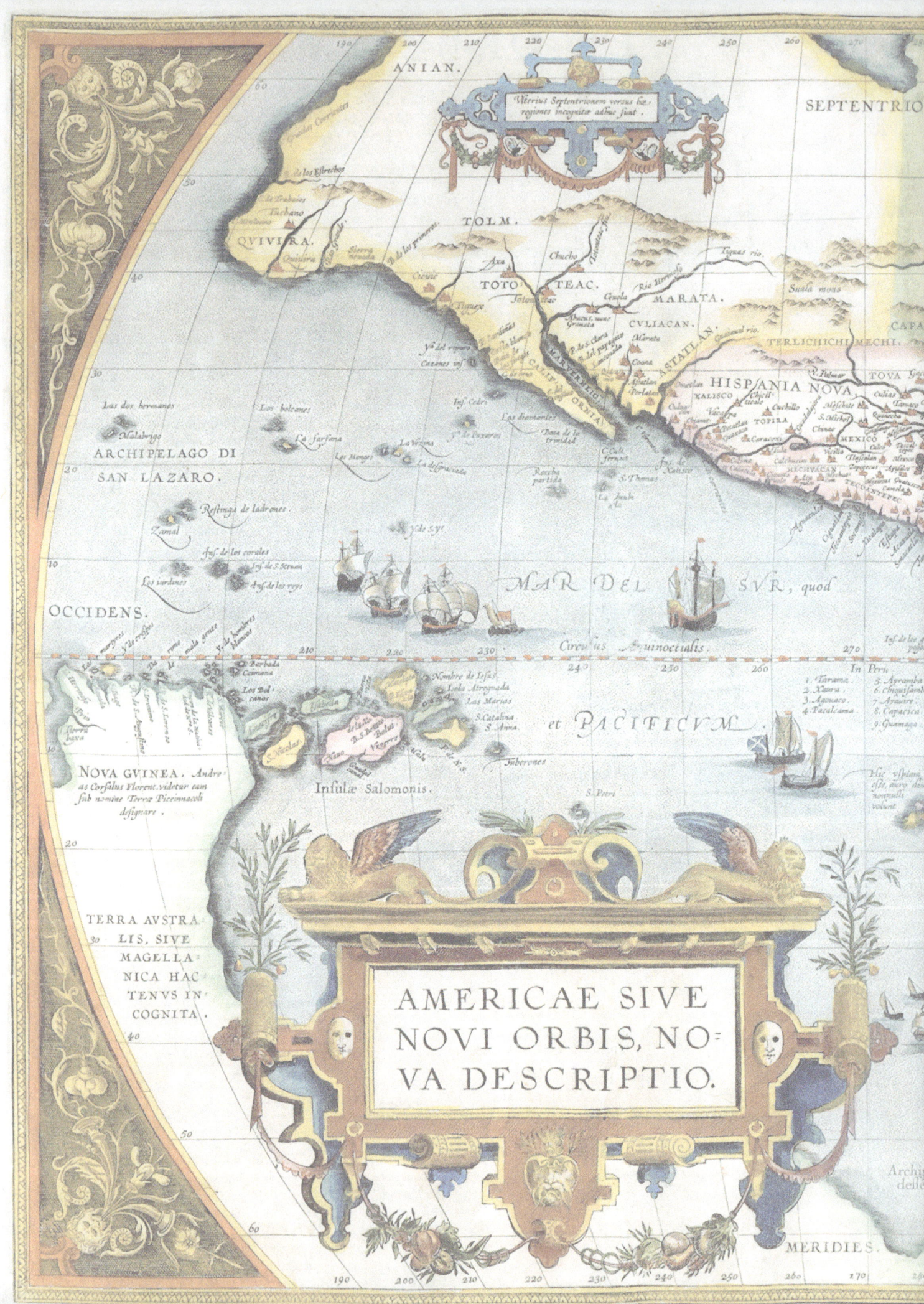

Table of Contents

Exhibition Themes 6

Acknowledgements 7

Foreword
   Dagmar Painter 9

Introduction
   Jennifer Heath 15

1. "The map is not the answer": Defining Homeland
   Aisling B. Cormack 25

2. Spaces of Memory and Reclaiming Palestinian
   History: John Halaka, Hani Zurob and Mary Tuma
   Valerie Behiery 33

3. Art and Activism: Native American Perspectives
   Phoebe Farris 43

4. Spinning Quiet Yarns:
   "The Silent Language of Textiles"
   Farah Mébarki 54

5. Walls and Mirrors: Identity in Art
   Germán Gil-Curiel 59

6. Journeys of Survivance
   John Halaka 67

7. The Unresolved Grief of a California Indian Tribe
   Valentin Lopez 75

8. Sharing the Burden: Solidarity
   Through a Recognition of Injustice
   Rawan Arar 81

9. Place-making: Mapping Territories,
   Landscapes, Lives
   Nessa Cronin 89

Notes 97

Selected Bibliography 100

Artists' Biographies 103

Contributors' and Curators' Biographies 110

Exhibition Checklist 112

Exhibition Themes

TERRITORY / MAP
Moonstone, 3200 BC, East Chamber, Knowth .... Tom Quinn Kumpf
Battles, Deeds, Fields, and Swords .... Sherry Wiggins
God Save the Queen .... Scott Benesiinaabandan
Currency .... Mick O'Kelly
Palestine Dublin 2012 .... F. Al-Tamimi and L. Johnson
Forgotten Survivors .... John Halaka
Rock of Palestine in Basel .... Najat El-Khairy
Epitaph for a Roadmap .... Rajie Cook
Flying Lesson #04 .... Hani Zurob

OCCUPATION / WALL
Crowded .... Norman Akers
Free D .... Rawan Arar
Territory .... Rita Duffy
Abu Dis – The Wall at Dusk .... Michael Keating
Child's Play, North Belfast .... Tom Quinn Kumpf
Solidarity Flag Derry .... Scott Benesiinaabandan
Border Tunnels .... Jane McMahan
Undocumented .... Malaquias Montoya
Stealing a Ride on the White Man's Bus ...... Neal Ambrose-Smith
Abu Nidal .... Vivien Sansour

CONFLICT / RESISTANCE
Police Station .... Rita Duffy
Flying Lesson #07 .... Hani Zurob
Rend .... Susanne Slavick
Birth of a Nation .... Rajie Cook
That old Tune of "GARRYOWEN" .... Michael Elizondo, Jr.
The Second Intifada .... Michael Elizondo, Jr.
Flags of Our Fathers .... Scott Benesiinaabandan
Irish History Lessons #1 .... Alan Montgomery

LAND / FOOD
Burren Pony, Co. Clare .... Tom Quinn Kumpf
Don Alonzo Lopez .... Vivien Sansour
Emilio .... Vivien Sansour
Lucky Can't Find a Piece of Land .... Mona El-Bayoumi
Cross Slabs of Cill Rialaig .... Kerry Vander Meer
Untitled Potato Prints .... Kerry Vander Meer
Hex XX, Hex XXXIII, Hex XLIV, and Hex IX ..... Andrew Ellis Johnson
Crumbs of Land: Khobz, a Word for Freedom #4 .... Claudia Borgna
Candles for Water .... Vivien Sansour
Flying Lesson #03 .... Hani Zurob

OVERLAY / IDENTITY
Seeing Each Other .... Melanie Yazzie
Fraternal Bonds .... Najib Joe Hakim
Killamery High Cross, Co. Kilkenny .... Tom Quinn Kumpf
Tatanka Ska Oyate, White Buffalo Nation .... Nadema Agard
Woven in Exile .... Helen Zughaib
Weight of the Discussion .... Neal Ambrose-Smith
Difference Machine, 1822 .... Matthew Egan
Hands of Time .... John Halaka
Lingering Presence .... Mary Tuma
Palestinian I Am .... Rula Halawani
Daughters of Palestine .... 6+: a women's art collective

HOME / DIASPORA
Passports to Exile .... Najib Joe Hakim
Clearing .... Rita Duffy
Repercussion .... Susanne Slavick
House and Home .... Jaune Quick-to-See Smith
Displaced .... Elena Farsakh
Diaspora .... Manal Deeb
Divergence, Convergence and Apparel .... Matthew Egan
Going Where No Man Has Gone Before ..... Neal Ambrose-Smith
Mohegan Wigwam .... Phoebe Farris
Abandoned I, II, III .... Michele Horrigan
Passport.Palestine .... Manal Deeb

WORDS / PERSISTENCE
Small Note from the North of Ireland .... Scott Benesiinaabandan
Anishinabe Republic .... Scott Benesiinaabandan
Beit/Salaam .... Helen Zughaib
Irish History Lesson #2 .... Alan Montgomery
Baby Bird Brain .... Neal Ambrose-Smith
Shaping the Enemy .... Grace Woodward
Parallel Paths-Three Poets .... Nora Collom
Uncharted .... Wahsontiio Cross
Hozhonahaslii: Stories of Healing the Soul Wound .... Donna Schindler

Acknowledgements

I must first and foremost thank the artists who made *"The Map is Not the Territory": Parallel Paths-Palestinians, Native Americans, Irish* such a vibrant and vital exhibition. They and the brilliant scholars who contributed to this catalogue have taught me a great deal, not least that I have much more to learn.

And then there are Dagmar Painter and the Jerusalem Fund Gallery Al-Quds in Washington, D.C. ...:
A few years ago, the artist Mary Tuma asked if I would curate an art exhibit addressing the similar circumstances experienced by Palestinians and Native Americans. It was an intriguing idea that fit right into the kind of social justice activism, writing and curation on which I base my career. Mary is irresistible – how could I say no? So I looked into it.

I found that the idea had already been explored several times in varying ways in recent years, perhaps partly inspired by Steven Salaita's powerful 2006 volume, *The Holy Land in Transit: Colonialism and the Quest for Canaan*. I did not want to be redundant. Nevertheless, the concept haunted me and it resonated with my studies about Ireland, past and present. Combining the three cultures would make, I realized, an even richer and more widely relevant exhibition. A catalogue like this one could give the project greater substance, credibility and endurance.

Still, I sensed that such an exhibit would never fly if it did not have a launch pad. What's more, my acquaintance with Palestinian artists was minimal. Helen Zughaib, another extremely talented artist with whom I'd worked earlier, kindly introduced me to Dagmar, whose gallery is the only one in Washington, D.C., specializing in the work of Palestinian and Arab artists.

Dagmar generously took the project on, rounding up artists with whom she works, helping to design and refine the exhibit and, with breathtaking energy, hanging the show, publicizing it, creating a stellar poster and a splendidly extravagant brochure, hiring musicians, sending invitations and confronting D.C. VIPs, all of which resulted in a Standing Room Only opening night. The exhibit has since taken on different threads of life, but without Dagmar's vigorous co-curation, *"The Map is Not the Territory"* might never have happened.

The support and encouragement of Firyal Alshalabi, Samirah Alkassim, David Barsamian, Claudia Borgna, Ghada Kanafani Elturk, Jim Faris, Soma Honkanen, Collin Heng-Patton, Bernice Hill, Lucy R. Lippard, Donna Schindler, Karin Elise Sturm, Mary Sweet, Sherry Wiggins, Andrew Wille and Ashraf Zahedi has been invaluable. And there are many more, too many to name, friends and family whose reassurances motivate me and return me to good cheer when the going gets tough.

This is not only an exhibit of "art for art's sake," but one that deals with bitter, challenging histories not of interest to many galleries. Thanks to Jordan Elgrably of the Levantine Cultural Center, Katherine Hanna and Michael Maria of the Boston Palestine Film Festival, Najib Joe Hakim, Yahya Zaloom of London's P21 Gallery and the Arab American National Museum, *"The Map is Not the Territory"* continues and the artists are receiving some of the visibility they deserve. May we tour on to other brave and beautiful venues.

Finally, my beloved husband Jack Collom. It is impossible for me to express how grateful I am for his sustained love and unrelenting support – materially, emotionally and spiritually – through this and all my projects.

Jennifer Heath

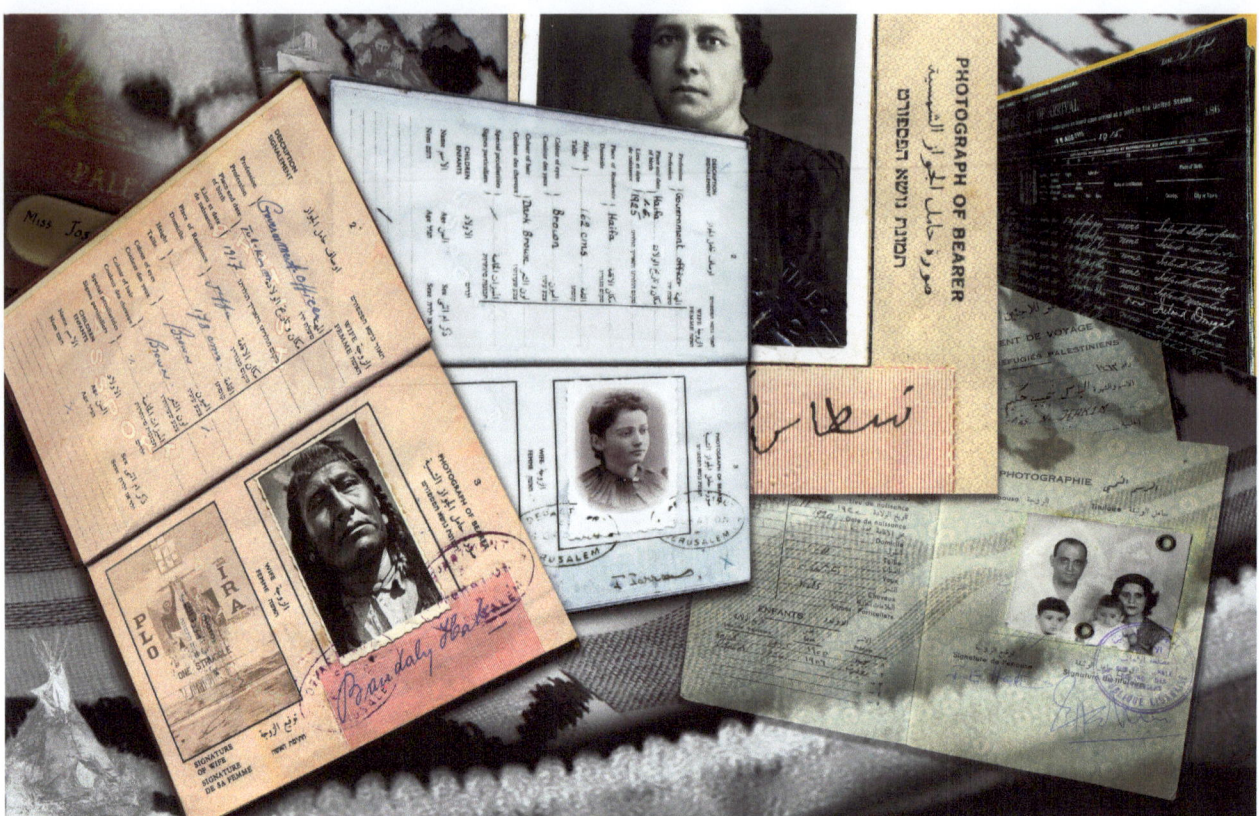

Passports to Exile, Najib Joe Hakim

We Native Americans, Irish, and Palestinians are a particular subset of the Family of Man. Our narratives in the 19th, 20th and 21st centuries ebb & flow like the threads of a gently tossed *kaffiyeh*. I appropriated documents and images, and assembled them in a casual stream-of-consciousness way. The juxtaposed elements of the images float over each other like quiet memories, mostly remembered, partly faded and often jumbled. A Native American shares a Palestine passport with a poster proclaiming the common struggles of the IRA and the PLO – all notarized by my uncle's signature and colonial British stamps. In another passport a fading image of a native Noatak family emerges through my Palestinian family's photo like some ghost of repeated history.

—Najib Joe Hakim

Foreword

Dagmar Painter

Pablo Picasso once said "Art is not made to decorate rooms; it is an offensive weapon in the defense against the enemy." The thirty-nine contemporary artists whose work defines *"The Map is Not the Territory": Parallel Paths—Palestinians, Native Americans, Irish* have wielded their weapons of paint, ink, emulsion and paper to great effect. These artists, most of whom have never met, were set the task of looking outside their personal fields of reference to identify similarities of struggle, both historically and contemporaneously with two other cultures besides their own, and to make art reflecting that new viewpoint. For some, these parallels had informed their work for some time, for others it forged new pathways to consideration of how the issues of conflict and resistance, lost territory and heritage, identity and the definition of home has had an analogous effect on cultures they might not previously have considered as comparable to their own. Perhaps most importantly, it enabled them to examine their own cultural struggles through a new lens.

Printmaker, painter and sculptor Melanie Yazzie, who contributed the digital print *Seeing Each Other,* speaks of the levels of friendship she shares as a Native American with the Lebanese artist May Hariri Aboutaam, pictured in her work. She bifurcates the image, introducing herself and her friend facing each other, each accompanied by objects of personal meaning, separate,

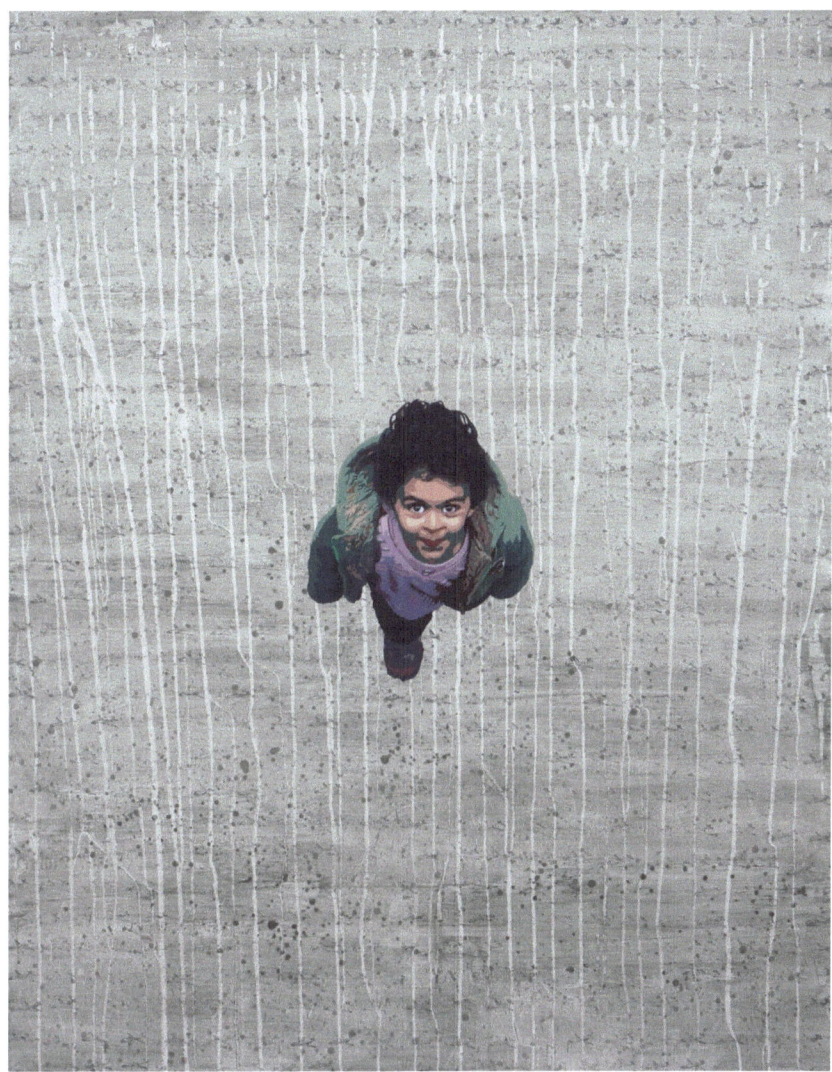

Flying Lesson #07, Hani Zurob

yet sharing a common historical connection "that many people do not see."

Palestinian photographer Najib Joe Hakim has been working for some time on the theme of family albums, the family in question being the family of man. Here he juxtaposes an old photo of his brother playing "Indian" with the appropriated image of the Salish boy in Edward Curtis's Flathead Child. A second piece interprets territory from the perspective of passports — those who have them and those who do not. Spectral images of Irish, Palestinian and Native Americans hover over documents seeking to define the undefinable. Are we who our papers say we are? Can we define ourselves by imposed borders?

Several artists used passports and books to rewrite history, correct history, remake history and define themselves and their people through their art. Wahsontiio Cross provided a hand-

(continued)

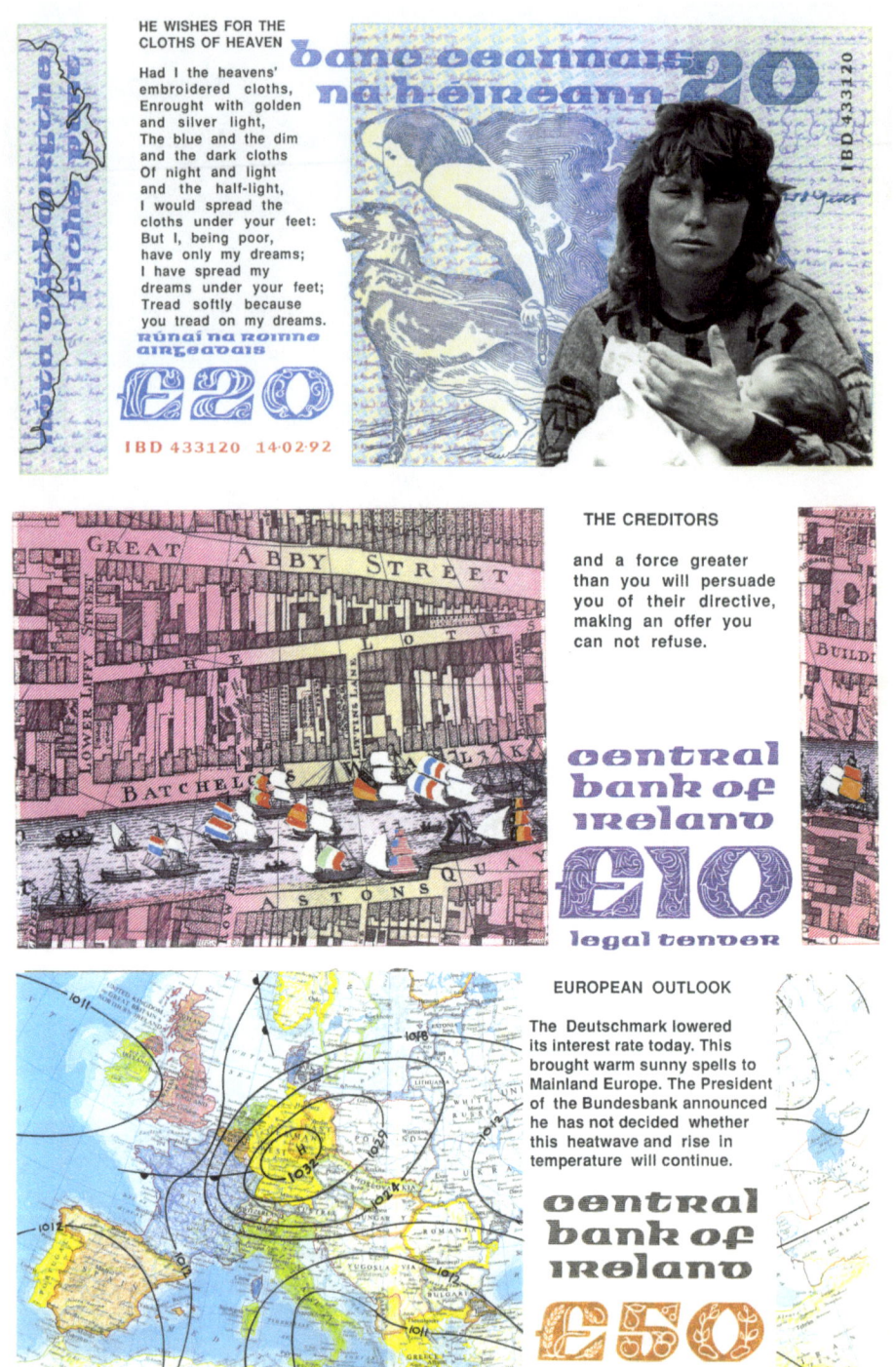

Currency, Mick O'Kelly

The forces of globalization have been about space and territory. We live in times of economic collapse, political conflict and societal fragmentation, discontinuities and deregulation on a global scale. Notions of sovereignty are challenged by systems of capital and the market place, equally formal and informal economies generate new conditions for mobility and labor across transnational spaces in which one maps out and understands identity. *Currency* is a response to the construction of identity. Its aesthetic celebrates cultural and political value within the milieu of spaces of social encounter and cultural complexity.

—Mick O'Kelly

stitched book, titled *Uncharted Territory,* whose drawings tell the story of the Kanien'kehá:ka (Mohawk) people. Rewriting the historic narrative through her art, she offers a revised perspective that eerily foreshadows some contemporary Palestinian history, as when she writes on one of her pages "Reservation System established…we are quarantined and separated from home."

Hani Zurob's poignant series, *Flying Lessons,* examines the implications of exile through the eyes of his small son. His paintings, conceived on a grand scale on canvas, retain their power even translated into the prints he made for this exhibition. A vast space divides a tiny boy from the empty jetway of a departed airplane his father will never board. Zurob's use of texture, line and perspective emphasizes the little boy's endless hope of finding a way out of this dilemma.

Some of the artists used this opportunity to explore the depths of their own cultural myths and heritage. Neal Ambrose-Smith's prints from monotypes are charming, humorous evocations of Salish petroglyphs eliciting cultural memes (and, in one instance, creating them). Using the characters *Baby Bird Brain,* he gently skewers those narrow-minded people uninterested in cultures other than their own, while in *Stealing a Ride on the White Man's Bus,* he addresses his Native American compatriots, urging them to accept change to effect progress. And in *Going Where No Man Has Gone Before,* he creates his own science-fiction Native American hero, standing in for the artist himself, always exploring new ideas. The softly textured prints he produced remind one of ancient images chalked onto cave walls, with collaged graffiti of the modern world superimposed through the passage of time.

A Small Note from the North of Ireland, Scott Benesiinaabandan

Words have become a common component of contemporary art, just as the ancient art of calligraphy became an acceptable stand-in for the figurative imagery unacceptable in certain traditions. And so words are an important component in our artists' rendering of their responses to "the map is not the territory." From photographs contrasting a flag-flown Free Derry mural with Free Dheisheh graffiti, to proclamations, poetry and product labels, these artists used their words, and the words of others, to make us look and look again.

In Rita Duffy's *Territory,* the "peace walls" in Northern Ireland become a tragic jigsaw of intersecting squares marked by the poetry of the late Seamus Heaney, the words seemingly scratched into the textured orange squares like abstracted scars of the walls themselves. Mona El-Bayoumi and Mick O'Kelly both address globalization and commodification of culture, O'Kelly with his constructed *Currency,* with its textual catch phrases, and El-Bayoumi with her collage painting of the food

(continued)

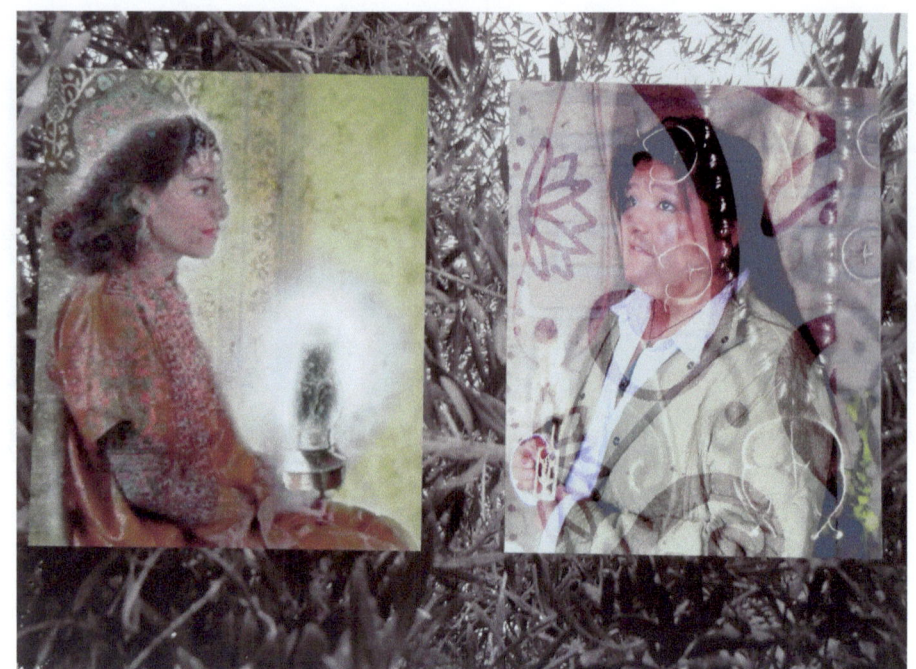

Seeing Each Other, Melanie Yazzie

There is a shared history our people have with the United States government and it connects us in ways many do not see. The print speaks to the many levels of our friendship as two women from different yet similar lands.

—Melanie Yazzie

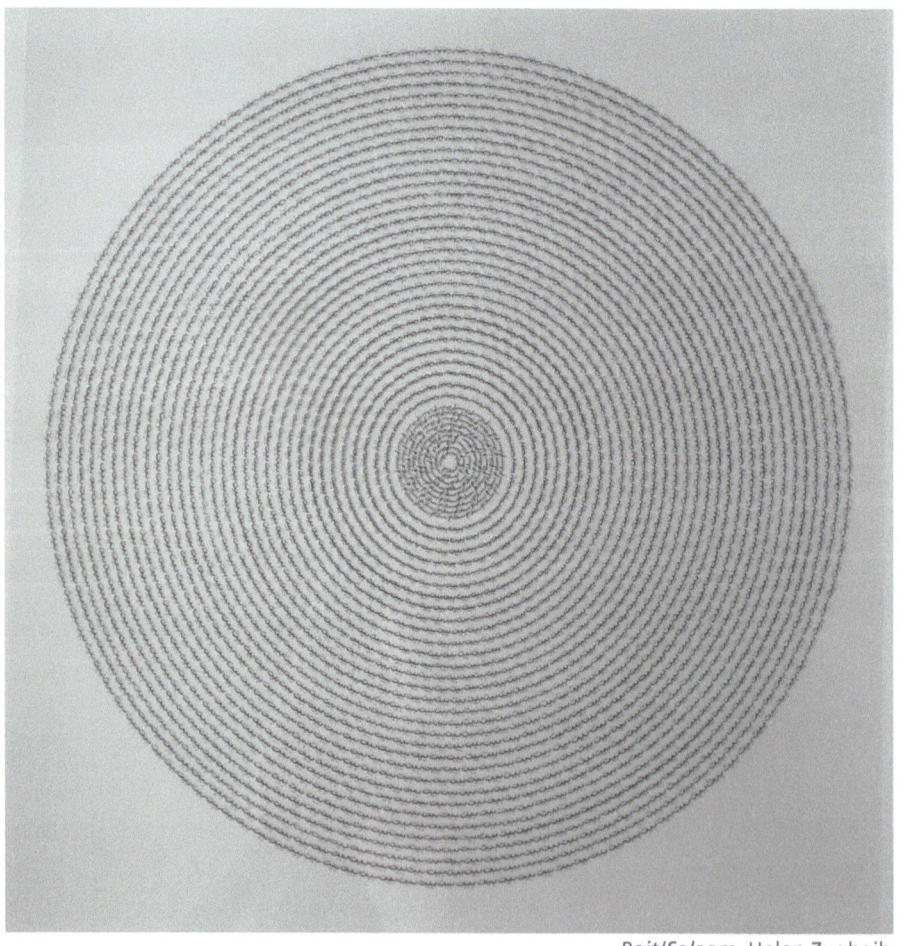

Beit/Salaam, Helen Zughaib

Beit/Salaam —
Circling round and round,
as if in meditation, calling
Peace/Home, Home//Peace

—Helen Zughaib

pyramid (a nod to her Egyptian heritage), with its appropriated cultural symbols creating an advertisement for imperial expansion, where *Lucky Can't Find a Piece of Land to Sit and Eat His Falafel Peacefully.*

But words can also calm and nourish in a conflict-ridden world. Helen Zughaib's *Beit/Salaam* calligraphy creates a meditative mandala in which circles of peace lead inevitably to home.

The great Palestinian intellectual Edward Said famously said, "Let the power of culture triumph over the culture of power." In making art for *"The Map is Not the Territory,"* thirty-nine artists discovered and shared a depth of synchronicity that defined the power of culture for them. They tapped into their deepest feelings about loss, of identity, of home, sometimes even of life, and created powerful art that will triumph over the culture of power for all who experience this exhibition. ∎

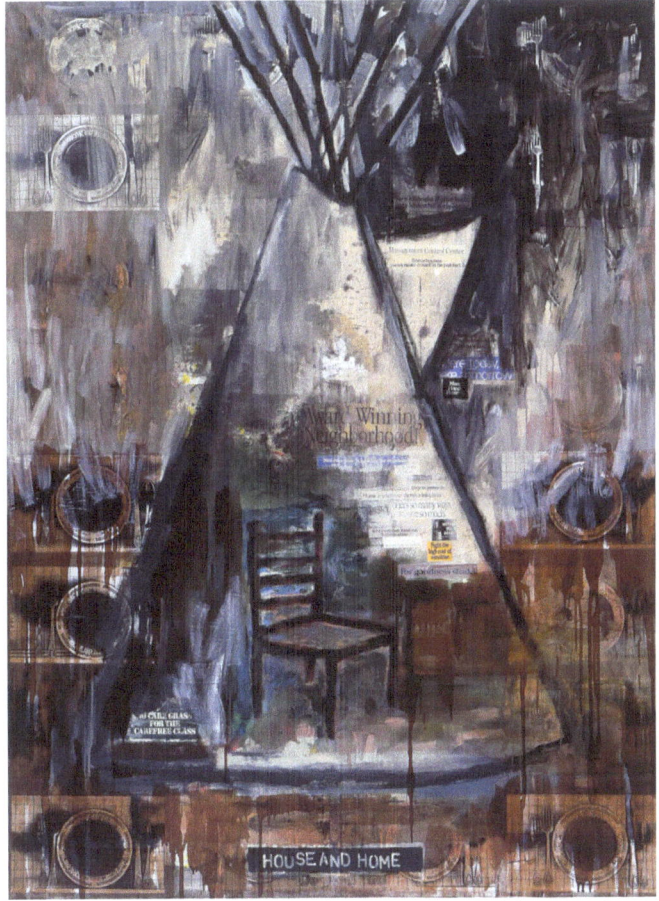

House and Home, Jaune Quick-to-See Smith

Human habitations come in all shapes and sizes. People live in one-room homes and sixty-room homes. Homes with no walls and walls two-feet thick. Homes dug into the ground and homes on stilts. Homes that are permanent and can last for 1,000 years or homes that are portable or temporary. People live in homes made of natural materials, such as mud, sticks, wood, animal hide. They live in homes of manmade material such as steel, bricks, rubber tires, aluminum beer cans, glass bottles and woven canvas. People still live in caves or dugouts or treetops or houseboats on the water and, believe it or not, many Native Americans still live in portable *tipis.*

When attending Medicine Lodge ceremonies in Montana with my family, we live in tipis for the duration of the ceremonies. We have such household goods as our bed rolls, a hanging mirror for doing our hair, some pots and pans and kitchen tools, a wash bowl for cleaning and our clothes and blankets hang on the tipi liner. It's a home away from home or sometimes it is in the backyard behind our winter cabin home.

I painted a chair inside the tipi, because on a rainy day, we might sit with visitors around a fire inside the tipi or on a sunny day sit just outside the tipi flap so we can visit with passersby. In the summer, on the reservation, you will see tipis raised behind the Indian cabins. The cabins are the winter homes and the tipis are the summer homes, especially for sleeping because they are cool at night and allow one to listen to crickets, night birds, a wolf, an owl. On rare occasions, a cougar will scream. Tipis are so well engineered, they will hold heat and stay warm. With movement of the ear flaps, it's possible to have fresh air moving through for a refreshing sleep at night. In a rainstorm, the inhabitants stay nice and dry. In violent thunder storms, tipis stand erect through high winds and driving rain. They shudder, make a loud noise and the ground shakes beneath the bed, but they are so well designed they remain standing and dry inside. The Salish peoples especially love being in nature and a tipi offers that incredible experience. A tipi is not a home of the past, it is a practical, well-designed home that is still used today and it is ecologically friendly.

—Jaune Quick-to-See Smith

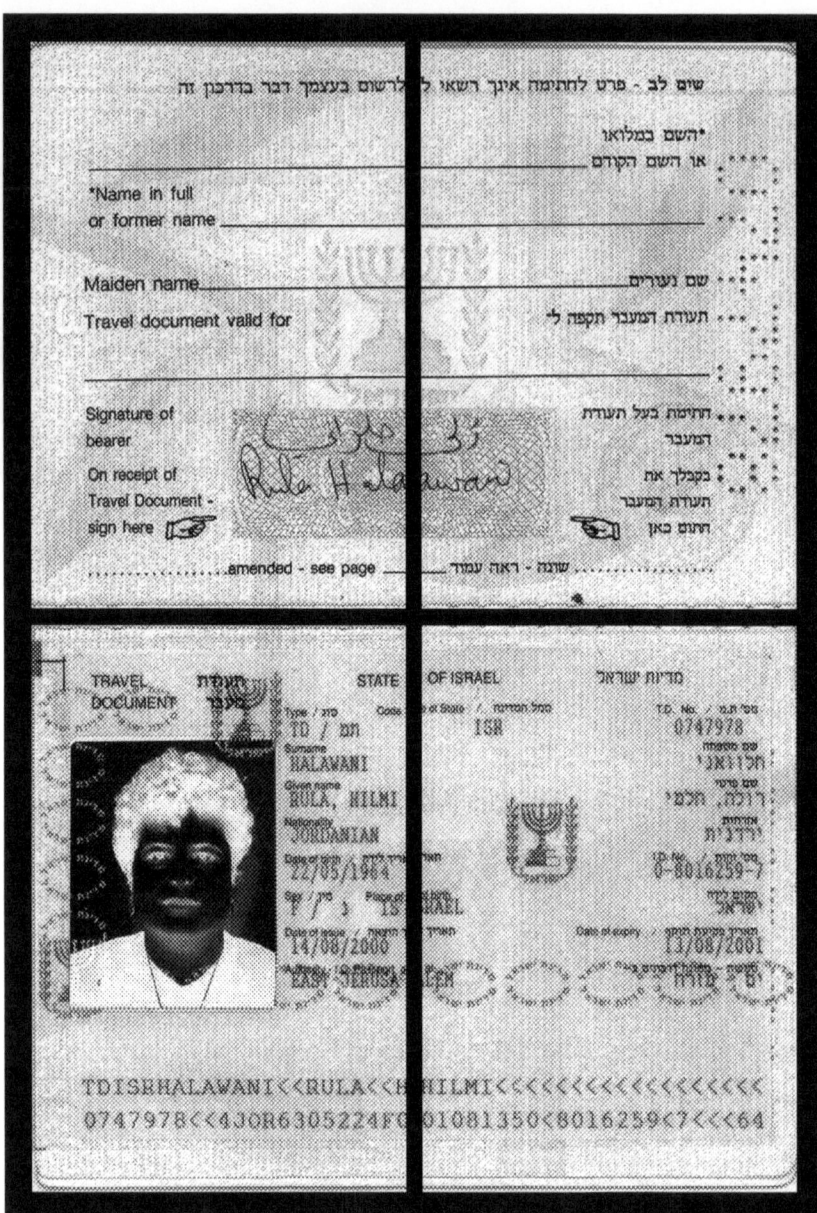

Palestinian I Am, Rula Halawani

Everyone wants to have an identity. This is the right of every individual. An individual has the right to choose who they are. The Israeli authorities believe there is no such thing as a *Palestinian.* In many ways identity is the most fundamental thing in each subject's life and gives every person a feeling of belonging and location. For me, my nationality is my identity, my land is my identity.

On 7 June 1967 the Israeli army completed its occupation of East Jerusalem and the West Bank. Ignoring the United Nations and the international community's position and violating international law, the Israeli government decided unilaterally on 25 June 1967 to annex occupied East Jerusalem. Israel considers Palestinians who live in Jerusalem as mere residents in the state of Israel and not citizens. Thus, they have no rights as citizens, but have to shoulder the burden of residency.

When I was eighteen years old, I applied for my first travel document; I filled an application form where I stated my nationality as a Palestinian. When I received my travel document back from the Israeli authorities, it had been changed to Jordanian. To this day, I have no choice but to carry a travel document with a nationality that is not of my choosing and one that, I feel, does not represent me.

—Rula Halawani

Introduction

Jennifer Heath

"The Map is Not the Territory" is a touring art exhibition that looks at relationships and commonalities in Palestinian, Native American and Irish experiences of invasion, occupation and colonization – not as novelty or polemic, but as history and current world events. Although many peoples worldwide have suffered long and brutal intrusions, Palestinians, Native Americans and the Irish have intersected for centuries in specific and often unusual ways. What are some of these intersections and how do contemporary artists examine and process them through their own lives and visions?

The phrase "the map is not the territory" was coined by philosopher/scientist Alfred Korzybski, who proposed that humans have access to desires and sets of beliefs which we confuse with direct knowledge of reality. The territory of the existing inhabitants – reality – is not necessarily synonymous with the maps and boundaries – desire – drawn by colonizers.

The images in this exhibition come together to shape vibrant and penetrating narratives. These thirty-nine contemporary artists – most of them from the three groups – confront history, investigate personal and political dialogue and reflect the multiple truths in Korzybski's dictum. The nine essayists – scholars who come from the Americas, Palestine, Ireland and Continental Europe – also explore "the map is not the territory" in diverse, creative ways, through realms of poetry, cartography, memory, film, music, and more. Rather than line up the artists' statements at the end of this book, in the customary fashion of exhibition catalogues, their abridged commentary has been distributed throughout. All the artist statements are displayed in full in the exhibition. It seems essential that the artists bear witness not only with their images, but with their own words juxtaposed alongside those of the writers, so as to make a more rhizomatic whole.

These are vast, complex histories (a selected bibliography is provided for those interested in pursuing them further). Many of the links, past and present, between the indigenous peoples of Palestine, the Americas and Ireland, have overlapped and continue to overlap elsewhere – for example (to name a few), in the worldwide slave trade, the ongoing abysmal treatment of aboriginal Australians and African Americans, the current rape epidemic desolating First Nations women in Canada and with genocide, racism, hunger, landlessness, imprisonment, disease, disappearances….

"The Map is Not the Territory" considers seven general themes (see page six) under which the images are displayed in the exhibition, where they are presented as wall texts designed to provide brief context and historical data in order to elucidate and

(continued)

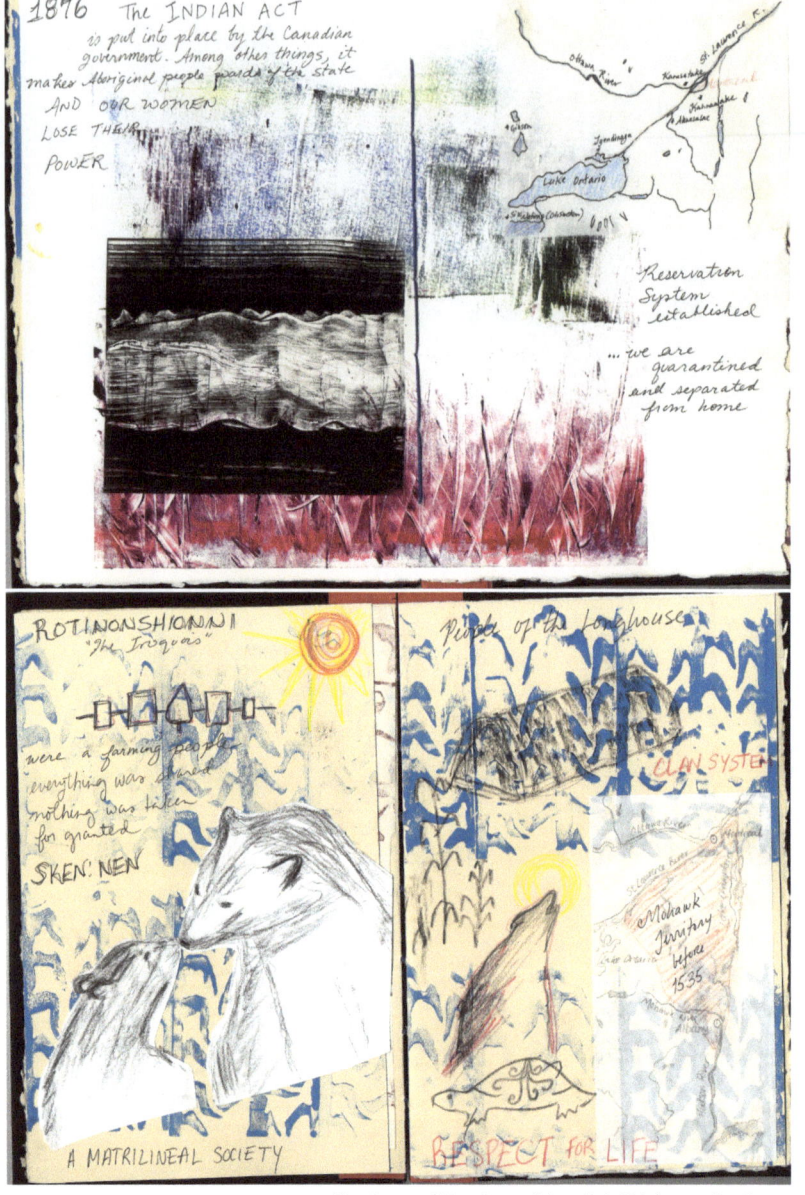

Uncharted Territory (details), Wahsontiio Cross

Historical events that are seen as integral to the identity of the United States and Canada – such as the arrival of Samuel de Champlain and Jacques Cartier in the 16th and 17th centuries are "corrected" in *Uncharted Territory*, which intends to disrupt the popular narrative and replace it with the Native perspective. Myth is replaced with fact. Maps with stories and images further illustrate this narrative. These maps and histories have been integral to the land claims sought by the Kanien'kehá:ka and Haudenosaunee (Iroquois) from Montreal, Québec to Albany, New York.

—Wahsontiio Cross

thread together the exhibition's overall investigations of the parallel sufferings of Palestinians, Native Americans and Irish, as well as of their potent encounters with one another. It's inevitable that some of these encounters have been hostile – consider, for instance, that many settlers in the American West and Canada were Irish, who, along with other white invaders, seized Native lands; yet, in the early colonial era, intermarriage and friendship regularly and quite naturally took place. There have been and continue to be myriad occurrences of assistance, camaraderie, familial bonds and empathy between Palestinians, Native Americans and the Irish offer us all hope. In the words of the great historian Howard Zinn, "Human history is a history not only of cruelty, but also of compassion, sacrifice, courage, kindness…."

"The future," Zinn said, "is an infinite succession of presents, and to live now as we think human beings should live, in defiance of all that is bad around us, is itself a marvelous victory."

Territory / Map

Flags are symbols of unity. Nationalism. At worst: jingoism and shrouds for caskets. To plant a flag is to claim the place – whether justly or not. To protest with the flag of another expresses solidarity, empathy – for the protestors may have experienced similar injustices. Flags declare borders. Maps delineate them.

Maps offer directions, guide us to our destinations, show the road or compass the skies. Maps are also distortions. Hypnotic. Fantastical. Wishful. Oversimplified. They contour the geographies of power, money, commercial globalization. Roadmaps to "peace" can be empty topographies.

Palestinian territory – the area now defined as Israel, the West Bank, and the Gaza Strip – has been occupied variously since before the birth of Christ. Among the many: the Great Seljuk Empire (1073-1098) … Crusaders (1099-1187) … the Ottoman Empire (1516-1917) … the British Empire (1917-1947) … the State of Israel (1948-present).

Fluid, fragmented maps.

Irish territory was partly occupied by the Anglo-Normans in the 12th century (and later by the British during the Tudor period), for nearly 800 years. Finally, freedom in 1922, but part of North stayed behind with the creation of Northern Ireland. Partition.

A sliced map.

In 1492, Columbus sailed the ocean blue – though some believe that, long before, Irish monks paddling little round *curachs* paid a visit to Turtle Island, said hello, and then went home. Columbus planted a flag and drew a map that each subsequent invader and every generation has enlarged across the continents, north and south. The territory diminished.

To the victor belongs the map.

Occupation / Wall

Oc·cu·pa·tion: possession, settlement, or use of land; the act of occupying; the state of being occupied.

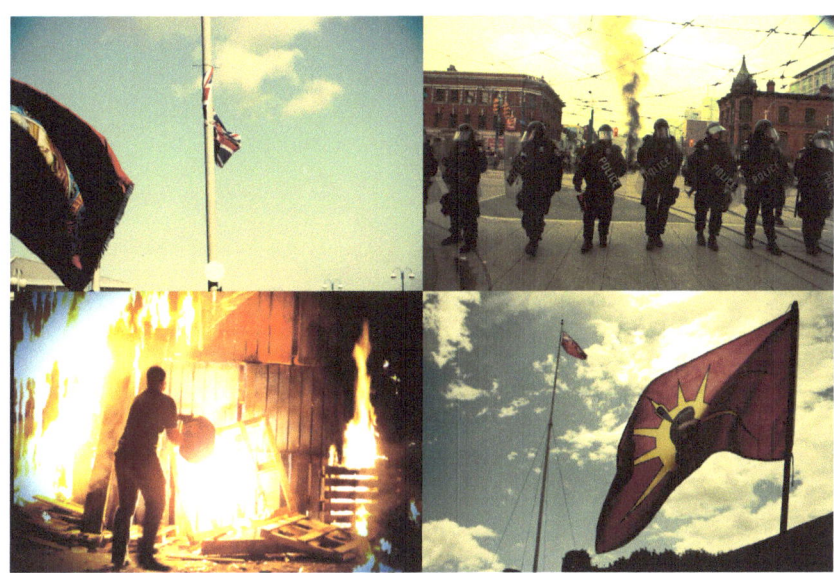

Flags of Our Fathers, Scott Benesiinaabandan

My work centers on cultural crisis/conflict and their political manifestations, located and contextualized around issues of Indigeniety from a global perspective. More broadly it seeks to address the continuing development and creation of a deeper personal cosmology, the impact of relationships and familial/communal ties, non-conventional ways of knowing (i.e., dreaming, intuition, blood memory), underlying threats and the danger inherent in searching for truth, and how these impacts radiate into wider communities.

—Scott Benesiinaabandan

A·part·heid: Apart-hood. A policy or practice of separating or segregating groups; the condition of being apart.

Hadrian's Wall. China's Great Wall. Berlin Wall. Walls are an ancient tactic, accelerating in our time. Separation walls – with soft euphemisms like "fence" or "line" – are constructed in Northern Ireland, Palestine and the United States.

The Peace Walls, Northern Ireland, aka "peacelines" began in 1969 during the Troubles, separating Catholic (nationalist) and Protestant (unionist) neighborhoods to minimize inter-communal violence. The forty-eight walls reach as high as 25 feet (7.6 m). Some have

gates (staffed by police), closed at night. Although the Troubles are thought to have ended in about 1998, these originally temporary structures have become wider, longer, increasingly permanent.

The Israeli-West Bank Wall was begun in 2000, to separate Israelis from Palestinians. Upon completion, the wall will be approximately 430 miles (700 km) long. Its route substantially penetrates the Occupied Territories and annexes Palestinian land. The International Court of Justice resolved that "Israel cannot rely on a right of self-defense or on a state of necessity in order to preclude the wrongfulness of the construc-

(continued)

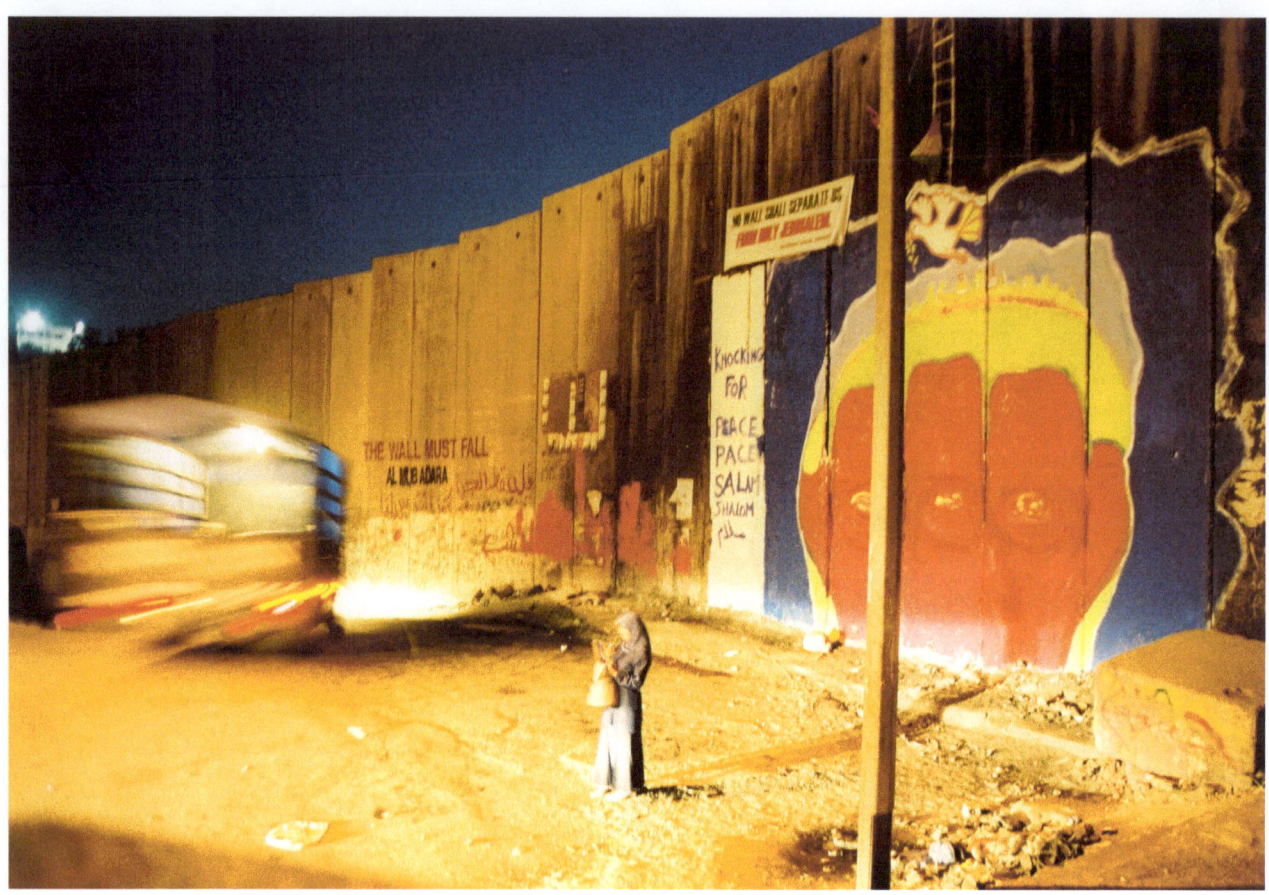

Abu-Dis – The Wall at Dusk, Michael Keating

My photography springs from the straightforward street photography of the 1970s. Perhaps the greatest pleasure of that approach (besides the pleasure of surprise) is to be presented (and to present) an image that is direct and irrefutable. *Abu Dis—The Wall at Dusk* is such an image. It forbids the excuse, the finesse, the lie. And yet, wrapped in the horror, there is an incredible beauty and strength.

—Michael Keating

tion of the wall … [which is] contrary to international law." Additional walls isolate Gaza, now a prison camp.

The Mexico–United States Walls, California, Texas, Arizona, New Mexico, were designed to prevent illegal movement across the Mexico–U. S. border. The walls jeopardize the safety of immigrants – 5,000 deaths in thirteen years. Environmentally hazardous, they destroy animal habitat, prevent wildlife from reaching water, and disturb migration patterns. In 2009, there were more than 580 miles (930 km) of walls. Construction is still under way, with proposed additions of Unmanned Aerial Vehicles ("drones") and other forms of militarization.

Are there cracks in the walls? Any escape? Tunnels, murals, and graffiti challenge concrete blockades and announce unity among the oppressed. "You are entering Free Derry" in Ireland and "You are entering Free Dheisheh" in Palestine proclaim defiance. An Anishinabe flag stands in proud solidarity.

Conflict / Resistance

Resistance takes many forms. Slaughter is often met with slaughter.

Centuries of massacres: Drogheda 1649, Gnadenhutten 1782, Sand Creek 1864, Wounded Knee 1890, Deir Yassin 1948, Bloody Sunday 1972, Sabra and Shatila 1982, Jenin 2002 … and more.

Years of uprisings: Irish Rebellion 1641, Easter Rising 1916, Intifada 1987 to 1993 and 2000 to 2005, Wounded Knee 1973 … and more.

Times of non-violent resistance: Cherokee Removal 1838, Palestinian Tax Strike 1919, Irish Non-Cooperation Movement 1919 … and more.

"It's not those who inflict the most, but those who endure the most, who will prevail." – Terence MacSwiney – Sinn Féin Mayor of Cork during the Irish War of Independence, imprisoned by the British on sedition charges, died in 1920 while on a hunger strike.

1981 – Bobby Sands and later nine other Provisional Irish Republican Army volunteers died on a hunger strike at Northern Ireland's Maze-Long Kesh prison protesting British injustices. As Sands lay fasting, he was elected to the House of Commons, but his term lasted less than a month. He died, aged 27, on the sixty-sixth day of his strike.

2011 – Palestinian Khader Adnan, imprisoned in Israel without charge or trial, went on hunger strike. On his sixty-sixth day, in immediate danger of death, he was released for fear he would, like Sands, become an icon and release a torrent of further resistance.

2012 – Attawapiskat First Nation Chief Theresa Spence went on hunger strike to protest a government push to terminate First Nations treaty rights throughout Canada. Her forty-three-day fast highlighted the grassroots Idle No More movement for North American Indigenous sovereignty, Indigenous rights, and respect for the – frequently broken – treaties.

Palestinians, Native Americans, and the Irish (with the Bobby Sands Trust) honor one another and offer each other support, solace, and strength in their common search for justice.

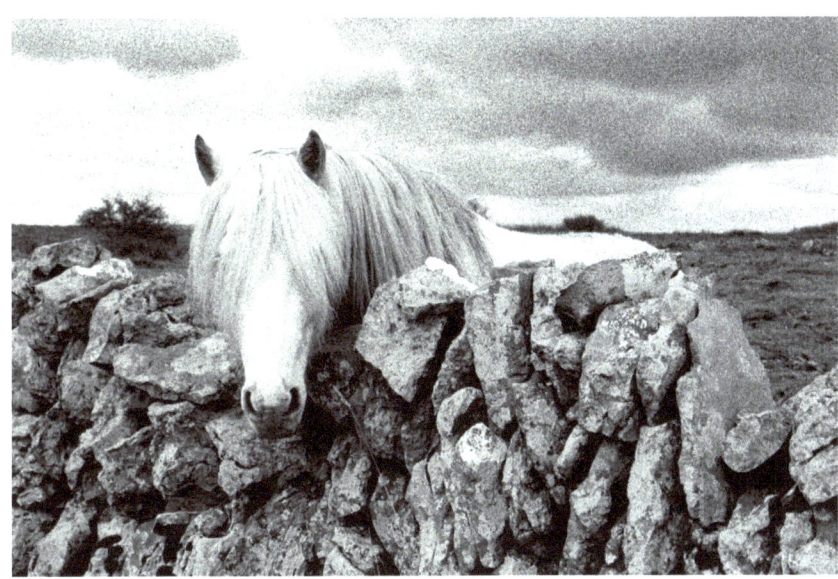

Burren Pony, Co. Clare, Tom Quinn Kumpf

Land / Food

Palestinians, Native Americans, and the Irish share deep reverence for the land. To justify the theft of those lands, occupiers not only postulate the racial, religious and cultural inferiority of those they are subjugating, they also reach back to the Roman law of *res nilius,* "unoccupied or underutilized land," considered wasted until someone – the colonizer – placed it under "proper use." Thus Roman and future colonizers could convince themselves that no human beings inhabited the coveted territory.

The English invasion of Ireland was a dress rehearsal for their incursions into North America. In Ireland, colonizers decimated forests, plowed over hunting grounds, and confiscated modest, sustainable homesteads, transforming them into huge plantations. A familiar scene. In the Americas, remaining indigenous people were restricted to reservations, where those who had once been nomadic hunter/gatherers were now forced to farm. Others, like the settled Mayan people of Guatemala, were left with only steep mountainsides to terrace for meager cultivation. Illegal Israeli settlements on Palestinian land double annually, and with the settlers comes deliberate destruction of ancient olive trees – 7,500 in 2011 alone – essential to Palestinians for livelihood and nourishment.

Food is a weapon of suppression. Its lack brings starvation and disease.

In Ireland, *An Gorta Mór,* The Great Hunger (1845 to 1851), was caused when the potato crops – on which the people relied almost entirely – were infected with fungus and rotted. Roughly one million Irish died. British rulers made few if any adequate efforts to aid the starving, instead evicting thousands from their homes. Food was in fact abundant, but landlords exported it to markets abroad.

(continued)

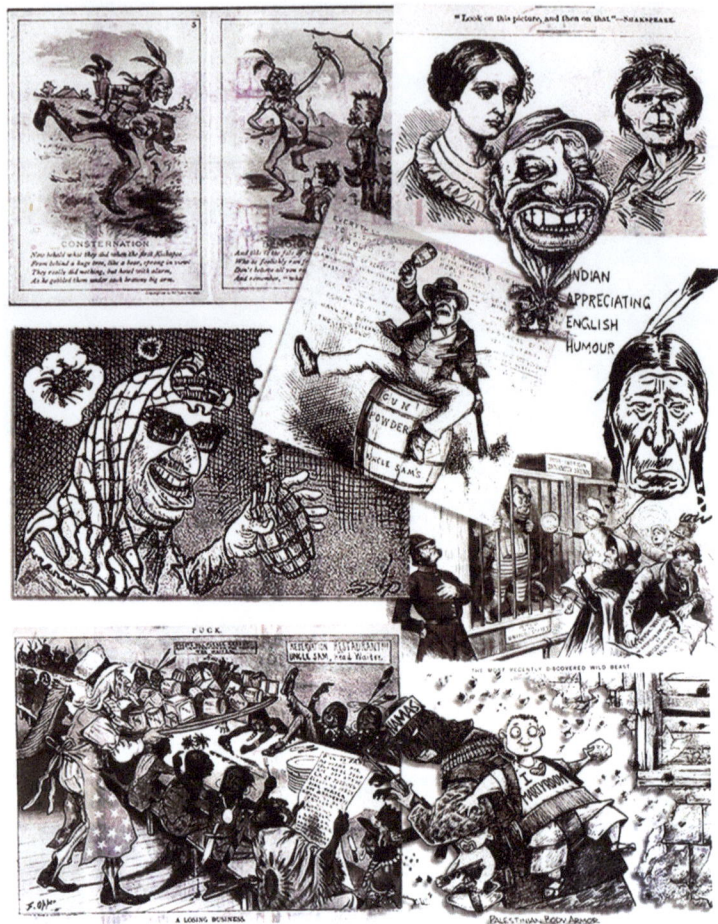

Shaping the Enemy, assembled by Grace Woodward

Ugly racist cartoons serve to demonize and bestialize the conquered peoples, thus justifying the actions of the conqueror, making it easier to hate, easier to erase the so-called "enemy." It is notable how alike the content and the caricatures are, despite the fact that the cartoons range from the 19th century into the 21st.

In 1847, the Choctaw Nation collected $170 (worth thousands today) and donated it to Irish Famine Relief. The empathetic Choctaw understood eviction, starvation, cold and disease having been forcibly sent in 1831 from their ancestral lands in Mississippi to what is now Oklahoma. In 1992, the Irish repaid the Choctaw by trekking the 500-mile Trail of Tears, which brutally exiled Choctaws, Cherokees, Chickasaw, Muscogee (Creek) and Seminole tribes from their homelands in 1831, an event similar to the Palestinian forced exodus called the *Nakba* (The Great Catastrophe). A plaque in Dublin dedicated to the Choctaw reads:

Their humanity calls us to remember the millions of human beings... who die of hunger and hunger-related illness in a world of plenty.

In 2014, a sculptor in the Irish city of Cork created a large public work to commemorate Choctaw generosity.

The land-and-sea blockade and frequent bombing of Palestine's Gaza Strip have created massive economic devastation, with supplies of food, medicine and other commodities dwindling. The Irish Ships to Gaza, part of the Ireland Palestine Solidarity Campaign and the international Freedom Flotilla Movement (including, among many others, North Americans, Turks and Israelis), was established in 2010 to send large Irish contingents – representing all elements of civil society – to help break the siege and deliver urgently needed humanitarian aid.

Overlay / Identity

A common claim among white North Americans is an "Indian princess" ancestor. While there were no European-style princesses (though there are countless prominent tribal women), in the colonial period, Native Americans often intermarried with traders and agents, many of whom were Irish. The children of these unions usually inherited the best of both worlds. The massive and violent white expansion that began in the early 19th century drastically changed these relationships.

Interlocking histories; memory, time, and place coincide; connections persist.

In 1743, Mary Jemison was born aboard a ship heading from Ireland to the colonies. During the French and Indian War, when she was fifteen, Mary was captured by a Shawnee raiding party and sold to the Seneca, who adopted and renamed her Dehgewa-

(continued)

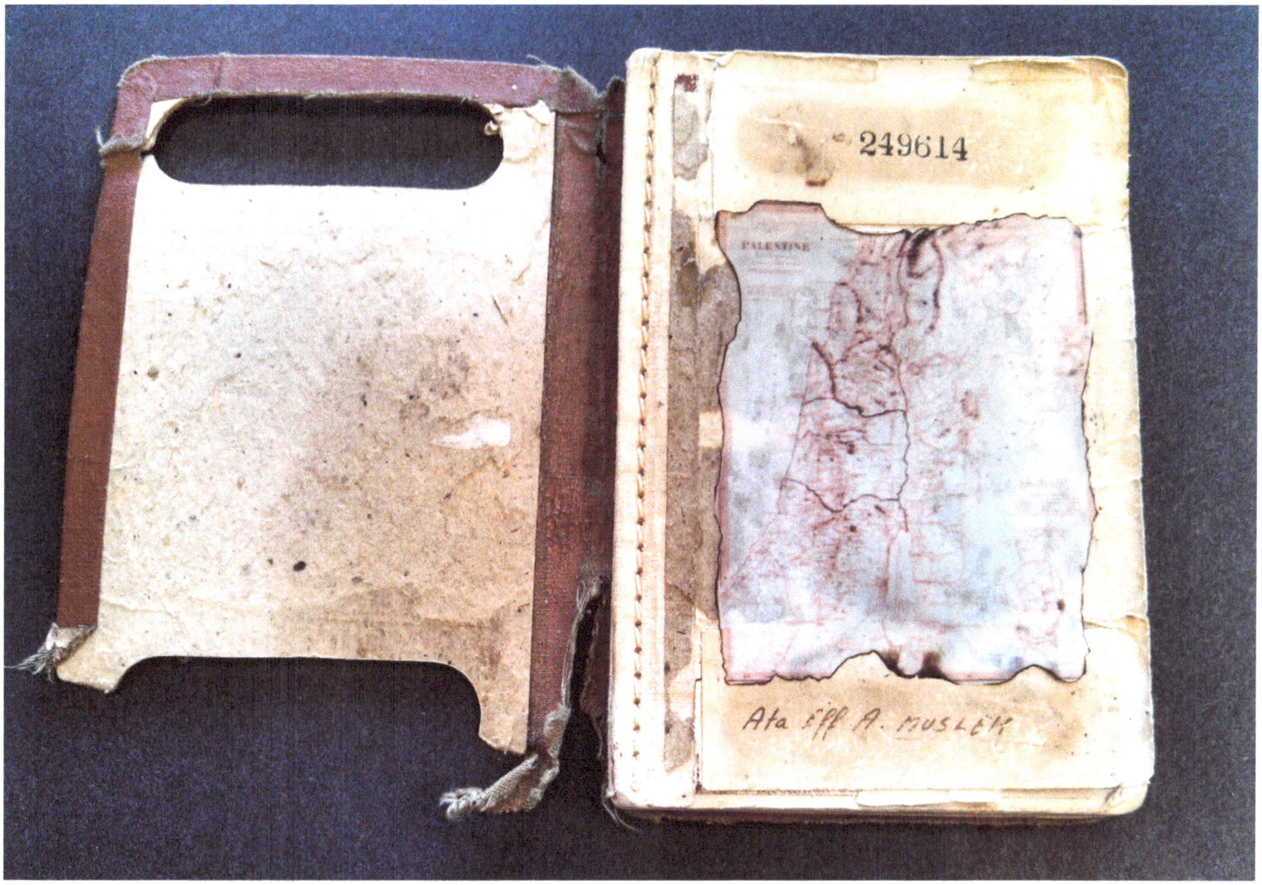

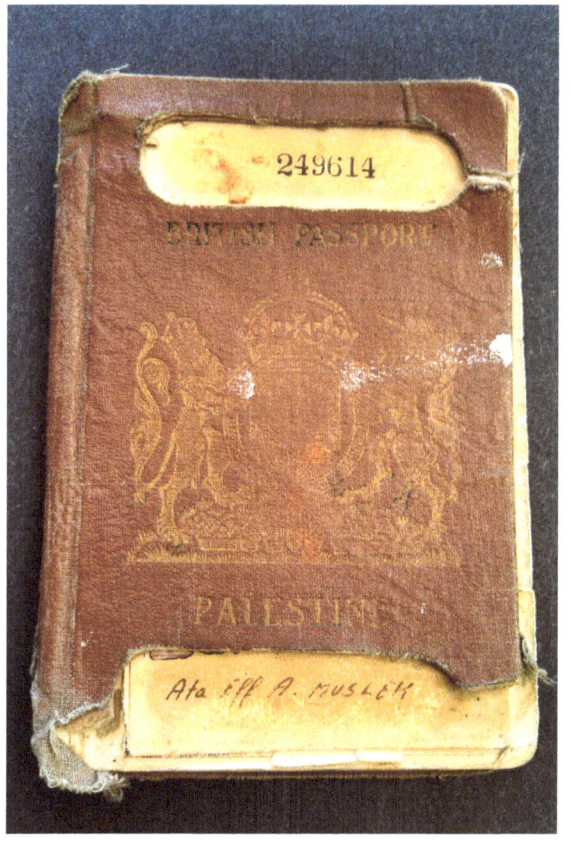

Passport.Palestine (details), Manal Deeb

Passport.Palestine presents the actual passport of my grandfather, Atta Ahmed Musleh, who passed away in 1975. As shown in the passport, he was born in Deir Tarif (the suburbs of the city of Lud, which no longer exists, around Tel Aviv) and was an orange grower, with the clear nationality status of Palestinian Citizen. The passport was issued on the 28th day of August 1947 just a few months before the 1948 *Nakba* (The Great Catastrophe). Here, the passport is represented with a map of historical Palestine (the same map used to issue the passport), along with images of Palestinian outcry, pain, destruction and exodus as a result of displacement in 1948 and 1967. The actual passport pages illustrate that the bearer could enter countries and obtain visas without the restrictions that are imposed on Palestinians today both inside and outside their own land. *Passport.Palestine* thus represents the history of Palestinian territory now imposed on a fictitious map.

—Manal Deeb

nus, "Two Falling Voices." She married twice and had seven children. Although there were attempts at "rescue" by whites, Dehgewanus refused to leave her people and became an effective negotiator on their behalf. The "Old White Woman of the Genesee" died in 1833 and is immortalized with a statue in New York's Letchworth State Park.

In the 1970s, a group of Palestinians found refuge in New Mexico. Many have intermarried with Navajos (Diné) and some Diné have even converted to Islam. Despite inevitable tensions, according to various reports, thanks to the Palestinian traders, business for artisans is booming. For the Diné, the Earth is Mother. For the Palestinians, the New Mexico landscape is a fond reminder of home.

In 2012, a group of Diné women in solidarity with Palestine opposed Navajo President Ben Shelly's visit to Israel to explore the use of chemical fertilizers. The pacifist group is in favor of sustainable agriculture and draws numerous parallels between Palestinian struggles and their own historical traumas. They take as their axiom:

"Every policy the Palestinians are now enduring was practiced on the American Indian.... American Indians are the Palestinians of the United States, and the Palestinians are the American Indians of the Middle East,"
—Russell Means, 2009

…

Palestinians, Native Americans, and the Irish are renowned for their skills in music, dance, storytelling, and poetry, for their contemporary and traditional arts and crafts, for their cuisine and hospitality, their wit, their wisdom and for their profound spiritual awareness and love of beauty. Despite invasion, occupation, colonization, displacement and all the resulting trials and tragedies, for the most part, Palestinians, Native Americans and the Irish have never lost their cultural identities.

Home / Diaspora

"Where we love is home – home that our feet may leave, but not our hearts."
—Oliver Wendell Holmes

The Irish have been leaving home since the 17th century. Having taken the land, the British rented it back to the Irish in a feudal arrangement that disallowed possession or free access. In the 1840s and '50s, evictions took place on a large scale and house demolitions were common. Throughout the British occupation, troops raided homes indiscriminately. With the Great Famine (1845 to 1851), millions of traumatized people fled the island. Soon, emigration became an established practice as men and women sought opportunities abroad. They were often sent off with an "American wake," not expected to be ever seen again. Emigrants traveled cheaply by sea in "coffin ships," so deadly with disease, thirst, hunger and overcrowding, that sharks were said to follow in their wake to catch the dead tossed overboard.

Diaspóra na nGael, *Irish diaspora, spread 100 million people (fifteen times the population of today's Ireland) around the world to every continent. The United States took in the overwhelming majority. With the death of the "Celtic Tiger," a period of rapid economic growth that lasted from 1995 to 2008, the Irish are on the move again.*

From the moment Europeans set foot in the Americas, Indigenous peoples began to be displaced. Bit by bit, lands were commandeered, forests leveled, homes burned. Unfamiliar diseases (especially smallpox), from which they had no immunity, killed Native Americans by the millions, as did war, hunger and malnutrition. The U.S. government used treaties to dispossess Indians of tribal lands, reinforced by the Removal Act of 1830 (signed into law by President Andrew Jackson, whose parents had fled from Ireland's County Antrim). In 1831, the forced relocation called The Trail of Tears sent members of the Muskogee, Seminole, Chickasaw, Choctaw and Cherokee nations (among others) from their autonomous homelands in the Deep South to present-day Oklahoma. All suffered exposure, disease and starvation. Sixty thousand of the 130,000 Cherokee died. (Their chief, John Ross, known as "Cherokee Moses," was part Irish.) In 1864, the Navajo were forced on The Long Walk to Bosque Redondo (New Mexico). Fifty-three other forced marches occurred between 1864 and 1866.

There are 334 reservations in the United States today, where almost a third of American Indians live. In 2010, the poverty rate on reservations was 28.4 percent. All have low education and employment levels, poor health services, substandard housing and inadequate infrastructures.

Large-scale emigration of Palestinian

My tribe's millennia-old petroglyphs abound in the Plateau region of Montana, Idaho, Washington and Oregon. Sometimes, I enliven them by making them dimensional, thus giving them an Anime appearance. Americans know very little about the history of Native Americans, yet the First Americans offer a rich and varied array of cultures. I strive to commemorate our Native history, but Bird Brains are narrow-minded thinkers uninterested in the histories of other peoples. Our global world must share this cultural knowledge to create more understanding and fewer wars.

—Neal Ambrose-Smith

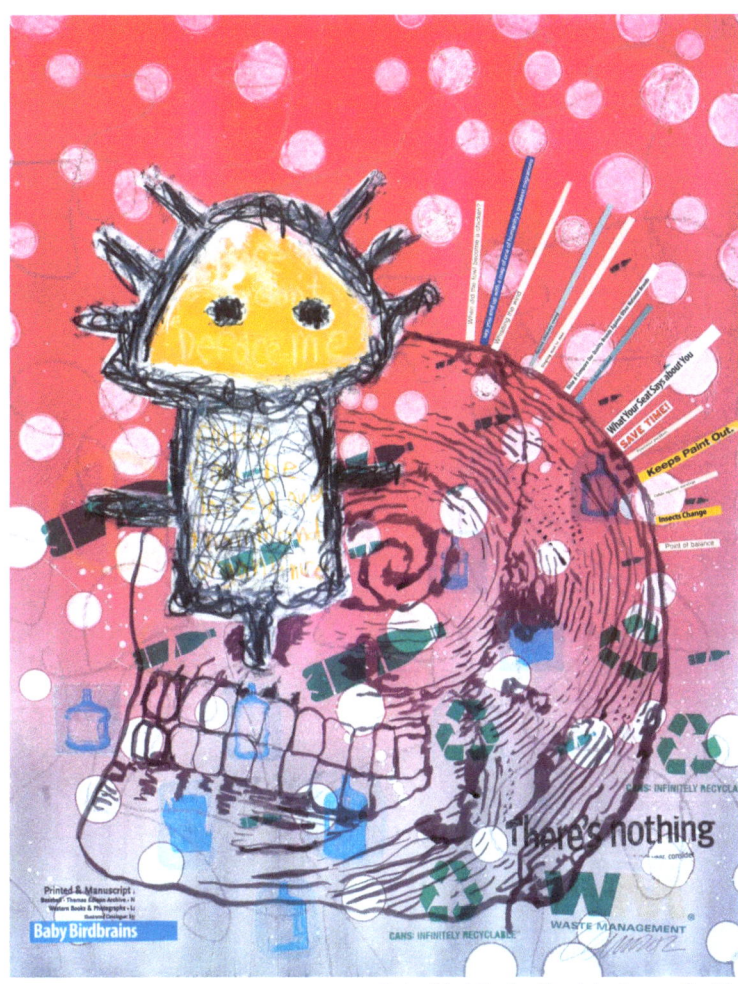

Baby Bird Brain, Neal Ambrose-Smith

Christians escaping Ottoman oppression began in the mid-19th century. After more than 700,000 Christian and Muslim Palestinians were expelled by Israel in the 1948 Nakba and forbidden to return to their homeland, an Absentee Property Law was enacted stating that uncultivated farmlands, idle businesses and empty homes would be appropriated. An ongoing policy of displacement has resulted in millions of exiles around the world, the majority located in the Middle East. The numbers of dispossessed continue to rise, as troops raid homes, houses are demolished and illegal settlements are built on Palestinian lands. Draconian restrictions on movement are dangerous, impoverishing and exhausting. Palestinians are not entitled to a "right of return," though it is a long-held and continuing hope.

One-third of registered Palestinian refugees, as many as 5 million, live in fifty-eight recognized camps in Jordan, Lebanon, Syria, the Gaza Strip and the West Bank, including East Jerusalem. Conditions in refugee camps are poor and densely populated and like Native American reservations, have inadequate facilities and infrastructure.

Words / Persistence

Listen: Sticks and stones – guns and bombs – may break our bones, but words have far wider powers to pierce, to hurt, to devastate … or to charm. Every word is an expression. Destructive. Constructive. Persuasive. Dissuasive.

troubled by speech, the only remedy is speech. —Dennis Formento

Listen: Words heal. Our stories are anchors that teach us to remember, to endure, to act courageously, to look adversity in the eye and maintain our faith that justice must and can prevail. To embrace hope. To aspire. To be persistent in a world that longs to forget, and turns away in denial.

Palestinians, Native Americans and the

(continued)

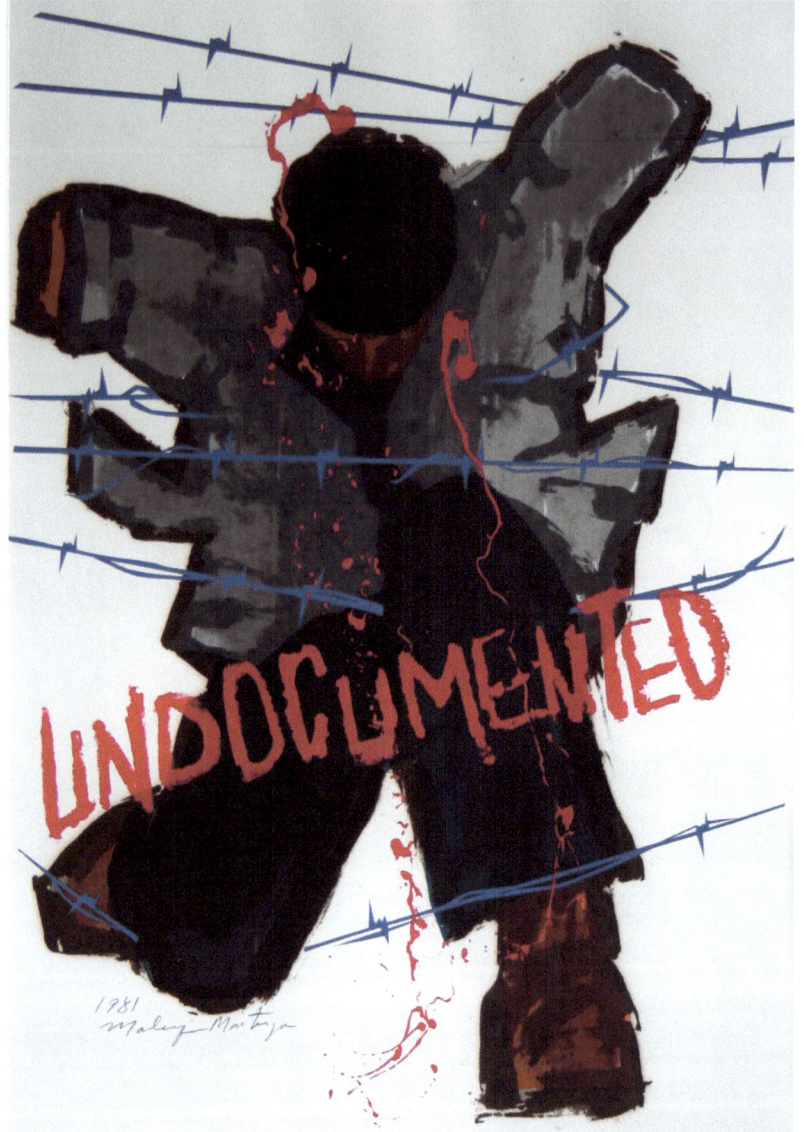

Undocumented, Malaquias Montoya

My inspirations come from the struggling collective. My work is collaborative. Three prominent themes run through it: *injustice, empowerment* and *international struggle*. I try to illuminate with clarity the defects of social and political existence.

My images of empowerment intend to confront the multitude of images of disempowerment fed to us by our daily media, disguising reality, manipulating consciousness and lulling the creative imagination to sleep. I pay tribute to those who struggle on a daily basis. I pay homage to workers and aggrandize their efforts. I celebrate small and large victories of the human spirit. As Bertolt Brecht said, "Art should not be a mirror of reality but a hammer with which to shape a new reality."

Images of international struggle are important to our community and offer solidarity. My work attempts to serve as a bridge, to offer us a better understanding of our world and show us that we are not an isolated, failed culture, but that we share common antagonists that make it necessary for us to unite. From Angola to Central America, from Palestine to the barrio, my images speak to the disenfranchised. They bear the imprint of contemporary Chicano art which reaches beyond the confines of the barrio. My images, art historian Ramon Favela notes, "... are of a dispossessed humanity restrained and shackled by an incomprehensible and nefarious political condition."

My work is often referred to as propaganda art. I don't mind being labeled as such since I feel all work is propagandist in nature, it just depends who you want to propagandize for. From cave painting to the present, art has always spoken on someone's behalf. We must not fall into the age-old cliché that the artist is always ahead of his/her time. No. It is most urgent that we be on time.

—Malaquias Montoya

Irish have experienced and shared sorrows and joys through centuries. Their narratives meet again and again across the circular boundaries of time, space and culture. In these narratives we can discover our own stories, as well as the stories of others.

There is growing urgency worldwide to understand who we are, where we've been, what we've done, where we are going. The knowledge of history and the contexts in which it took place provide strategies for change. So does an understanding of time.

The artists in *"The Map is Not the Territory"* live close to the surfaces of their personal histories. They bravely confront vestiges of the past and reshape them in unexpected ways. Their images are details of a larger picture that stands for all who have suffered everywhere … and will one day triumph.

Look. And listen. ■

CHAPTER I

"The map is not the answer" Defining Homeland

Aisling B. Cormack

The name of this art exhibition derives from Alfred Korzybski's famous assertion, "The map is *not* the territory."[1] For Korzybski, the relationship between map and territory is the same as the relationship between any language and the thing it represents. The map (like language) is *"similar in structure"* to the actual territory (or the external or internal phenomena) it represents; however, it is not identical nor does it represent all the characteristics of the territory (phenomena).[2] The true nature of the territory or phenomena remains nonverbal and unspeakable. According to Korzybski, "[W]hatever we *say* something *is*, it *is not.* Statements are verbal; they are never *it.*"[3] Although Korzybski admits that his statements about the non-identity and *"non-allness"* of the map-territory and language-fact relationships are "quite obvious," he believes that they are needed to counteract "silent" and even "vicious" Aristotelian assumptions, which conflate "verbal statements or judgments about the facts with the actual facts" and treat these "verbal generalizations" as true "for all time to come."[4] He believes that such assumptions are dangerous, being responsible for "dogmatism," "absolutism" and even "neurosis or psychosis."[5]

The map-territory relationship, as set forth by Korzybski, has obvious significance in the fields of linguistics, philosophy and psychology. However, his straightforward assertion, "The map is *not* the territory," also has political, historical and artistic relevance, particularly when thinking about regions with histories of colonization, occupation and dispossession. Korzybski's statement has the power to undermine the legitimacy of maps of these historically troubled regions by suggesting the often arbitrary and fragile nature of boundary lines and place-names. Yet, although Korzybski's proposition destabilizes the validity and permanence of territorial maps, his analysis of the map-territory relationship also highlights the dangerous power of dogmatic and absolutist representations to structure reality. That is, although inherently false, an official map has real effects on the inhabitants of a region. Nevertheless, those whose homelands have been occupied and transformed – sometimes leaving no trace of what came before – have the capacity to redraw the maps or, in other words, to challenge the narratives and ideologies of the powerful. This essay looks at writers and artists from Israel/Palestine and the Irish and Mexican-American borderlands. I look specifically at representations of homeland that prompt us to see past the illusory stability and tidiness of official maps to the fragility and messiness of territory itself and the web of emotions, memories, and visions it sustains.

The Palestinian writer Mahmoud Darwish offers a compelling variation on Korzybski's assertion, "The map is *not* the territory." After posing the question "What is homeland?" in *Journal of an Ordinary Grief*, Darwish first explains what is not homeland: "The map is not the answer."[6] When his family returned to their hometown of Al-Birwa after over a year spent in exile in Lebanon – having fled in 1948 when the village was occupied by Israel Defense Forces during the Arab-Israeli war – Darwish found that he could no longer utter the simplest answer to the question of homeland: "[M]y homeland is where I was born."[7] For, when Darwish returned to his birthplace, he "found nothing."[8] The village of Al-Birwa had been razed to the ground, its name officially changed, and his grandfather designated a "present-absentee" with no rights to his land.[9] According to Darwish, what really defines homeland is power – the power of not only the military to occupy and retain land but also the teacher to disavow the violent foundation of the Israeli state and memories of lost Palestinian homelands: "The history teacher is still telling you that they did not drive anyone out."[10]

In the face of dispossession, Darwish concludes, "The map does not constitute an answer because it is very much like an abstract painting."[11] Like Korzybski, Darwish sees the map as a form of representation that expresses the beliefs and desires of the mapmakers rather than the actual territory. The official map of the State of Israel and the occupied Palestinian territories – on which Al-Birwa no longer appears – reflects the political and economic interests of the governing powers as well as the whims of the surveyor. Yet, as with an abstract painting, a map is open to a multiplicity

(continued)

Abu Nidal, Vivien Sansour

Abu Nidal is going through a dark tunnel built by the Israeli army in order to reach the graves of his family. A farmer, who still offers his guests the sweetest fruits, Abu Nidal lost his land and trees but fought in court to keep at least his parents' and grandmothers' tombstones. It is hard to call this tunnel a victory, but Abu Nidal is proud that he was at least able to save a few meters to guard those he loved the most. "There is no life without hope and no hope without life," he says. "They consider my parents' graves, my grapes, my olives and my old pine tree a problem. But the problem is the occupation. They may be surrounding me by a wall now but the reality is that they are surrounding themselves."

—Vivien Sansour

of interpretations. The reception of the map is as vulnerable to the experiences and desires of former inhabitants as the abstract painting is to the divergent interpretations of generations of art lovers and critics.

Darwish explores the intersection between geographical and psychic maps, which trace the inner territory of memory and emotion, in his poem "And we have countries…":

And we have countries without borders, like our idea of the unknown, narrow and wide—countries whose maps narrow to a gray tunnel as we walk in them and cry out in their labyrinths: "And still we love you."[12]

Through language, Darwish creates imagined terrains that extend without limit or constrict to labyrinthine tunnels. Darwish's poem evokes the territory of the "heart and imagination," which he calls "reality's terrain, the only true place."[13] Because the landscape of this place is inextricably bound to the "soul" of the poet – "A lake widens north of the soul. Wheat spikes / spring up south of the soul"[14] – it eludes mapping. The countries described by Darwish – "that grow / by tossing us into the unknown"[15] – are like the *real* "unspeakable" territory described by Korzybski, which may correspond to a physical map but ultimately exceeds it.

In this poem and other works, Darwish portrays the pain of the exile, which can neither return home nor find belonging in the new state. The Palestinian literary theorist Edward Said attributes the plight of the exile to the troubled territories created by the transfer of power in the 20th century from former colonies to new states:

> As the struggle for independence produced new states and new boundaries, it also produced homeless wanderers, nomads, vagrants, unassimilated to the emergent structures of institutional power, rejected by the established order for their intransigence and obdurate rebelliousness. And in so far as these people exist between the old and the new, between the old empire and the new state, their condition articulates the tensions, irresolutions and contradictions in the overlapping territories shown on the cultural map of imperialism.[16]

For Said, the map of imperialism only highlights the impossibility of mapping the new territories without conflict and uncertainty; like the map described by Darwish, it can provide no definite answers for those lost in the borderlands between the old and new orders.

The writers and artists discussed in this essay work to define what homeland means to those living within territories whose borders have been redrawn, contested and muddled in the aftermath of imperialist invasion and occupation. The people of Israel/Palestine and Ireland, in particular, share histories of partition following the withdrawal of British imperial powers. Ireland was the first of several British colonies, including the Indian subcontinent and Palestine, to be partitioned in 1922. This was followed in 1947 by the adoption of a United Nations resolution, still unrealized, to partition the British Mandate of Palestine into independent Arab and Jewish states. These partitions were intended to grant the right of self-determination and ensure a smooth transfer of power to two territorially discrete and internally homogeneous populations. However, partitioning (or attempting to partition) the former British colonies along sectarian lines led to years of violent conflict and population shifts, as well as disputed maps and histories.

What Said calls "the tensions, irresolutions and contradictions in the overlapping territories shown on the cultural map of imperialism" are at the center of much literature from the borderlands between Ireland and Northern Ireland. Like Korzybski and Darwish, many writers from this border region explore disjunctions between maps and territories. For example, Shane Connaghton, in his novel *The Run of the Country*, describes the impossibility of mapping the imbrication of territories north and south of the geographical boundary line: "The land was impervious to maps. What appeared plain on paper was on the ground an orgy of political and geographical confusion. [Counties] Cavan and Monaghan in the South were locked into Fermanagh in the North, like two dogs trying to cover the one hot bitch."[17]

Other writers similarly expose the geographical ambiguity of the border region through their representations of territory. In Patrick Quigley's novel *Borderland*, a character asks, "But where is the Border?" Another character replies, "There are no traces of it here. No checkpoints or observation towers. Sometimes it's just a stream, sometimes just a hedge between fields."[18] The writer Patrick McCabe describes the "geographical border" as "drawn by a drunken man, every bit as tremulous and deceptive as the one which borders life and death."[19] Paul Muldoon uses the figure of a "wall of glass" to describe the insubstantial nature of the border in his poem "The Boundary Commission."[20] Muldoon also suggests, like McCabe, the illogical and arbitrary course of the border, as it was drawn by an appointed commission following partition: "*You remember that village where the border ran / Down the middle of the street, / With the butcher and baker in different states?*"[21]

The border may sometimes elude maps; however, its dire repercussions for the inhabitants of the Irish borderlands are undeniable. Eugene McCabe, a writer whose farm lies a few hundred yards from the border on the southern side, describes it as follows: "Clearly an obstacle to normal contact and communication, a hindrance, a hostile, unfriendly, defensive thing."[22] Since the partition of the island in 1922,

(continued)

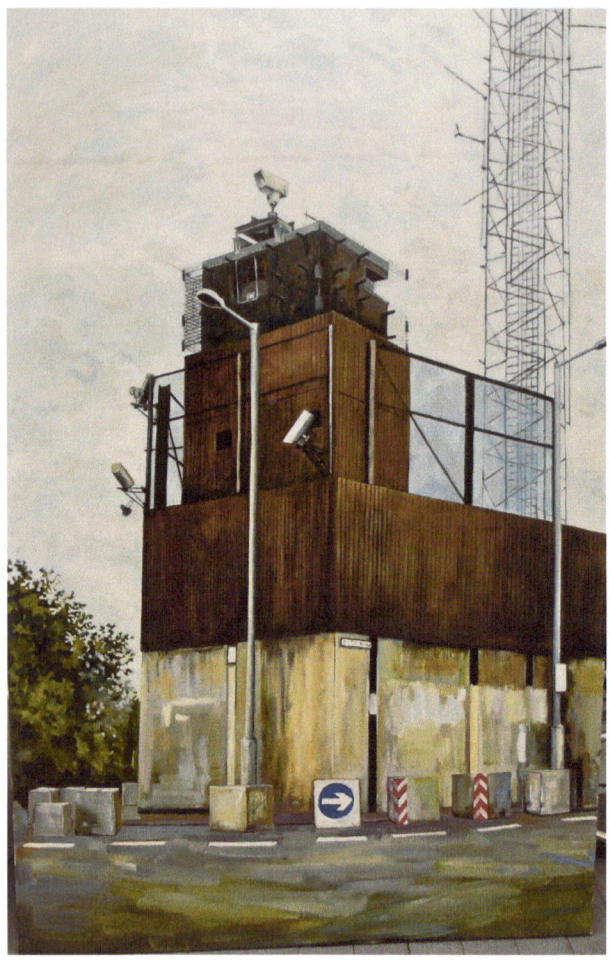

Police Station, Rita Duffy

borderland inhabitants have lived through tense periods of violence by paramilitary and security forces; the closure of cross-border railways, roads and bridges, which cuts off ties with social and economic hinterlands; and subjection to interrogation, searches, checkpoints and surveillance.

Military watchtowers built to monitor and regulate movement across the Irish border during the so-called Troubles in Northern Ireland substantiated the nebulous boundary line's presence. A collection of paintings by the Belfast artist Rita Duffy serves as a visceral reminder of the state of constant surveillance under which many Northern Irish inhabitants lived. These paintings represent the heavily armed observation posts and forts built by the British Army near border crossings and at police stations. *Watchtower II* depicts a drab tower that is reminiscent of the military posts that guard the border between Israel and occupied Palestinian territories as well as its border with adjacent states. It is surrounded by a corrugated metal wall and topped with a massive surveillance camera that affords a view of rolling green hills and fields. In his poem "Rita Duffy: *Watchtower II*," Paul Muldoon describes the tower as follows: "From here it looks as if the whole country is spread under a camouflage tarp / rolled out by successive British garrisons / stationed at Crossmaglen...."[23] Crossmaglen is a border town in South Armagh, an area which was a center of resistance to British rule during the conflict and therefore home to the biggest concentration of watchtowers. A menacing army observation post dominated the small town's police station. In his poem, Muldoon connects his experience growing up in a heavily militarized, nationalist enclave in County Armagh – under permanent scrutiny by British "scanners scanning our hillsides"[24] – to histories of occupation and resistance shared by Native Americans and Palestinians

> One of our neighbors, interned for selling An Phoblacht
>   [a political newspaper], learned we're not the first tribe
>   to have been put down or the first to have risen
> against our oppressors. That's why we've always sided
>   with the Redskin
> and the Palestinian....[25]

Duffy portrays another persistent reminder of oppression in Northern Ireland, as well as in Palestine and the United States, in her painting *Police Station*: the militarization of the police. This work features an imposing, angular fortress, which is fortified by high concrete walls and fences, a rust-colored watchtower, and surveillance cameras aimed in all directions. It represents the now-demolished Andersonstown Police Station, a notorious landmark during the Troubles commanding a looming presence at the junction of the Falls and Glen Roads in West Belfast. Duffy's paintings emphasize the dual role of watchtowers: both to guard and monitor "troubled" regions and, perhaps more crucially, to make visible not only the state border but also internal partitions in cities like Belfast and Derry. In these cities, "peacelines" – or physical barriers constructed to minimize intercommunity violence – have separated working-class Protestant unionist from Catholic nationalist neighborhoods since 1969.

It is perhaps the intractability and continued impact of these partitions that move artists and writers to offer their own alternative topographies, as Duffy does in her painting *Territory*. The painting consists of three rows of five 24" x 30" panels of layered and sanded paint; on the top layer of each panel, a detailed map of one of fifteen different "peacelines" in Belfast has been drawn in graphite. Each map stands in no relation to the others, suggesting the manner in which these borders produce an urban landscape fragmented and disjointed by fear of tension and violence. The total effect of the fifteen panels echoes the description of Belfast's peacelines by Jon Calame and Esther Charlesworth: "No overarching logic guides their placement with respect to the city as a whole; rather, the walls are built in direct response to specific and chronic episodes of local violence. They all correspond to segments of interfaces where residential areas occupied by rival communities meet."[26]

Spread over the fifteen panels of *Territory* are the following stenciled phrases, which Duffy appropriates from Seamus Heaney's poem "Act of Union"

> his heart beneath your heart
> is a wardrum
> and ignorant little fists already beat at your
> borders
> your tracked and stretchmarked body
> the big pain

The title of Heaney's poem refers to the Act of Union of 1800, which formed the United Kingdom of Great Britain and Ireland. Heaney represents the Act of Union as a sexual act between an "imperially Male" Great Britain and a passive, feminine Ireland.[27] The poem recalls the tradition of *aisling* poetry in which Ireland, personified as a woman, calls Irish men (or foreign Catholic rulers) to liberate her from the power and violence, often sexual in nature, of English invaders.

In "Act of Union," the sexual act – the violence of which is conveyed in the lines "The rending process in the colony, / The battering ram, the boom burst from within" – produces offspring fated to perpetuate the violence.[28] Heaney describes the fetus as an enemy within – "an obstinate fifth column" – whose heart beats like a "wardrum" and whose "fists already / Beat at your borders" and are "cocked / At me across the water."[29] The "fifth column" is a metaphor for both nationalist and unionist paramilitary forces. Nationalists have tried to dismantle the border in order to achieve a united Ireland free of British rule. Unionists – suggested by the "wardrum," which evokes images of the large drums used in unionist street parades – historically "[b]eat at your [Ireland's] borders" to break free of "her" control. (For example, the unionist-led Northern Irish government opted out of the Irish Free State created by the Anglo-Irish treaty of 1921.) Given that the offspring of the centuries-old Act of

(continued)

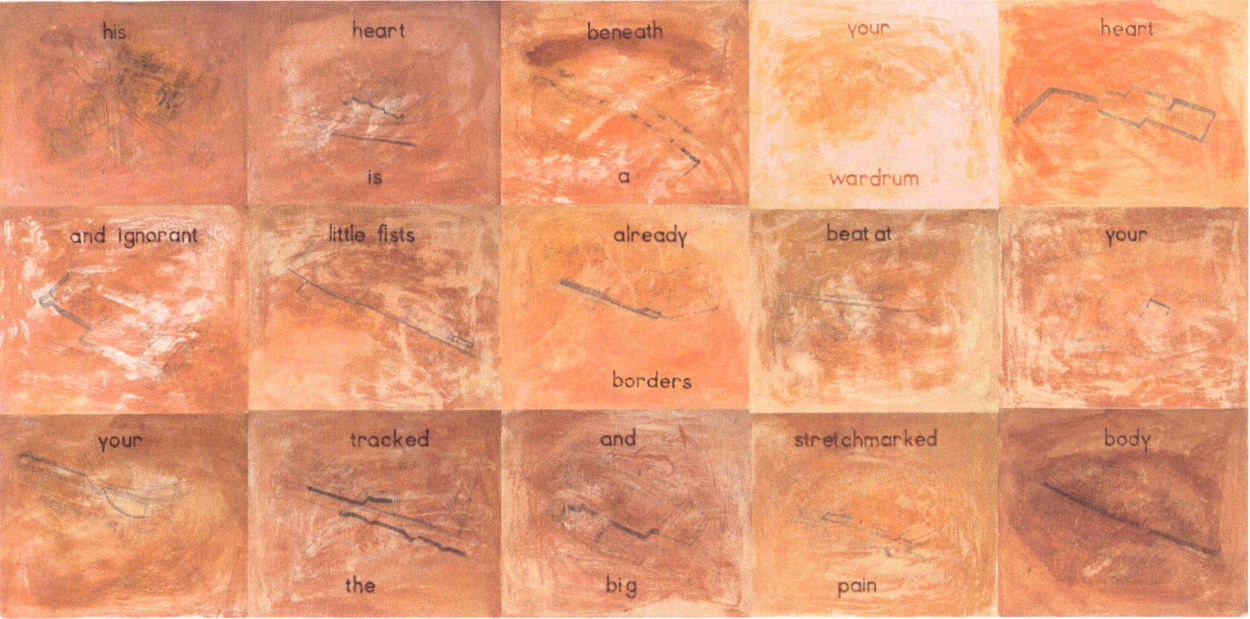

Territory, Rita Duffy

Union continue to clash – even after Ireland is allowed her "half-independen[ce]" – the speaker of the poem (Great Britain) laments

> No treaty
> I foresee will salve completely your tracked
> And stretchmarked body, the big pain
> That leaves you raw, like opened ground, again.[30]

The manner in which Duffy incorporates phrases from Heaney's "Act of Union" into her painting *Territory* results in a crucial shift of perspective: from that of the "imperially Male" Great Britain to the invaded, feminine Ireland. By eschewing references to the "I" of Heaney's poem – the agent of sexual violence – Duffy prompts the viewer to identify with the "you," the victimized and occupied woman. Furthermore, Duffy excises fragments of the poem, disrupting the rhythm and rhymes of Heaney's original sonnet form. The artist's arrangement of these verbal fragments on the fifteen panels achieves a new form: one which not only mirrors the fragmented and disjointed traces of Belfast's peacelines but more crucially produces a tense and thought-provoking synthesis between the words and images.

In *Territory*, the "borders" and "tracked and stretchmarked" body become that of Belfast, with the graphite traces on the layered and sanded paint creating the impression of incisions on tender and mottled skin. The internal borders constructed to maintain peace in the city instead become tools of violence scarring the urban territory. Duffy suggests that the "big pain," the trauma facing many inhabitants of the city, is caused not only by the never-ceasing threat of intercommunity violence but also by the "peacelines" that perpetuate the existence of "ignorant little fists" beating at their borders.

The painting – produced in 1996, two years before the Good Friday Agreement that at least provisionally ended the Troubles – suggests that landscapes, like bodies, can retain the scars of conflict long after peace has been declared. The tracks and stretch marks – "the big pain" – etched in the internally partitioned territory represented by Duffy find an analogue in the open wound that separates the United States and Mexico, according to writer and scholar Gloria Anzaldúa. In her seminal text *Borderlands/La Frontera*, Anzaldúa writes, "The U.S.-Mexican border *es una herida abierta* [is an open wound] where the Third World grates against the first and bleeds. And before a scab forms it hemorrhages again, the lifeblood of two worlds merging to form a third country—a border country."[31] For Anzaldúa, the borderland is both the site of trauma that eludes representation and a space where friction between clashing territories can spur creative production. She writes

> Living in a state of psychic unrest, in a Borderland, is what makes poets write and artists create. It is like a cactus needle embedded in the flesh. It worries itself deeper and deeper, and I keep aggravating it by poking it. When it begins to fester I have to do something to put an end to the aggravation and to figure out why I have it. I get deep down into the place where it's rooted in my skin and pluck away at it … making the pain worse before it can get better. Then out it comes…. That's what writing is for me, an endless cycle of making it worse, making it better, but always making meaning out of the experience, whatever it may be.[32]

Anzaldúa positions herself as an exile, lacking a country as a *mestiza* (a woman of mixed racial ancestry) and cast out of her homeland and disowned by her people as a lesbian.[33] However, writing of her wounds and exile allows Anzaldúa to reclaim her *tierra natal*, her homeland: the "borderland between the Nueces and the Rio Grande" that "has survived possession and ill-use by five countries: Spain, Mexico, the Republic of Texas, the U.S., the Confederacy, and the U.S. again."[34] Darwish, like Anzaldúa, also writes of his homeland in order to make meaning out of traumatic past experiences. "Do not write a history now," he urges his reader. "When you do that, you leave the past behind, and what is required is to call the past to account. Do not write a history except that of your wounds. Do not write a history except that of your exile."[35]

The need to "call the past to account" is driven by what Anzaldúa describes as "psychic unrest." Yet, to struggle through art to give shape to hitherto unspeakable experiences is to end this state of unrest, even if only provisionally. In other words, writers and artists can construct a map capable of making sense of a troubled geographical or psychic territory, even if the map cannot be the decisive answer to a question like "What is homeland?"

Two projects included in this art exhibition – the film *Hozhonahaslíí: Stories of Healing the Soul Wound* by Donna

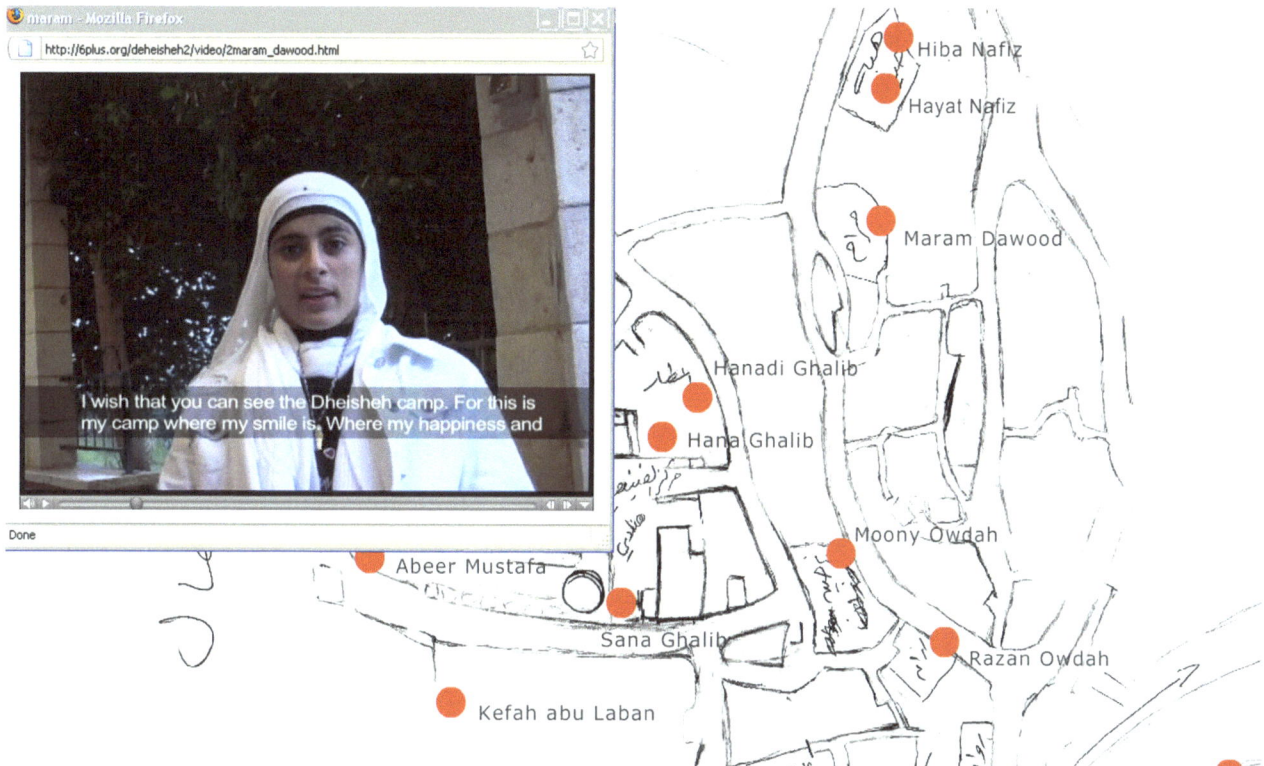

Daughters of Palestine: Personal Narratives from the Young Women of the Dheisheh Refugee Camp, 6+: a women's art collective

Schindler and the web-based project *Daughters of Palestine*, launched by 6+: a women's art collective, in collaboration with the Al Feneiq Cultural Center in the Dheisheh Refugee Camp in Palestine – answer this need to make sense of experiences like occupation, dispossession and dislocation through writing, or in the case of *Hozhonahaslíí*, through oral narratives. In *Hozhonahaslíí*, members of the Navajo Nation (the Diné) share memories and stories of colonization, genocide and forced assimilation, which according to the film "have left a scar on Native people throughout the world…" The Diné believe that not only their people bear the scars of their traumatic history – which they call "soul wounds" – but that the territory itself where Native Americans were massacred bears "blood memories."

The film documents the traumatic legacy of colonization and imperialism; furthermore, it works to heal wounds that have been transmitted intergenerationally in Native-American communities, causing physical and mental illness as well as domestic violence and addiction. Anzaldúa also describes illness as the toll of trauma, which can only be healed through working undigested images into narrative: "Because writing invokes images from my unconscious, and because some of the images are residues of trauma which I then have to reconstruct, I sometimes get sick when I *do* write…. But, in reconstructing the traumas behind the images, I make 'sense' of them, and once they have 'meaning' they are changed, transformed."[36]

The *Daughters of Palestine* project empowers twenty young women from the Dheisheh Refugee Camp and the town of Bethlehem to similarly transform traumatic images from their past into meaningful narratives. In December 2007, the women collaborated to create a multimedia map of the refugee camp through video footage and photographs of their homes and fellow inhabitants. The participants' narratives about their experiences as refugees, which are connected on the online map to their homes or other relevant locations, result in the overlapping of geographical and psychic topography. Some tell stories of their love for the Dheisheh Refugee Camp, which is the only home they have known and where the necessity of living close together means that

(continued)

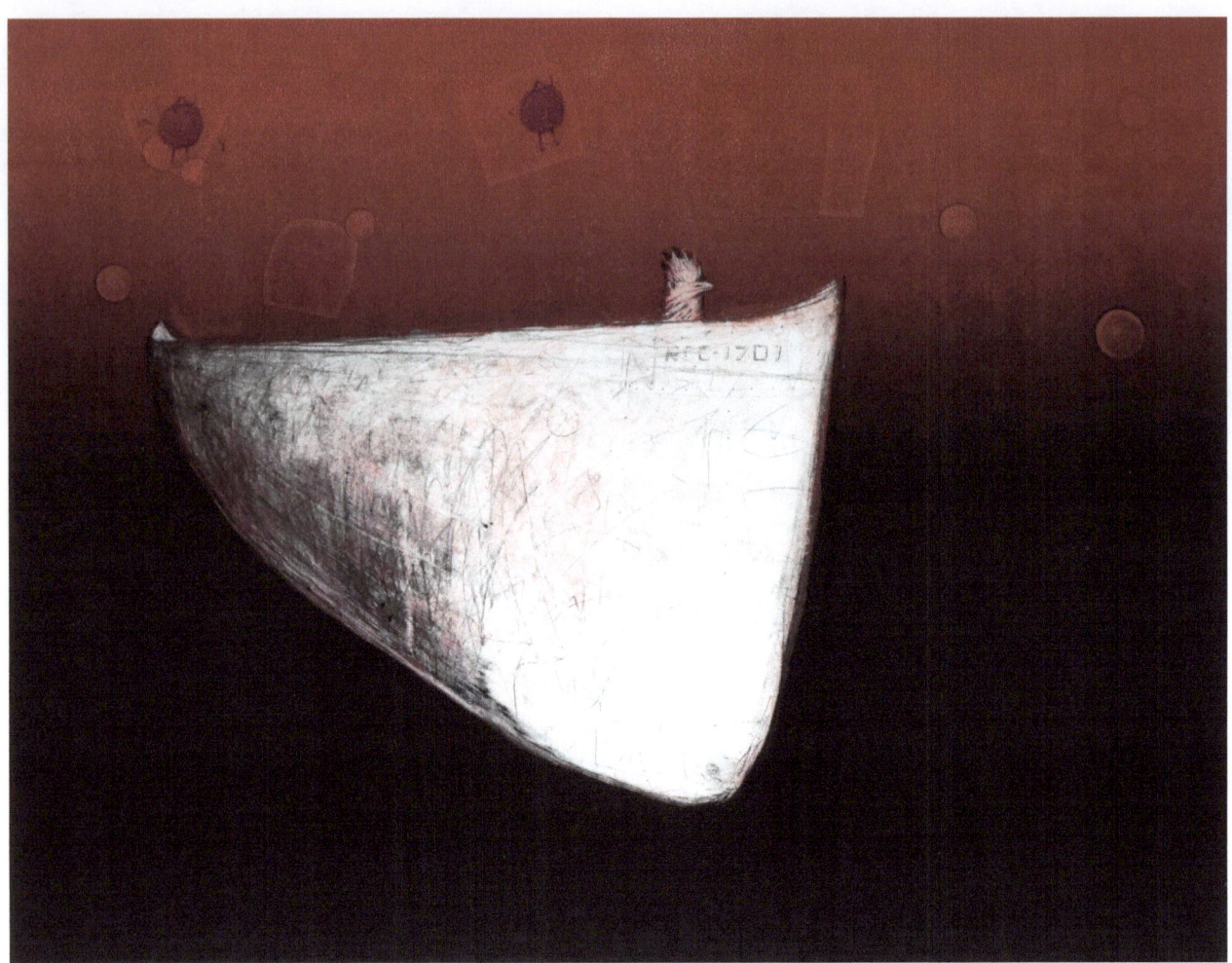

Going Where No Man Has Gone Before, Neal Ambrose-Smith

everyone knows and looks out for his or her neighbors. Others recount experiences of profound unrest and loss: of homes searched in the middle of the night by Israeli soldiers; homes fired upon by tanks or rockets; curfews imposed; streets lined with pictures of martyrs; family members interrogated and arrested; and deaths of loved ones witnessed.

As the young women describe these disturbing events, the viewer intuits depths of trauma that cannot yet be contained by their narratives. One refugee, Wafaa Hassan, tells a story of how Israeli soldiers blew up a wanted man in a car parked outside her house, injuring and killing others nearby, and in the end demolishing her house after clearing out the family and neighbors who had sought shelter. She tells the camera, "Everybody was upset. Nobody is living in this world. Life has become burden after burden.… People cry over their condition.… This is a very sad story."[37] However, one also sees in the participants the desire and vision to define their own homeland, even in the face of permanent exile. Maram Dawood (al-Mahsiri), a sixteen-year-old who has lived in the refugee camp since birth, says, "I pray to God that I will see even a small glimpse of my original home, Beit Mahseer. However, I will not relinquish my residence here, the Dheisheh Refugee camp. I wish that you may know how much I love and cherish this camp. For each people there is a homeland where they live. As for me and us we have a homeland that lives in us." ∎

CHAPTER 2

Spaces of Memory and Reclaiming of Palestinian History

John Halaka, Hani Zurob and Mary Tuma

Valerie Behiery

The victors write history. They make it nearly impossible for alternative historical narratives to enter the public arena, transform public opinion and, most significantly, restore the countless lives erased by the pen of power. Today's huge, undemocratic mass media normalizes the colonial versions of history, alleging the inferiority or barbarity of their colonized subjects. Silenced and dehumanized, occupied peoples from different periods and places have much in common. The commonality of their experiences forms the premise of the touring exhibition, *"The Map is Not the Territory: Parallel Paths-Palestinians, Native Americans, Irish."*[1] The means used to subjugate them have been the same: forced displacement, destruction of the economy and culture, theft of resources and perennial imprisonment, torture and murder.

Despite the violence and injustice inherent in the colonization of the Americas, Palestine and Ireland, anger is not the chief characteristic of the art exhibited in *"The Map is Not the Territory."*[2] The artists resist rather than confront, and do so largely through the articulation of cultural, topographical and personal memory. While this certainly reflects a curatorial decision, recourse to memory as a strategy for minoritized artists to gain visibility and voice is a tendency seen worldwide. Since the demonstration by Michel Foucault, Edward Said and others of the ideological nature of history, a shift has taken place from the privileging of history to the gathering of memory as a tool to maintain culture and redress history's caveats.[3] Consequently, although I focus on the role memory plays in the specific works of three Palestinian artists participating in the *"The Map is Not the Territory"* – John Halaka, Hani Zurob and Mary Tuma – readers and viewers will find correspondences with the work of artists from other communities.

The idea that memory can play a critical role in reclaiming lost histories intends to highlight the diverse ways history can be represented, probe the intersections of individual and collective memory in contemporary Palestinian art and, of course, analyze its capacity to alter mainstream Western perceptions of Palestine and Palestinians.[4] Because the modern history of Palestine is largely one of displacement, the term Palestinian is here understood in its widest sense. Only one of the artists discussed – Zurob – was born and raised in Palestine and is of Palestinian descent on both his mother's and father's side. None currently live in Palestine and all three naturally have other factors informing their respective self-identities. As such, their work is poly- or transcultural and should be positioned not only within the context of Palestinian art but also that of Euro-American and global contemporary art more broadly.

The Case of Palestine: Culture as Crime

Some historically marginalized or colonized communities, for example African-Americans, have gained a bit of ground in mainstream culture by challenging the victors' version of history although the acknowledgment of the history of slavery has engendered political correctness rather than abolished structural racism. Palestinians, however, are still most often

(continued)

"We live in a world of suffering in which evil is rampant, a world whose events do not confirm our Being, a world that has to be resisted. It is in this situation that the aesthetic moment offers hope."

—John Berger
The Sense of Sight

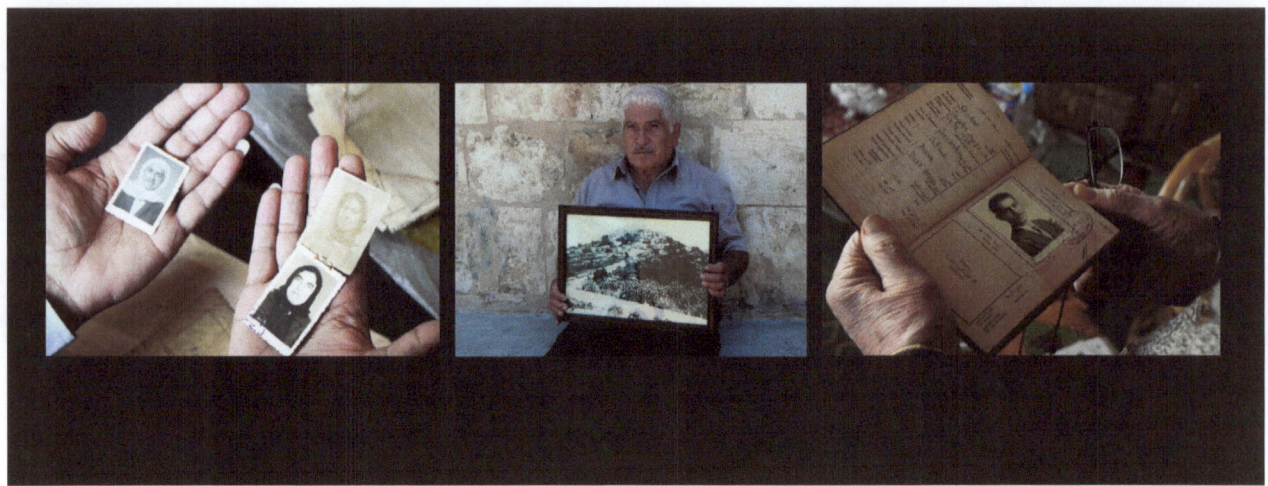

Hands of Time, John Halaka

ignored or misrepresented in North American mainstream media and political discourse. Palestine remains under occupation, while the Israeli nationalist narrative dominates the Western view of history and current events. Journalists or scholars who dare venture beyond "official speak" often pay a hefty price. And this same system of imposed silence or punishment also extends to the realm of culture. Jessica Winegar, in an article arguing that post-9\11 exhibits of Middle Eastern art in the United States generally reproduce the neo-Orientalism they attempt to counter, also discusses how "recent art events related to Palestine strikingly reveal the … political underpinnings of the category of art."[5] For example, the curator of the 2003 *Made in Palestine* exhibit held at the Station Museum in Texas had great difficulty securing other venues for the show.[6] That he was systematically told by museum directors that "they would lose their museum funding if they were to hold a show that was pro-Palestinian"[7] and by gallery directors that "showing Palestinian art would likely mean an end to their gallery"[8] effectively points to the art world's indebtedness to the politics of its funders.[9] Commentary on the show was also sometimes predictably hyperbolic with at least two officials claiming *Made in Palestine* was anti-American and anti-Israeli propaganda and a glorification of terrorism and murder.[10]

Not only is contemporary Palestinian art targeted, but, also – perhaps even more so – Palestine's historical and traditional art. Farah Munayyer, an important American collector of antique Palestinian and Syrian costumes, states for example, that "Israel keeps the finest collection of Palestinian costumes in the world under lock and key in a museum basement," underlining the desired invisibility of such collections.[11] Any affirmation of Palestinian cultural lineage and heritage counters the Israeli fable of "a land without a people for a people without a land."[12]

Palestinian culture and history are, from the perspective of Israeli nationalism, at the very least a threat, revealing the enmeshment of colonialism and (ethnic) nationalism both premised on the exclusion of difference. Yet the refusal to acknowledge Palestinian history and the attempts to erase it have actually endowed cultural and topographical signs with a political agency that they would not have had otherwise. The ongoing practices of cultural destruction, land expropriation and media censorship explains why memory – both collective and individual – remains central to contemporary Palestinian art and activism. While not infallible, memory is a space that can defy in varying degrees, the colonizers and their historical biases. As Lila Abu-Lughod and Ahmad H. Saidi state, "Memory is one of the few weapons available to those against whom history has turned."[13]

John Halaka: Documenting the Forgotten Survivors

John Halaka, Palestinian through his mother, was born in Egypt, but raised in the United States where he lives and teaches. Until recently, he worked essentially in painting and drawing, creating series of canvases that use simplified figures, objects, fragments and motifs as visual metaphors to articulate the many tensions at the heart of human experience between, for example, desire and denial, life and death, human strength and frailty, power and oppression, reality and illusion. For Halaka, identity is shaped by inseparable personal, cultural, historical and political factors. Some of his series specifically address the Palestinian issue, and through it, the universal issues of injustice, oppression, displacement and the violence of our blindness to them.

In the last few years, Halaka has felt compelled to document rather than merely evoke what he calls the "ethnic cleansing of Palestine." For example, in his series, *Landscapes of Desire* (2009-2013), he draws the ruins of Palestinian houses and villages destroyed in 1948, inserting and building forms textually by stamping words that read "remember," "resist," "return," "rebuild" and "forgive." Text here serves a double function. It provides these forgotten spaces and places with a voice. Once mute, they now speak: we can no longer pretend we don't see and know. The words also simultaneously emphasize and change the meditative, discursive filter underwriting these sites and images of Palestine. Constituting a bridge between art and viewer, they point to the possibility of seeing Palestine and Palestinians in terms other than those of the American mass media.

The documentary impulse in which reality takes precedence over metaphor culminates in Halaka's most recent series. *Portraits of Desire and Denial* (2012-ongoing) is an interdisciplinary social and artistic project focusing on Palestinian refugee families. It involves drawings, photography, videos and documentary film.[14] Color photographs are assembled into horizontal or vertical diptychs and triptychs featuring the men and women Halaka has interviewed along with images of objects, photographs, documents or land that act as synecdoches for the subjects' yearning for home. While the photographs are portraits of real people, they are not purely photojournalistic. Unlike in standard portraiture, each piece is here produced by combining and contrasting images to visually enact what is normally intangible: the personal narratives of the subjects as well as their relationship to Palestine.

The two photographs from *Portraits of Desire and Denial* exhibited in *"The Map is Not the Territory"* illustrate the artist's manner of rendering portraits from the inside, so to speak.

The central photograph of the horizontal triptych, *Hands of Time,* shows a late middle-aged man, Boulous Khoury, sitting on the ground. His back is straight and propped against the wall of what appears to be a traditional house made of hewn stone. Khoury is holding a framed black-and-white photograph about the same width as his torso, a landscape showing a path winding up a small, tree-rich mountain. Several elements converge to communicate the importance of the picture that seems to possess an almost talismanic quality for the subject. One: there is the mirroring situation of viewing a photograph both outdoors and within another photograph. Two: the man is not looking at the viewer, but gazing into space. Instead, it is the old photograph that looks back at the camera. Finally, the space delineated by the photograph, devoid of either a horizon line or any physical depth, is claustrophobic: the ground-and-wall backdrop provides no vista apart from the one seen in the keepsake image in Boulous Khoury's hands. Black and white, it speaks of the past, suggesting that the only opening, the only way out or forward lies in memory.

The image-in-an-image theme is repeated in the photographs on either side of the triptych's center. On the viewer's right, is a close-up of an elderly person's hands holding an aging passport showing, one guesses, Boulous Khoury as a young man. Viewers who know the history of Palestine immediately infer that this is a British Mandate Palestinian passport or, in other terms, an official document that attests to the existence of a nation.[15] The passport and hands take up most of the image, the hints of the chair, carpets, table and water bottle seen behind it revealing that we are in someone's home.

The image on the left is also a close-up of hands. These appear younger. Open palms hold three black-and-white identity photographs, one more yellowed and faded from age than the others. Here too, framing and the position of the hands convey that the two men and one woman portrayed play, or played, a central role in Khoury's life. The juxtaposition of images, objects and framing strategies, as well as of past and present, draws viewers into the work, inviting them to piece the image(s) together and, by extension, the subject's life. The passport and old photographs – or, in other

(continued)

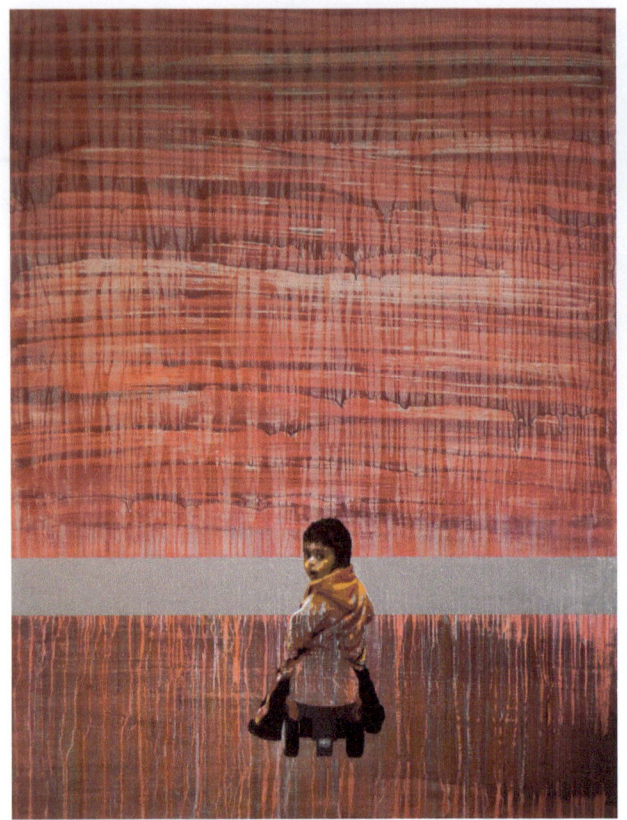

Flying Lesson #03, Hani Zurob

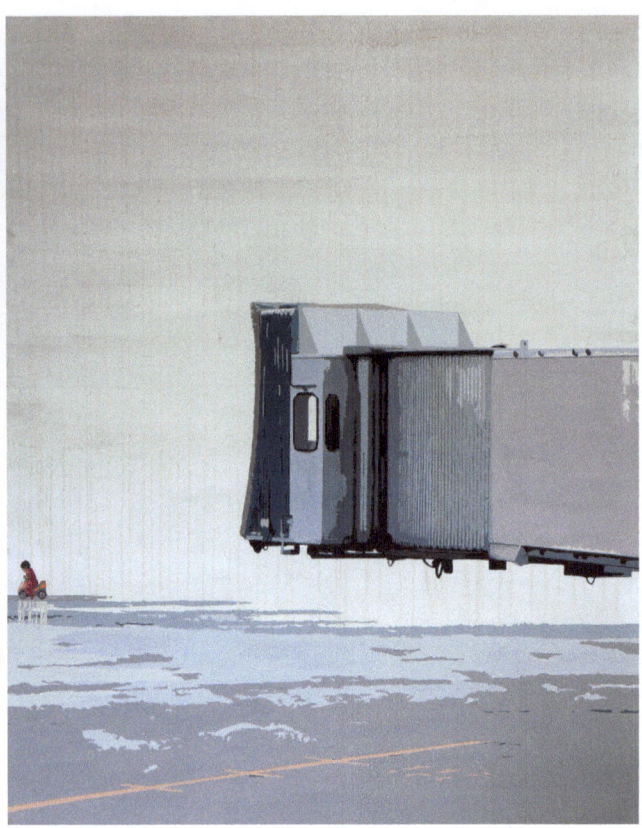

Flying Lesson #04, Hani Zurob

works, items such as bones or antique house keys – are mnemonic devices that succeed in conferring upon memory, usually impalpable, a visual and tactile dimension.

Memory is twofold in *Portraits of Desire and Denial*. The series is as much about documenting the life stories of elderly Palestinians, who still remember the 1948 *Nakba,* and of their descendants as it is about weaving the information into the fabric of the viewers' consciousness.

The second image featured in *"The Map is Not the Territory," Forgotten Survivors* (2013) is also produced through juxtaposition, but this time, the technique of multiple exposure allows for three images combined into one. The upper portion of an elderly woman's face fills the whole image. The top third of the photograph shows Rif'a AbedAllah El Kurd's wrinkled brow and bespectacled eyes whose gaze, although directed into space, is clearly turned inward. A map of Palestine overlays the left side of her face creating a vertical dividing line in the photograph. Superimposed over the lower part of the women's face, particularly her mouth, a scene of a refugee camp seems to silence her. The imaged voicelessness further intensifies the pain of exile and trauma marking her face and gaze: memory is here clearly a wound. The photograph, whose narrative content is stated less ambiguously than that of *Hands of Time,* is simple, direct and powerful.[16] Halaka, by realigning subject and homeland, offers hope to Rif'a AbedAllah El Kurd and defines memory itself as a territory to be reckoned with as it lies beyond the reach of colonial appropriation. In this version of *Forgotten Survivors,* Halaka has fixed a screen overtop the image. As a distancing mechanism, it stresses how the images and lives of Palestinian refugees are not part of our Euro-American cultural imagery or what Kaja Silverman so aptly calls our "cultural screen."[17] The screen equally denotes imprisonment, adding a material and tactile dimension to "the conditions that trapped the refugees in a life of neglect and denial."[18]

Hani Zurob: Space and the Foreclosure of Memory

Zurob grew up in the Rafah refugee camp. His experience of the Occupation and of Palestinian art produced within Palestine, because direct, therefore differs from that of Halaka and Tuma, both of whom grew up and studied in the United States. Zurob is a painter whose work can stand without blush or shadow next to the best contemporary art, proving wrong those pundits and critics who enjoy periodically announcing the death of painting. His personal trajectory is unusual in that the proclivity he felt for painting as a young boy first manifested itself in adult life in the posters and urban graffiti he created during the 1987 Intifada. Later, he made his way from Gaza to the West Bank and completed an art degree in 1999 at the University of Nablus. In his professional career, Zurob has never adopted the nationalist and political symbolism that characterizes a central current of Palestinian modern art. Instead, he privileges a personal rather than collective space and language in his work, where self-portraiture is central.

Zurob's life changed when, in 2004, he received a grant for a residency in Paris, where he has lived ever since. His work, too, has undergone marked changes. Earlier series – bearing titles such as *Siege* (2004-6), *Exit* (2006), *Barrage* (2007) or *Standby* (2008), evoking exile and occupation – are characterized by oscillation between abstraction and figuration and by an expressionistic style in which the physical performance of painting and the materiality of paint work together to convey meaning and even, in part, the narrative content. The feelings accompanying exile – Zurob holds an identity card from Gaza and cannot travel back to Palestine – pain, deferral, incompleteness, loneliness and hopeless waiting, are conveyed through an almost violent brushstroke, contorted bodies and faces and the use of materials such as tar.

Flying Lesson #03, #04 and #07, exhibited in "The Map is Not the Territory," are prints from a painted series of the same name. The images were born of a simple question the artist's son Qoudsi innocently asked his father, not understanding the travel restrictions that have prevented Zurob from going "home" with his son and wife: "Daddy, why don't you come with us to Jerusalem?" Qoudsi is the sole figure in all the paintings, often lost in reverie, playing with toys of transportation. But as Zurob describes, the paintings are layered and the images of Qoudsi are also in a sense self-portraits

> Through the use of oil and acrylic paint, and other media, I try to create a world composed of three worlds: exile where the artist lives (the father), and who appears in the paintings as the sole living human being by the depiction of the son who is portrayed in a relatively small scale in contrast to his surroundings. The second world concerns Qoudsi himself, as he visually appears and shows his feelings through his interactions with his toys. The third world is one of space, where we come from, depicted through walls, and multilayered backgrounds, as symbolic traces of the complex life that prevents Qoudsi and me from meeting. Yet, it is in my construction of a virtual world where a space for such a meeting occurs.[19]

Zurob describes the painted planes of color, most evident in *Flying Lesson #03*, as functioning simultaneously as walls of separation and desired spaces of encounter. Throughout the series, Qoudsi is depicted realistically, but placed in a painterly no-man's-land. Here the child sits in a toy car heading into the painting. Only his face is turned back to look at his father and the viewer. The rest of the canvas is composed of long, woven, predominately red and orange brushstrokes. The painting is divided horizontally in two by a hard, solid grey line running across the canvas at the height of Qoudsi's shoulders, as if the simplified wall motif in other paintings has shrunk to recall the dividing line on a street or highway. The line provides a certain spatiality to the painting, placing Qoudsi closer to his father, and draws attention to the child's look of both trust and apprehension of leaving. The spaces of pure painting are unsettling, desolate, without context, yet they equally offer hope. The brushwork allows the wall-like expanses to dissipate and transform into sites of potentiality holding the seeds of a different life in which father and son can meet at will. Indeed, this red-and-orange interstitial space communicates how ultimately the intangible father-son relationship transcends the physical restrictions of colonial regulations and practices. Using very different means than Halaka's *Portraits of Desire and Denial*, Zurob's *Flying Lessons* also endow both personal narrative and, more significantly, the interpersonal – the space of the encounter – with the capacity of resistance. In the virtual, albeit embodied, world of paint, Zurob and Qoudsi are never apart.

Mary Tuma: Palestine and the Material Memory of Things

Mary Tuma, whose father is Palestinian and mother Irish-American, is an installation artist based in North Carolina.

(continued)

Her *Lingering Presence* displayed in *"The Map is Not the Territory,"* is a small, two-dimensional work, created of handmade paper, sewing patterns, thread and printed maps that reflects her training in textile and fashion design.

Straddling the vocabularies and processes of contemporary craft and conceptual art, Tuma's work probes the materiality of memory and its relationship to the body. Her material is in fact often the stuff of – personal – life, combined with realpolitik. Tuma's art is largely autobiographical. Like Halaka and Zurob, she avoids the pitfalls of self-absorption, but does so differently, by employing, consciously or not, two main strategies.[20] First, her concept of materiality encompasses her own body, suggesting that she considers "the material world … as woven into people's bodies, identities, and actions."[21] This underlying oneness of self (selves), objects and the world moves the work beyond the solipsistic. Second, the aesthetics of impermanence characterizing her work empties it of any hubris. Her installations often appear as part of a continuum rather than as finished, independent art objects, connected only through the inner logic of Tuma's nomadic perspective and the physical act of making. The word "votive" most aptly describes the process, aim, aesthetic and physical instability of her work. While ex-votos certainly form part of visual culture, and some are beautiful artefacts in their own right, their importance comes from the acts of request, gratitude and commemoration that they are thought to symbolize. Tuma's art shares much with ex-votos, premised as it is on the idea of the existence of an ethereal, even spiritual aspect of things, of a relationship between humans and larger cosmic forces and of a strong connection between objects and memory.

In works such as *Wind Collection* (2000) – composed of eleven transparent bottles transformed into containers of the air of Gaza, Bethlehem, Jerusalem, Hebron and seven other cities of historic Palestine – memory is cast as a significant archive and a soft weapon of political resistance in which tangible and intangible are intertwined. Tuma's best known work, *Homes for the Disembodied* (2000)[22] – five 9-feet-long dresses made of 50 yards of continuous black silk on hangers suspended from the ceiling – is also underwritten by a vision of cohabitation or inseparability of matter and spirit (or affect), and the idea of the space within objects as a receptable for the unseen. Both works are implicitly performative.

Lingering Presence, which Tuma made especially for *"The Map is Not the Territory,"* is set on white ground, a collage composed of a grid of fifty-one small squares. Torn bits of road map rest within all but five. These map fragments, placed right side up, upside down or sideways, are transformed into small abstract canvases, pleasing no longer for their accurate directions but for their shapes and colors. Tuma has machine- and hand-stitched various types of lines and designs on a number of them in bright, pinkish red thread, creating a loose network that softens the grid composition, even as it subtley heightens the visual unity of the piece. While some names of highways or places remain legible, including those of several American states, the work is not about a particular destination, but about the act of mapping, its instability, transformations and arbitrariness, thereby echoing the tripartite concept of *"The Map is Not the Territory."* "That these maps are of the U.S. isn't really important," she says. "It could be anywhere."[23]

Mirroring much craft-oriented contemporary art, Tuma works through ideas and political concerns by thinking with her hands: cutting, placing, pasting and sewing. As in other *works, it is the performed intent that links Lingering Presence* to Palestine. For Tuma, the dismantled map serves as a metaphor for the memory of Palestine, historical Palestine, as a physical presence that cannot be destroyed or ever wholly forgotten. This holistic worldview is rooted in all Tuma's work. Her optimism and the vision of memory from which it stems are best expressed in her own words

> The occupier can never really forget us since we will always be present…We are indelibly present, a part of the breeze, the horizon, the stones. We are a part of the fabric of the place, sewn in layers, patched and rewoven… our cells are part of the fruit and the sky. We will always be home, even as we long for home. [24]

Memory forms a necessary part of our everyday lives and is a cornerstone of our personal narratives, the stories we tell ourselves and others about ourselves. It holds a critical place in modern and contemporary Palestinian art whether produced by artists living in the West Bank, Gaza or Israel or those living in the diaspora. The examination of the role

(continued)

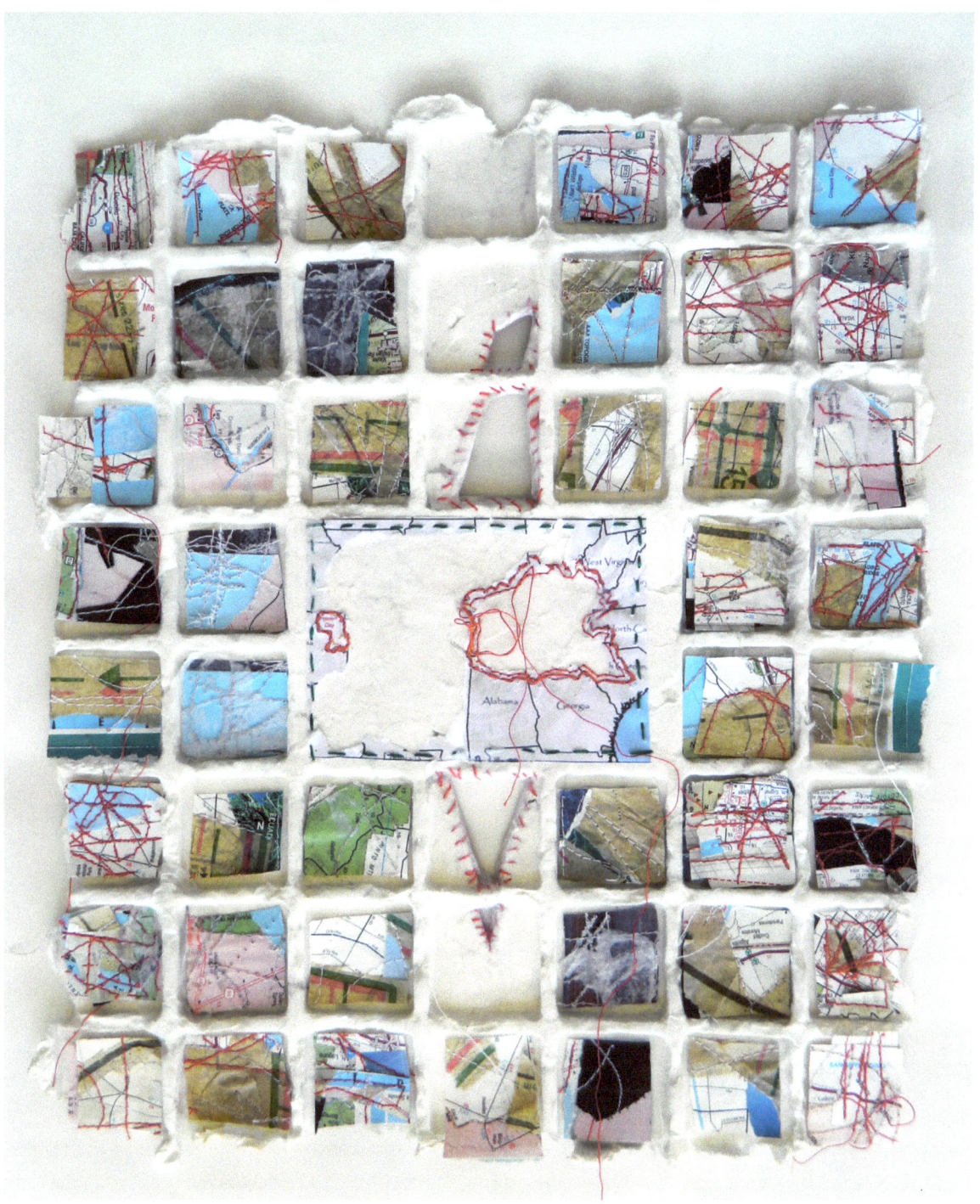

Lingering Presence, Mary Tuma

Even if we are driven all the way to the moon, our spirits will continue to fill the lands that were once our homes. The occupier can never really forget us since we will always be present. The land remembers us. The land is our witness and our record-keeper. We are indelibly present, a part of the breeze, the horizon, the stones. We are a part of the fabric of the place, sewn in layers, patched and rewoven … our cells are part of the fruit and sky. We will always be home, even as we long for home.

—Mary Tuma

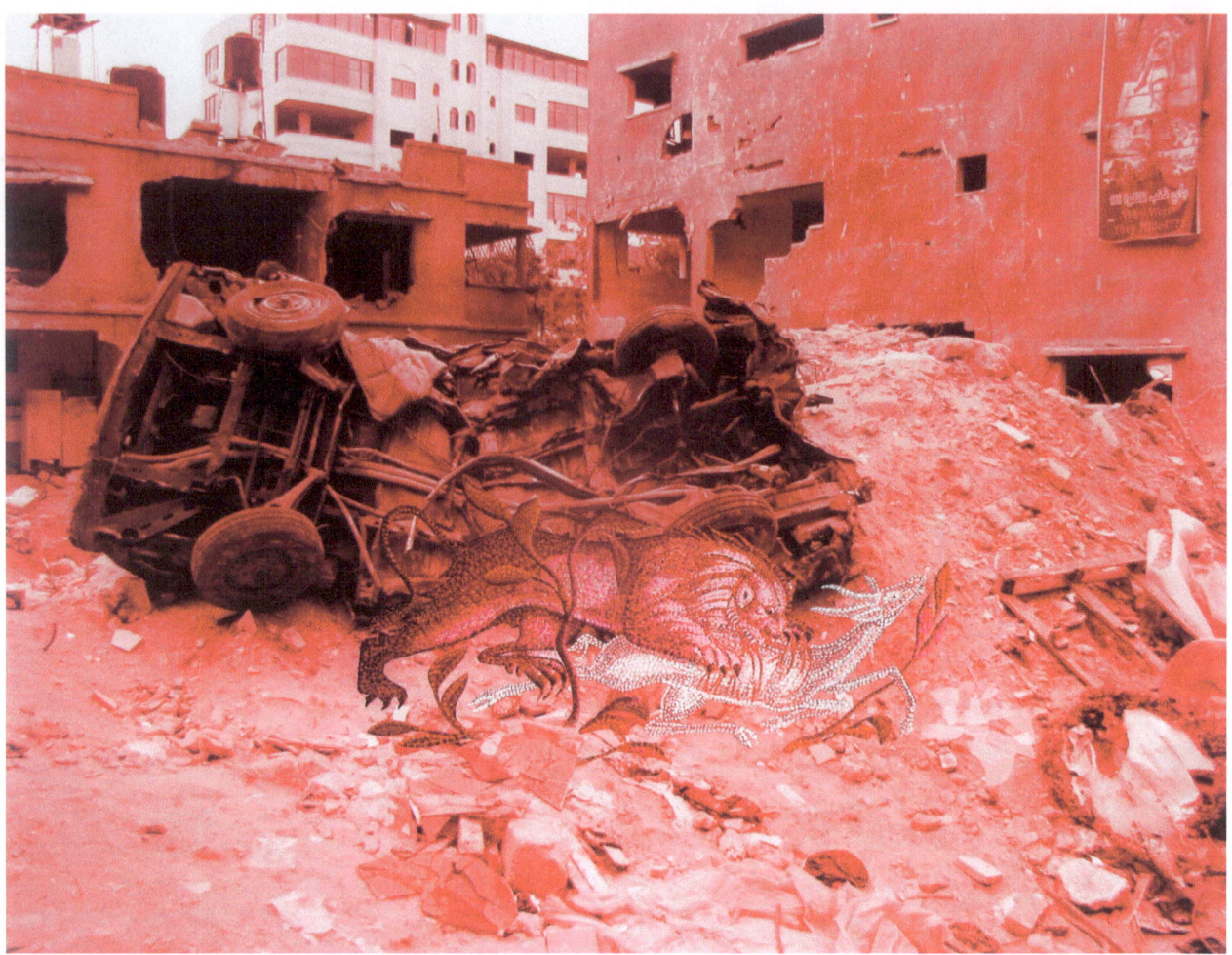

Rend, Susanne Slavick

Israeli "Pillar of Defense" military offensive in Gaza on November 12, 2012 that killed 72 people including four children in the Al Dalu home on Nasser Street; animal motif derived from a Tree of Life mosaic (8th c. Umayyad period) that depicts the mythical tree with two deer grazing peacefully on one side and a third deer attacked by a lion on the other, in the *diwan* of the bath complex at Khirbet El-Mafjar/Hisham's Palace in Jericho, West Bank (wrecked car in Gaza).

—Susanne Slavick

of memory in the work of artists exhibiting in *"The Map is Not the Territory"* is here limited to three Palestinian artists solely for reasons of length. Ideally, this essay would have equally considered the relationship between memory and art in the work of the other exhibiting Palestinian artists – Elena Farsakh, Manal Deeb, Najat el-Taji el-Khairy, Najib Joe Hakim, Rajie Cook, Rawan Arar, Vivien Sansour and 6+: a women's collective – as well as the non-Palestinian artists who address the question of Palestine, like Michael Keating, Andrew Ellis Johnson, Sherry Wiggins and Suzanne Slavick.[25]

Palestinian lineage consitutes the core of Halaka's, Zurob's and Tuma's identities and, in each case, the Nakba and its ensuing consequences directly inform their work whether it is visually evident or not.

Halaka's *Portraits of Desire and Denial* bridges personal and collective memory. It is an archival project concerned with recording and documenting – witnessing – critical elements in the oral and visual testimonies of Palestinian elders who still remember the catastrophe of 1948. Zurob's case is more

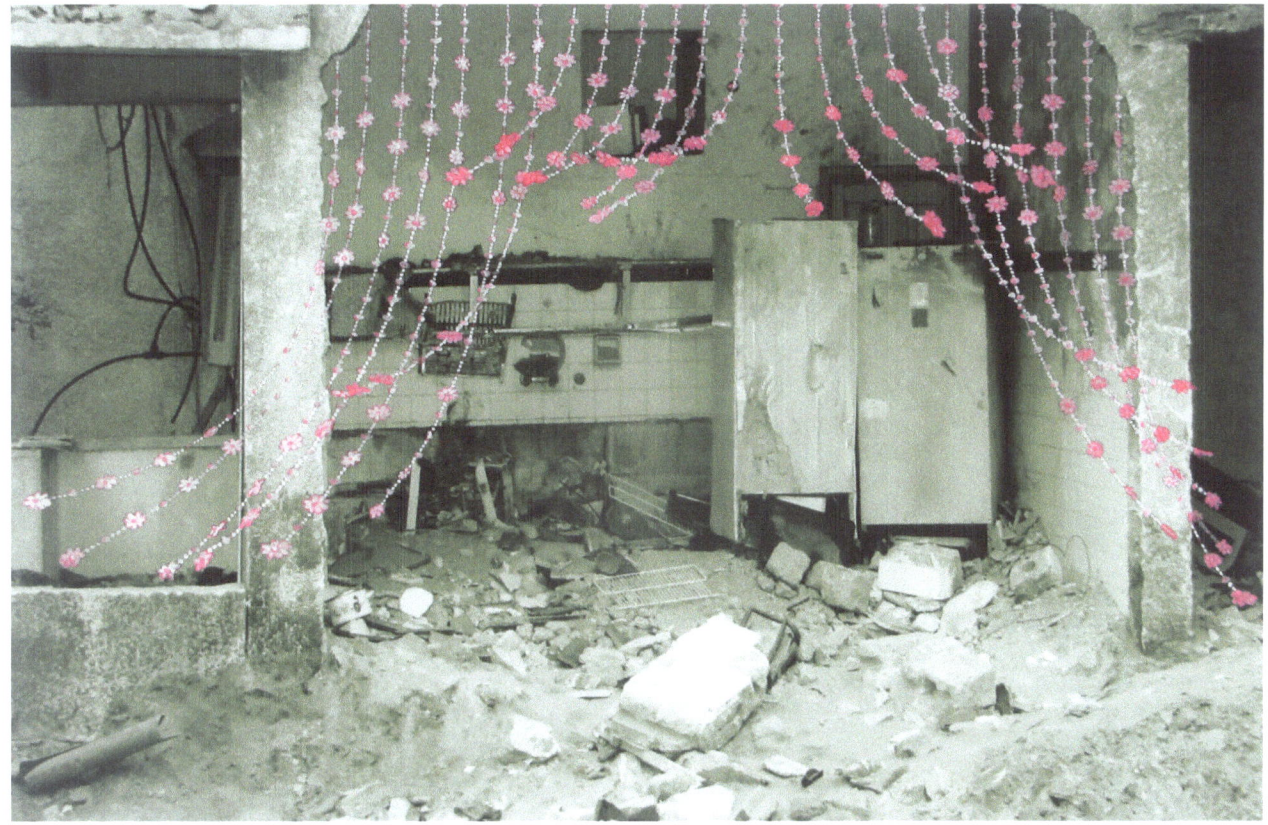

Repercussion, Susanne Slavick

Israeli "Pillar of Defense" military offensive in Gaza on November 12, 2012 that killed 72 people including Mzanar Abdallah, 20, and Amina Mznar, 80, an elderly woman in a wheelchair who was in the kitchen at the time of the bombing. Her wheelchair was found in the rubble (beaded curtains).

—Susanne Slavick

complex. As the sole artist here to have experienced Israeli aggression firsthand, his images consider how that aggression impacts and hinders his private life today. Nevertheless, his paintings confirm that Israeli tanks and bombs have not fully succeeded in effecting cultural genocide and amnesia. In Tuma's work, Palestine takes on a performative and poetic form. Her memory of it cannot be undone or hindered by war, theft, embargos, destruction, lies and the building of separation walls. Like Zurob and Halaka, Tuma addresses collective memory subjectively.

The most significant question is whether art and photography can deconstruct and recast mainstream North American Western perceptions of Palestine and Palestinians. Culture, as Immanuel Wallerstein and so many others have argued, is a profoundly ideological terrain explaining why power holders seek its control.[26] Alternative cultural and historical narratives challenging the status quo thus meet opposition, ridicule or censure. But power holders can never wield absolute power. The Palestinian perspective is increasingly finding its way into the cultural arena, providing opportunity for more people to become aware of the historical facts.[27] Although art and art exhibits may seem impotent in light of the many horrors of the Occupation, in fact, art can act as an agent for change. It offers, as John Berger suggests, hope, a vital element of human psychological and emotional health. It is hope that keeps Halaka, Zurob and Tuma making and exhibiting art despite the worsening conditions of life in the Palestinian Territories. They persist, resolute, in imaging Palestine – their Palestine – in order to resist a world, as Berger reminds us,[28] "whose events do not confirm our Being" and eventually help change the tide of history, or, at the very least, rebalance the archive.

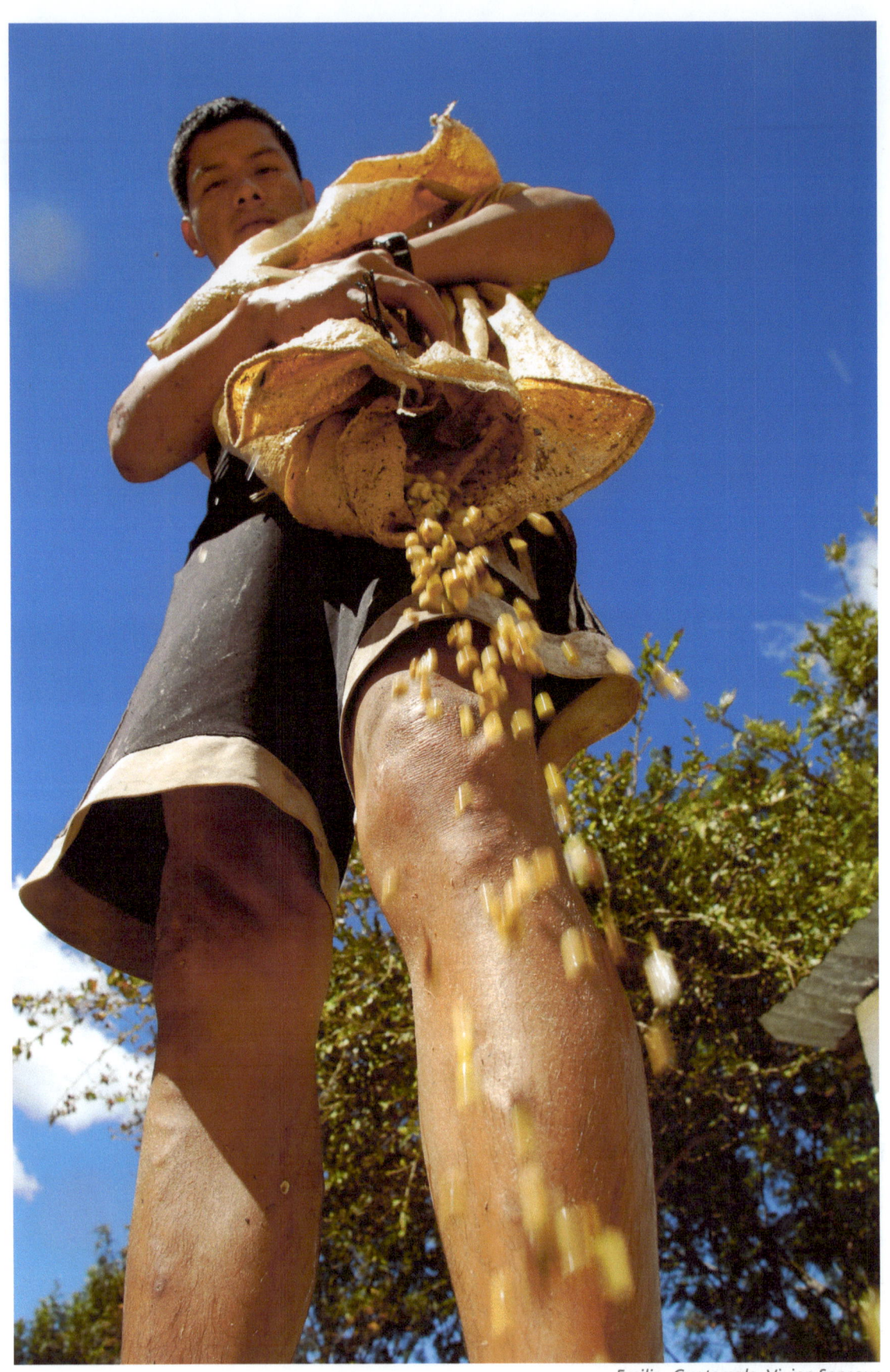

Emilio, Guatemala, Vivien Sansour

CHAPTER 3

Art and Activism
Defining Homeland

Phoebe Farris

Much of the non-Indian public is informed about the vast array of American Indian arts and crafts, especially those that fall within traditional, tribal heritages. However, few viewers are aware of our contributions as professors, museum curators and writers and the impact that this intellectual heritage has had on our development as visual artists/activists. Indeed, a feature of *"The Map Is Not the Territory": Parallel Paths-Palestinians, Native Americans, Irish*[1] is that it highlights the interconnections of being both a visual artist and an activist.

The artists participating in *"The Map is Not the Territory"* have diverse perspectives about the connections between visual art and social justice activism. Focusing on 21st-century art practices, our interests include the use of video and other new technologies to bridge crucial differences and similarities across cultures: resistance, the struggle for sovereignty and the right to perform traditional cultural practices, the evolution of indigenous art, the exploration of the concept of globalism and its effects on indigenous peoples and evolving Native identity in the self-styled pre-modern, modern, post-modern, post-colonial and post-racial worlds.

Contemporary art created by Native Americans, like that of many artists, reaches into the past for some of its influences, is very much a product of its times and is also visionary, reaching toward the future. Art is usually regarded by its Native American creators as an essential element of life, not a separate aesthetic expression. Five hundred years after the arrival of explorers and conquerors to the Americas, the cultural influences affecting Native American art continue to be varied and complex. Many aesthetic changes have taken place in the 20th and 21st centuries, as Native peoples began participating more fully in the dominant culture of globalism and incorporating artistic traditions from Africa, Asia and Europe into their own indigenous practices. Yet, as artist Jaune Quick-to-See Smith noted, "When Native Americans

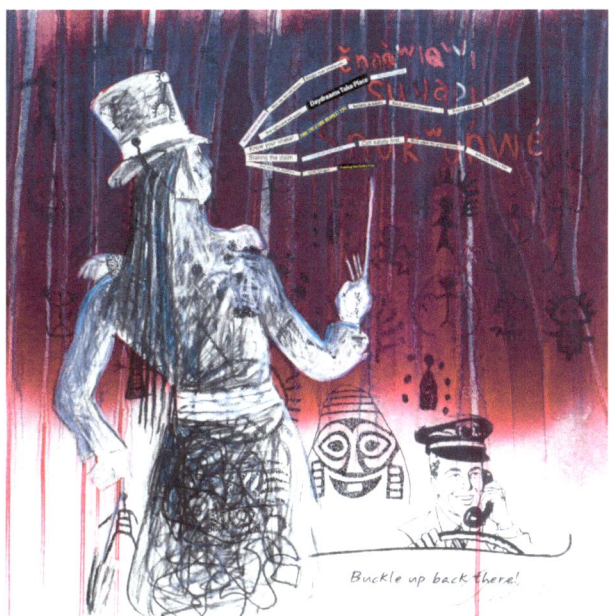

Stealing a Ride on the White Man's Bus, Neal Ambrose-Smith

I found this phrase in my Salish language dictionary and it is written in Salish in the background of this print. As Native Americans, we must not be reticent to get on the bus of progress and participate in society. Here I feature a Catlin figure of an Indian man dressed in 19th-century clothing pretending to be a modern man, but of course clothing doesn't make someone modern. We need education to become working members of society. I encourage my Native American students to participate in change and be more proactive.

—Neal Ambrose-Smith

refer to Indian art, it is automatically assumed to be 'traditional' by white critics, even when it transcends tradition and is mixed with Euro-American style."[2] Any insistence that Indian art remain "traditional" as a way of preserving culture is a form of cultural discrimination. Cultures are dynamic, not static.

Contemporary Native American artists, like those in *"The Map is Not the Territory,"* explore and often blend pre-contact art traditions, with styles developed during early colonialism and reservation confinement, so-called "traditional" painting taught in the early to mid-1900s primarily by white

(continued)

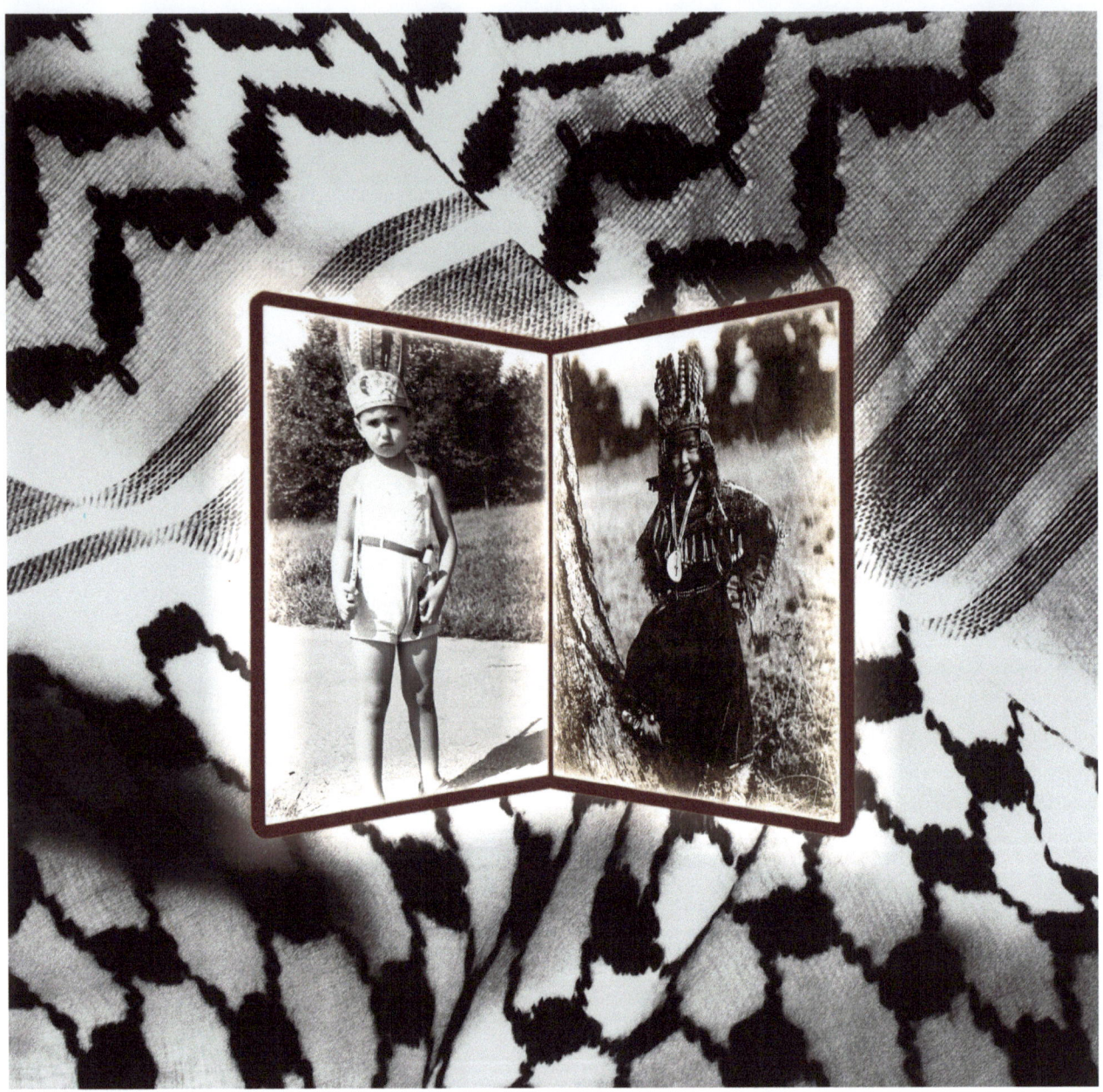

Fraternal Bonds, Najib Joe Hakim

instructors in New Mexico and Oklahoma that encouraged a flat-shaded treatment of historic Native imagery, as well as newer, often experimental art concepts. Their art frequently functions as social criticism by using content that expresses alienation from the dominant Western culture. Take for example, Neal Ambrose-Smith's visual cues in his digital print monotype, *Stealing a Ride on the White Man's Bus,* which parodies the well-known figure of an Indian man dressed in a 19th-century top hat and tails, from George Caitlin's painting, *Pigeon's Egg Head (The Light) Going to and Returning from Washington, 1837–39.* In Ambrose-Smith's monotype, the Indian faces the familiar character of a uniformed bus driver from a mid-20th-century advertisement advising us to "buckle up for safety." Whether Native American work is abstract or leans toward the representational, whether straightforward or subtle, it recurrently has a social context.

The 1960s are considered a turning point when many Native American artists broke away from flat-shaded painting styles to start developing their own contemporary art practices, often influenced by curricula offered by the Institute of American Indian Arts, founded in 1962 in Santa Fe, New Mexico. The IAIA continues to nurture many Native American artists and teachers, including one the artists in this exhibit, Norman Akers, a professor at the University of Kansas. In the 1970s, Native American art outside the southwestern region of the United States started receiving more recognition, and the work began to "graduate:" from ethnographic museums – where indigenous arts were inevitably relegated – into mainstream art institutions. The decade is also noted for increased representation by Indian women, such as Quick-to-See Smith.

For artists in the U.S. and abroad, public discourse in the 1980s centered on themes of post-modernism, post-structuralism, feminism, multiculturalism and other "isms," which impacted studio production. Many Native American artists, who were active during that period, were instead expressing concerns about the intersections of art, race/ethnicity, gender and politics in their work – long before these issues became trendy and commodified by the art market. In 1992, a common theme uniting Native American artists was the Quincentenary of the alleged "discovery" of the Americas by Christopher Columbus, which inspired Native visual and written protests against the celebration of invasion and occupation.

Artists who focus on Native American issues in "*The Map is Not the Territory*" are represented under the themes "Territory/Map," "Occupation/Wall," "Conflict/Resistance," "Land/Food," "Overlay/Identity," "Words/Persistence" and "Home/Diaspora." Norman Akers (Osage), Neal Ambrose-Smith (Salish), Scott Benesiinaabandan (Anishinabe), Wahsontiio Cross (Mohawk), Michael Elizondo, Jr. (Southern Cheyenne/Chumash), Melanie Yazzie (Navajo), Nadema Agard (Cherokee/Lakota/Powhatan), Jaune Quick-to-See Smith (Salish/Kootenai), Malaquias Montoya (Chicano) and I (Powhatan-Renape/Pamunkey) have indigenous United States, Canadian, and Mexican heritages.[3]

Of the non-Native artists in the exhibition, Palestinian photographer Vivien Sansour displays sensitive imagery of indigenous people in Chiapas, Mexico, and the Altiplanos of Guatemala. Filmmaker and psychiatrist Donna Schindler's video, *Hozhonohahaslii: Stories of Healing the Soul Wound*, shares aspects of the work she and Native American psychologist Dr. Eduardo Duran have done with the Navajo Nation and other indigenous groups regarding the historic trauma suffered by victims of occupation and dislocation.[4] Najib Joe Hakim's *Passports to Exile* describes shared oppression and resistance, while his *Fraternal Bonds* seems to parody the popular game of "cowboys and Indians," juxtaposing a picture of his brother at play with an image by Edward S. Curtis of a Flathead boy. Other artists in "*The Map Is Not the Territory*" incorporate Native American, Palestinian and Irish imagery in their work as a sign of solidarity regardless of their own racial/ethnic identity.

In *Seeing Each Other*, Melanie Yazzie, a Diné printmaker, chose to depict herself alongside a Lebanese friend – artist May Hariri Aboutaam – to honor Middle Eastern and Native American homelands and culture. Each woman selected objects that are important to them and Yazzie combined those images, creating dual portraits facing each other and surrounded by their respective cultural artifacts. Each portrait is enclosed in a floating rectangle with similar shades of red, pale green and brown tones. The women look more alike than not, emphasizing their "Overlay/Identity." A common sepia-toned background made with plant vegetation unites the two portraits, symbolizing a shared concern for the land. Indeed, in their work as printmakers, Both Yazzie and Ambrose-Smith echo Native American apprehensions about the destruction of the Earth (and the health of the artists) by avoiding the use of toxic inks.

Flags of Our Fathers, *Solidarity Flag Derry*, *A Small Note from the North of Ireland* and *Anishinabe Proclamation* reference Scott Benesiinaabandan's artist residencies and international collaborations in Canada, the United Kingdom and Ireland. Based in Canada, this Anishinabe mixed-media artist creates works that focus on global indigenous struggles. His flag photos include those that are not recognized by nation states: flags hung at half mast, flags being burned and, notably in *God Save the Queen*, unofficial flags being draped over government monuments by a protester, here blanketing a statue of Queen Victoria who presided over the vast British Empire that incorporated Canada and Ireland. It was thanks to colonialist Britain that Palestinians ultimately lost their land to Israel, with the Balfour Declaration of 1917.

(continued)

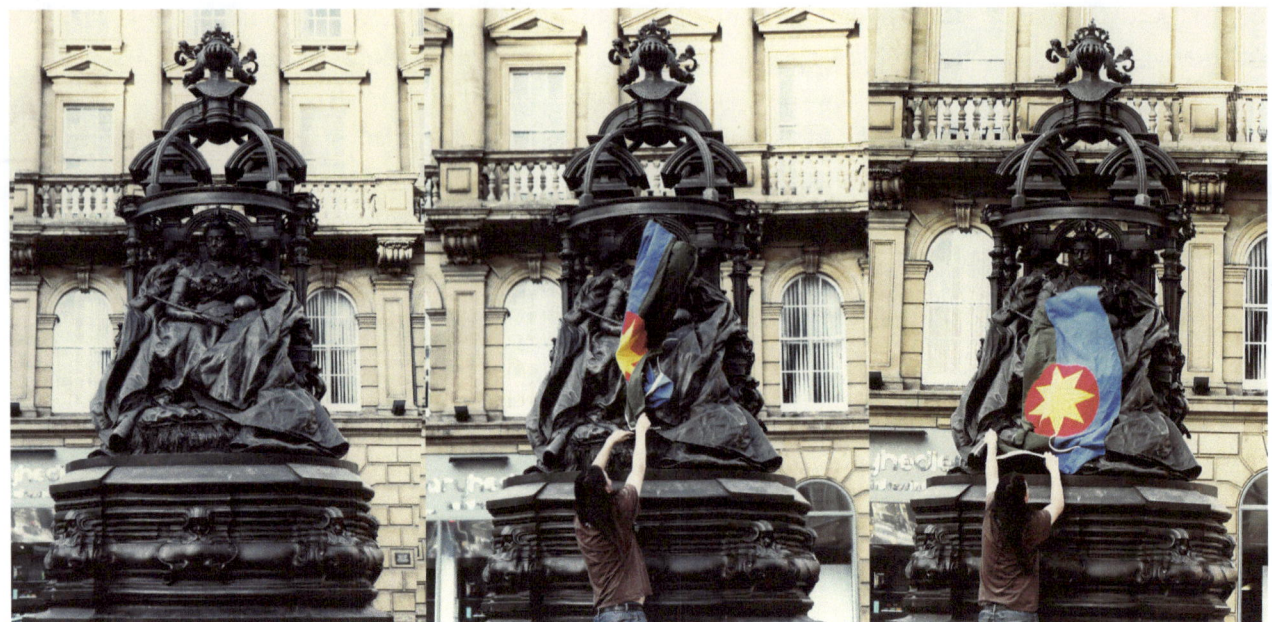

God Save the Queen, Scott Benesiinaabandan

Malaquias Montoya's ink-jet print titled *Undocumented* is a harsh reminder of the walls and fences created by nation states – in this context, the U.S. and Israel – to block indigenous peoples from entering lands that they historically inhabited. A clothed figure is trapped on a barbed wire fence with blood oozing from the body and the word "undocumented" splashed across it in red ink. Montoya is of Chicano (Mexican American) heritage,[5] so viewers may assume that his figure is trying to enter the U.S. from Mexico to join the ranks of people who are classified as illegal "aliens." Yet it could represent *mestizo* migrants trying to re-enter land that once belonged to their ancestors before European occupation, lands now called Mexico, New Mexico, Arizona, Texas and California. And as Montoya points out, his is an art of protest on behalf of the oppressed worldwide. He creates images of the disenfranchised "from Angola, to Central America, from Palestine to the barrio."[6]

Like Montoya's work, Norman Akers's *Crowded* is displayed under the exhibition theme "Occupation/Wall," and is based on his reflections of current events about immigration laws, national borders and boundaries. *Crowded* is concerned with defining and/or finding an indigenous space within the swarming U.S. landscape. An American Indian man, saturated in red, wearing Plains clothing and headdress, beats on a drum while gazing upward at black and gray birds flying across the digital print's surface, whose background is a partial map of North and South America. Meanwhile, the faces of U.S. presidents Abraham Lincoln and George Washington, as well as other white male historical faces found on U.S. currency, float across the landscape encased in space craft, a way of indicating that they, of course, are the real aliens. The lone Indian is increasingly pressed and pushed to the edge of the space.

Nadema Agard notes that the "*Map is Not the Territory*" is "unique" and "binding" of the three cultures. Her watercolor/pastel/mixed media, *Tatanka Ska Oyate/White Buffalo Nation* is dedicated to White Buffalo Calf Maiden who brought the Sacred Pipe to the Lakota Nation. The piece takes the form of a traditional rawhide *parfleche* bag, made of paper, which opens and is tied with a ribbon.[7] The work, Agard says, is about a "relational concept of nationhood that is not defined by maps but is the territory of the heart, spirit, mind, and body of the Oyate or The People."[8] Agard's parfleche is decorated with seven white buffalo (*tatanka*), moving through a reddish landscape located above a gold-and-white buffalo skull, another example of how the traditional and contemporary are incorporated.

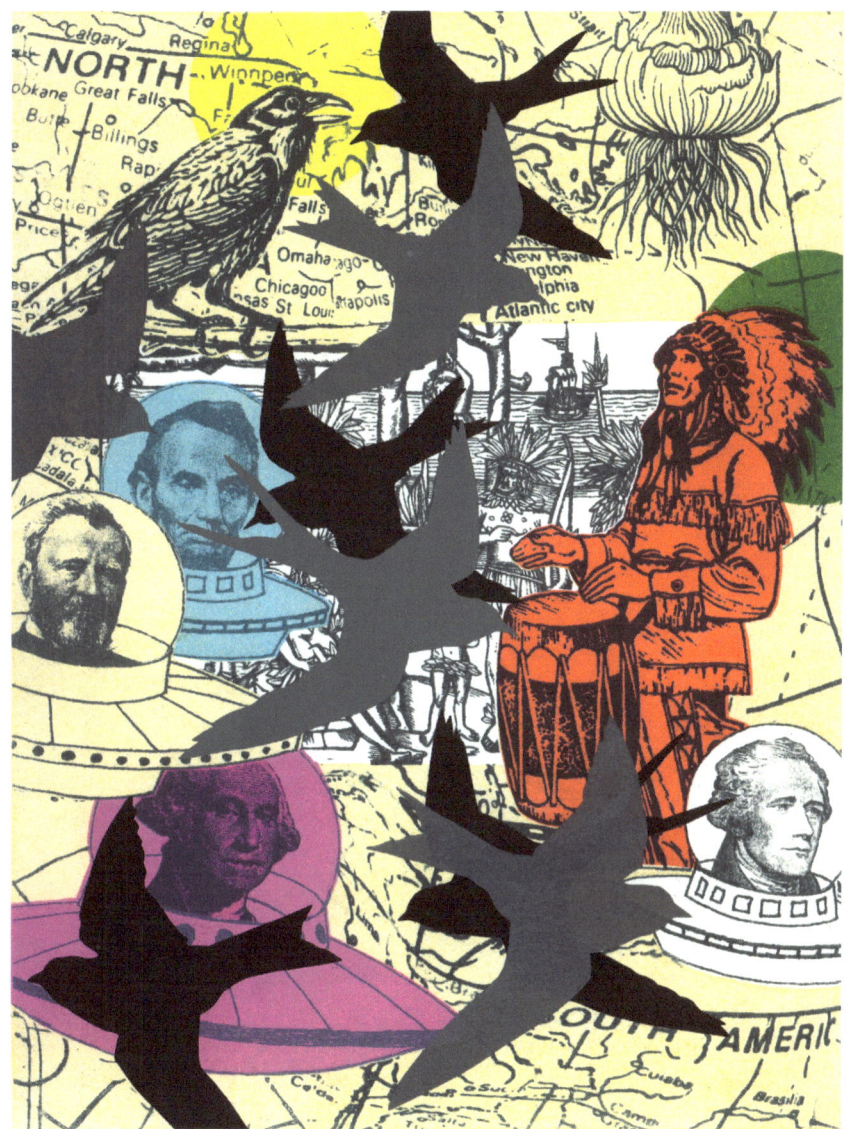

Crowded, Norman Akers

Current issues in the news about immigration laws and talk in public media about strengthening national borders is leading my work into a new direction. Questions about who is the "other" and terms such as indigenous, immigrant and illegal alien have entered my vocabulary. *Crowded* addresses the continuous movement of peoples across the Americas, and the need to define an indigenous place within this ever-changing landscape.

—Norman Akers

Jaune Quick-to-See Smith's pigment print, *House and Home*, is colored primarily in blue hues that wash across the surface in broad brush strokes. The image, displayed under the exhibition theme "Home/Diaspora," is of a tipi with – surprisingly – a European-style chair imposed on the center, but whether it is inside or outside of the tipi is a mystery. *House and Home*'s background includes several placemats with formal settings of silverware and dinner plates. In her artist statement, Smith explains that some Native Americans still live in portable tipis, especially in the summer. We learn that members of her Confederated Salish and Kootenai Nation of Montana occupy tipis while participating in Medicine Lodge ceremonies. The strength and durability of tipi architecture enables inhabitants to be comfortable in thunderstorms and in hot summer heat. In the 19th and early 20th centuries, as white settlers pushed farther and farther west into Indian lands, tribes were forced onto reservations and into cabins and houses. But many maintained their tipis nearby and used them for, among other things spiritual purposes. The juxtaposition in *House and Home* of formal place settings and the erect hardback chair with an Indian dwelling speaks to the continuity of traditional Native American homes and their adaptations in the 21st century.

My digital photo, *Mohegan Wigwam* – also displayed under the "Home/Diaspora" theme – gives homage to a type of

(continued)

architecture still prevalent among the Woodlands people from New England all the way down to the southern states and in mid-western areas that are now Indiana and Wisconsin. It is photographed from the interior and looks up at the small opening that allows for light and air enveloped by the bark and willow.

Like *Stealing a Ride on the White Man's Bus*, Ambrose-Smith's digital print monotypes, *Weight of the Discussion*, *Baby Bird Brain* and *Going Where No Man Has Gone Before*, use humor to portray Coyote stories about ethical behavior, his Salish tribe's millennia-old petroglyphs, Indian participation in modernity and the artist's desire to see Native American characters in science-fiction.[9]

Michael Elizondo Jr.'s acrylic paintings deal with similarities between his Southern Cheyenne and Chumash backgrounds and the plight of Palestinians, each at one time and another under colonial siege. For Palestinians, the colonial and military siege is ongoing. For the Southern Cheyenne, the centuries-long struggle against occupation has reduced their numbers to a mere 12,130. Elizondo's *That Old Tune of "GARRYOWEN"* references the marching song of the U.S. 7th Cavalry, famously the regiment of George Armstrong Custer, and originally an Irish tune, while *The Second Intifada* is named for the September 2000 Palestinian uprising against Israeli occupation. Both have flame-colored yellow/red/orange sunsets at approximately mid-level with flat black surfaces at the bottom. *Intifada* is a horizontal landscape dominated by a curled barbed-wire fence, another classic barrier to the reclamation of indigenous lands and an instrument of ground wars. *That Old Tune* is vertical with a large black helicopter in the center flanked by two smaller ones, reminiscent of modern confrontations from the 1973 Occupation at Wounded Knee to continuous assaults on Gaza to the Troubles in Northern Ireland, which began in the late 1960s. The landscapes in both paintings are decimated, with no signs of human, animal or plant life.

Vivien Sansour's digital photographs, *Emilio*, *Candles for Water*, *Don Alonso Lopez*, and *Abu Nidal* express profound compassion for the lives of farmers, displaced and struggling on the small plots of land left to them, in the highlands of Chiapas, Mexico, the Altiplanos of Guatemala and Palestine.

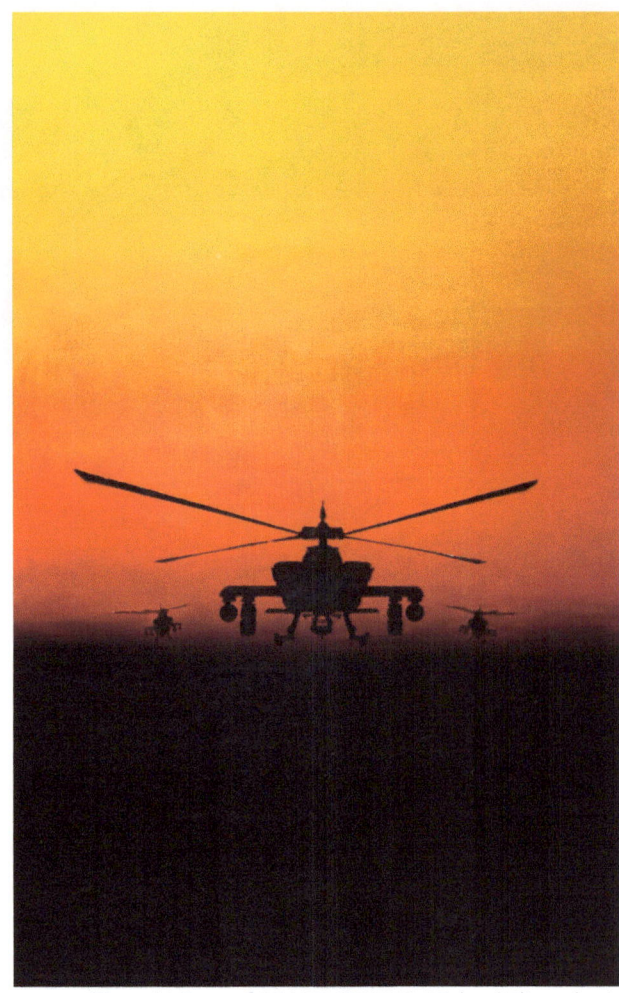

That old Tune of "GARRYOWEN", Michael Elizondo, Jr

Don Alonso Lopez beams as he shows us a large papaya grown without pesticides while other villagers stand in the fields behind him. Where once clean Native lands have been polluted by the poisonous chemicals used in agribusiness, Don Alonso's organic farming practices are empowering. *Candles for Water* is foregrounded by lighted candles placed in reddish clay near the bare feet of women and children, whose clothing, legs and feet are the same color contrasted against a lush green background. As natural resources are stolen, water among them, this age-old reverence seems more urgent than ever. *Abu Nidal* profiles a solitary male figure, a dark silhouetted shape, standing in a doorway open to the light. The rest of the photo is engulfed in rectangular darkness. Abu Nidal is passing through a dark tunnel built by the Israeli army to enable him to reach his family's graves and tombstones. His land and orchard were taken from

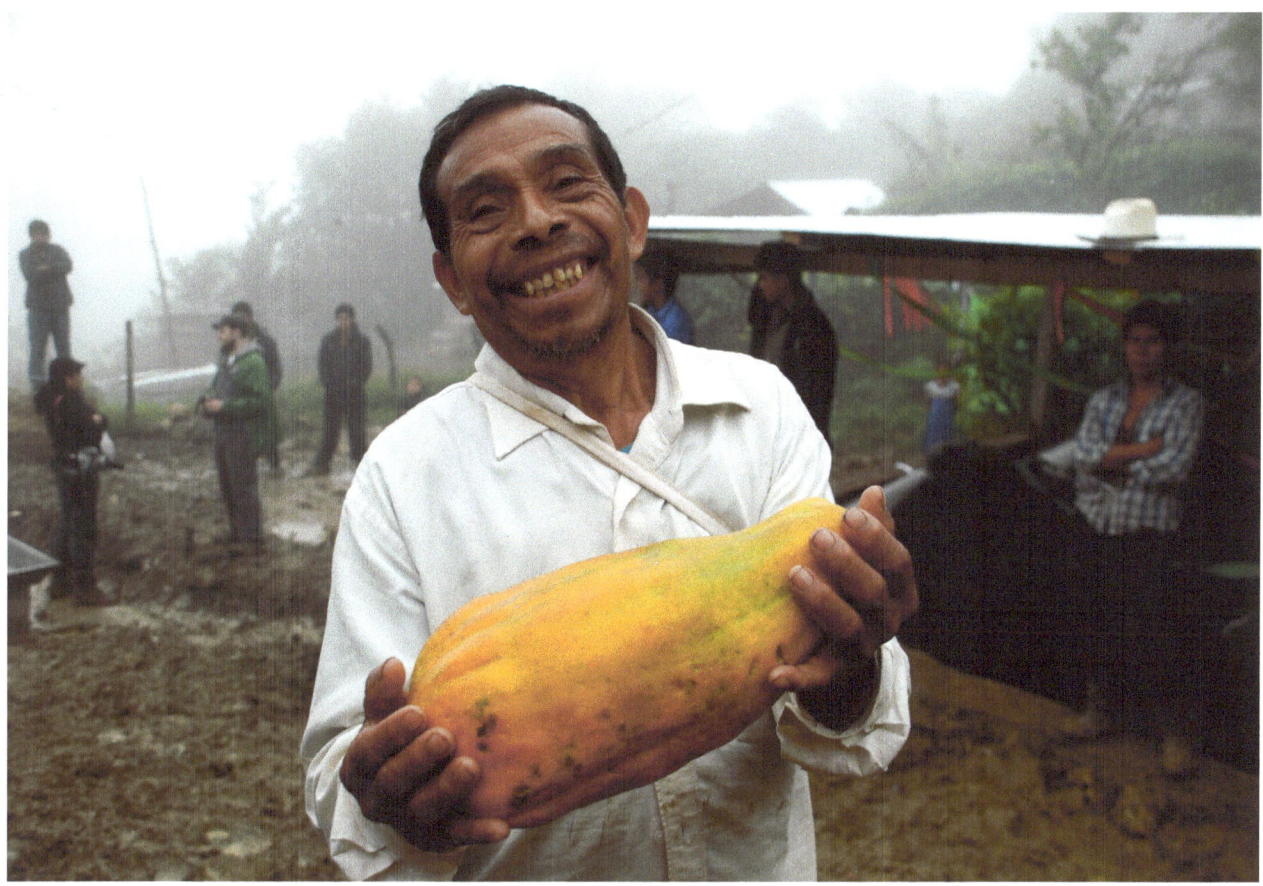

Don Alonso Lopez, Vivien Sansour

My work with farmers in Palestine allowed me to develop a better understanding of the deep connectedness of the struggle of farmers all over the world. Whether it is political oppression or gigantic corporations represented by agribusiness, indigenous communities are being forced to abandon their mother tongues and to forget their ancient ways of food production in order to become consumers rather than independent producers. Parallel to this grim reality is perseverance and beauty. Don Alonzo, a village elder, was photographed during a celebration by the people of Esquipulas to thank those who helped them build a water cistern. "I am proud to offer you a clean papaya," he said. "Like our grandfathers and mothers we respect Mother Earth. We do not use chemicals. Please accept this humble gift as a sign of our gratitude for helping us have water in our community."

—Vivien Sansour

him by Israeli settlers. He sued at least to keep his family cemetery, but an underground passage to access it is all that was granted, yet another incidence of forced separation from territory and family.

Wahsontiio Cross, a member of the Kanien' Keha':Ka (Mohawk) Nation in Quebec, exhibits a hand-stitched, hardcover book titled *Uncharted Territory,* in which she combines maps of the United States and Canada with stories that tell the Mohawk version of history with the arrival of 16th- and 17th-century European explorers. Her maps and stories document the establishment of reservations, the Canadian Indian Act of 1876[10] – still in force – of corn fields, the Turtle and Bear clans and the loss of women's power that is so integral in matrilineal societies.

Native American artists have survived colonialism, servitude, racial discrimination and rapid technological changes. Native artists/activists continually develop and revise the multiple meanings of our art and our heritages to suit our

(continued)

own concepts of American Indian/Native American/First Nations/Indigenous peoples. We undertake the evolution of these cultural concepts with the support and guidance of our elders, spiritual advisors, tribal leaders and community members. We realize the necessity of our art to be responsive to today's life circumstances. The Native American, Palestinian and Irish artists participating in "*The Map is Not the Territory,*" women and men from different tribal, racial and ethnic backgrounds, came together to honor their respective original homelands despite current occupations, to give voice to those who are silenced, to acknowledge their people's continuing existence and perseverance, despite centuries of physical and cultural genocide, and to celebrate their commonalities and diversities.

In the words of Melanie Yazzie, "It is through making art we are making a connection to people and each other. Many … fail to see the power art has to touch people in a way that words cannot. By sharing my work, I have many times gotten through to someone who is not an artist or who has a closed way of seeing, and the discovery is great. We are doing this type of hard work with '*The Map is Not the Territory.*'"[11]

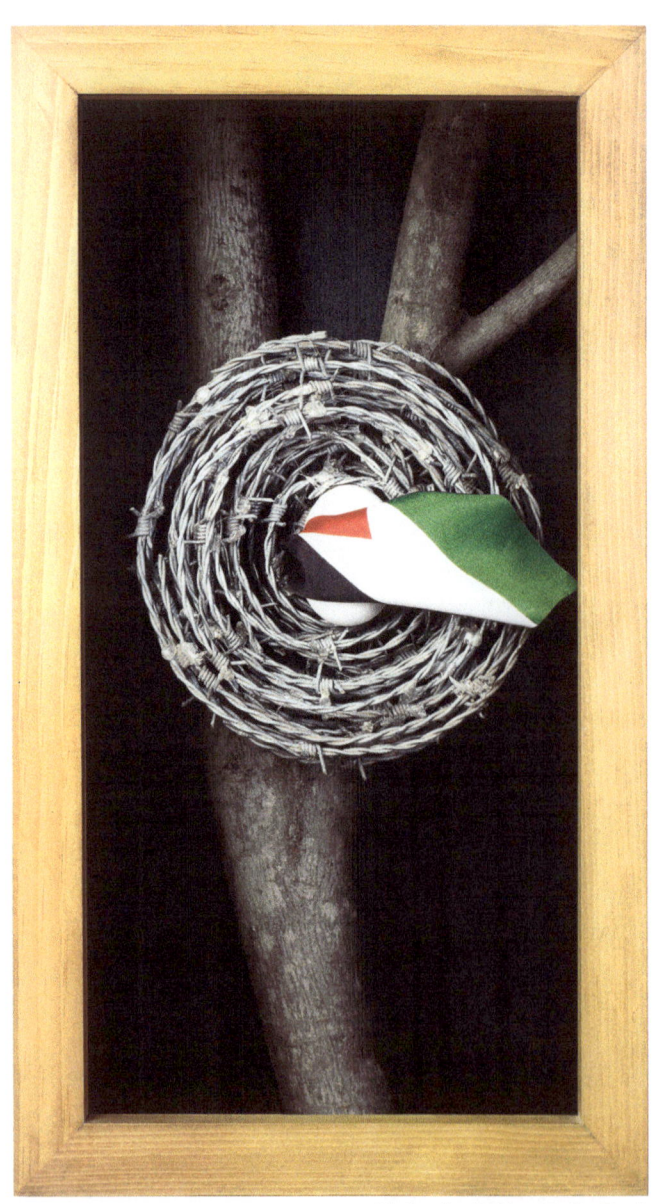

Birth of a Nation, Rajie Cook

During the late 19th century, British colonialists began meddling in every aspect of Palestinian life destroying local production and frustrating Palestinian aspirations to nationhood. By 1920, Palestine had become one of their colonies. Believing there was oil in the Negev, they encouraged and armed Jewish immigrants to be their agents. In 1948, a few years after brutally suppressing the 1936-39 Palestinian revolt, they handed the government over to the Jewish minority and thus the British colony of Palestine became Israel. A brief war ensued between the poorly armed Palestinians and the militarized Israelis, who executed a massive ethnic cleansing campaign. Palestinians' aspirations are alive, handed down through the generations.

—Rajie Cook

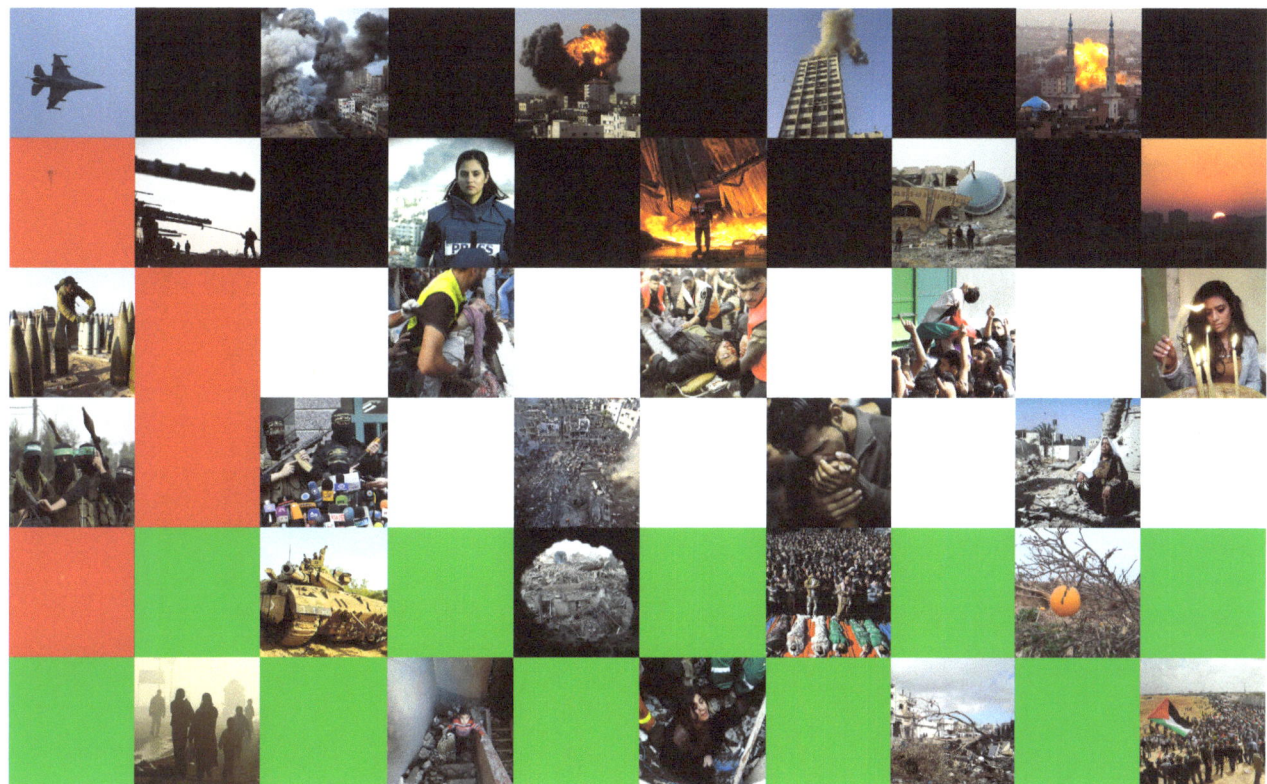

Battles, Deeds, Fields, and Swords, Sherry Wiggins

These Google Images taken during the Israeli wars on Gaza in 2009 and 2012 are inserted within the framework of the colors and design of the Palestinian flag. They portray the misery and destruction Palestinians in Gaza have endured while the whole world watches. The title *Battles, Deeds, Fields and Swords* are words taken from the poem by the 14th-century Arab poet Safi al-Din al-Hili that some say is the inspiration for the colors of the Palestinian flag:

> *Ask the high rising spears, of our aspirations*
> *Bring witness the swords, did we lose hope*
> *We are a band, honor halts our souls*
> *Of beginning with harm, those who won't harm us*
> *White are our deeds, black are our battles*
> *Green are our fields, red are our swords.*

—Sherry Wiggins

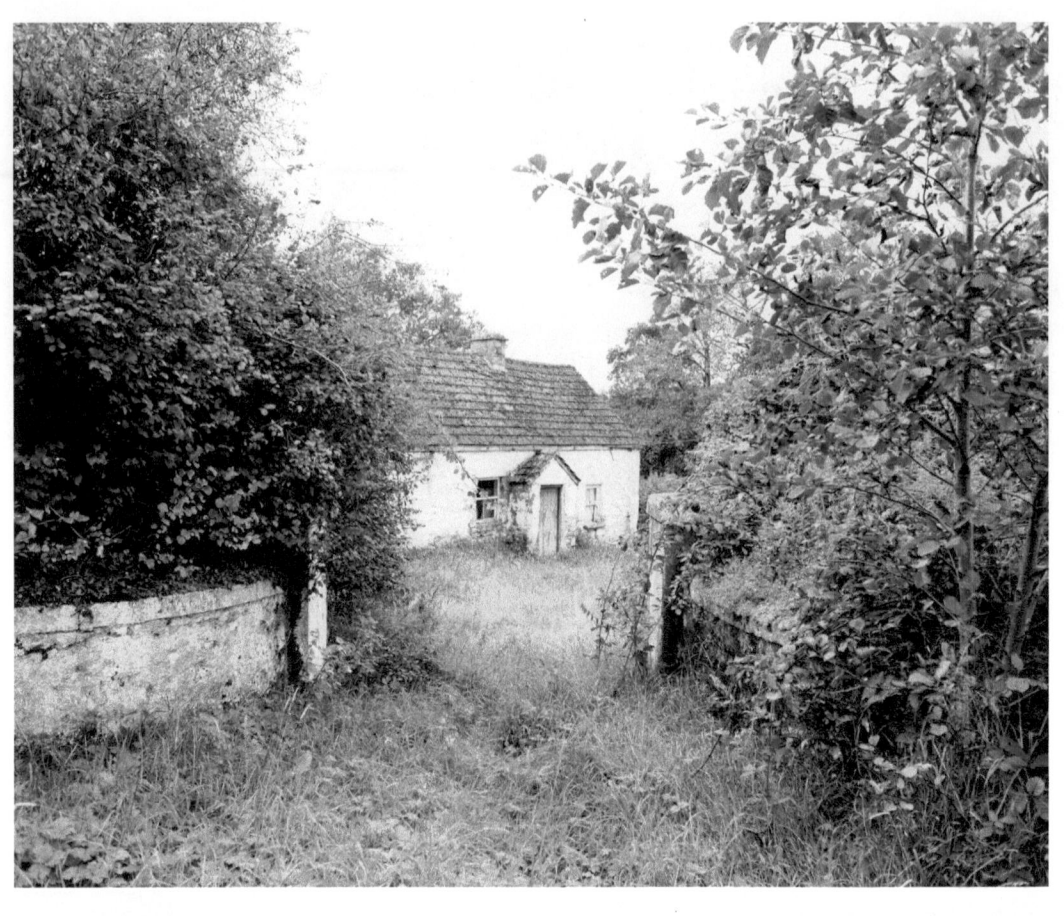

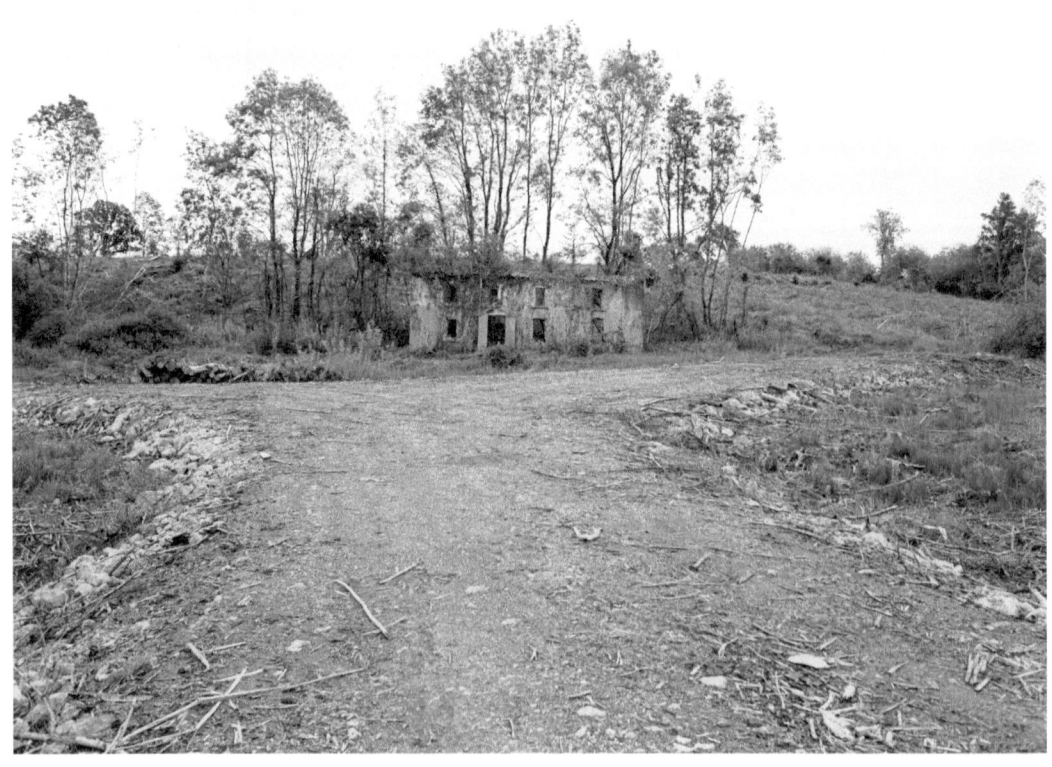

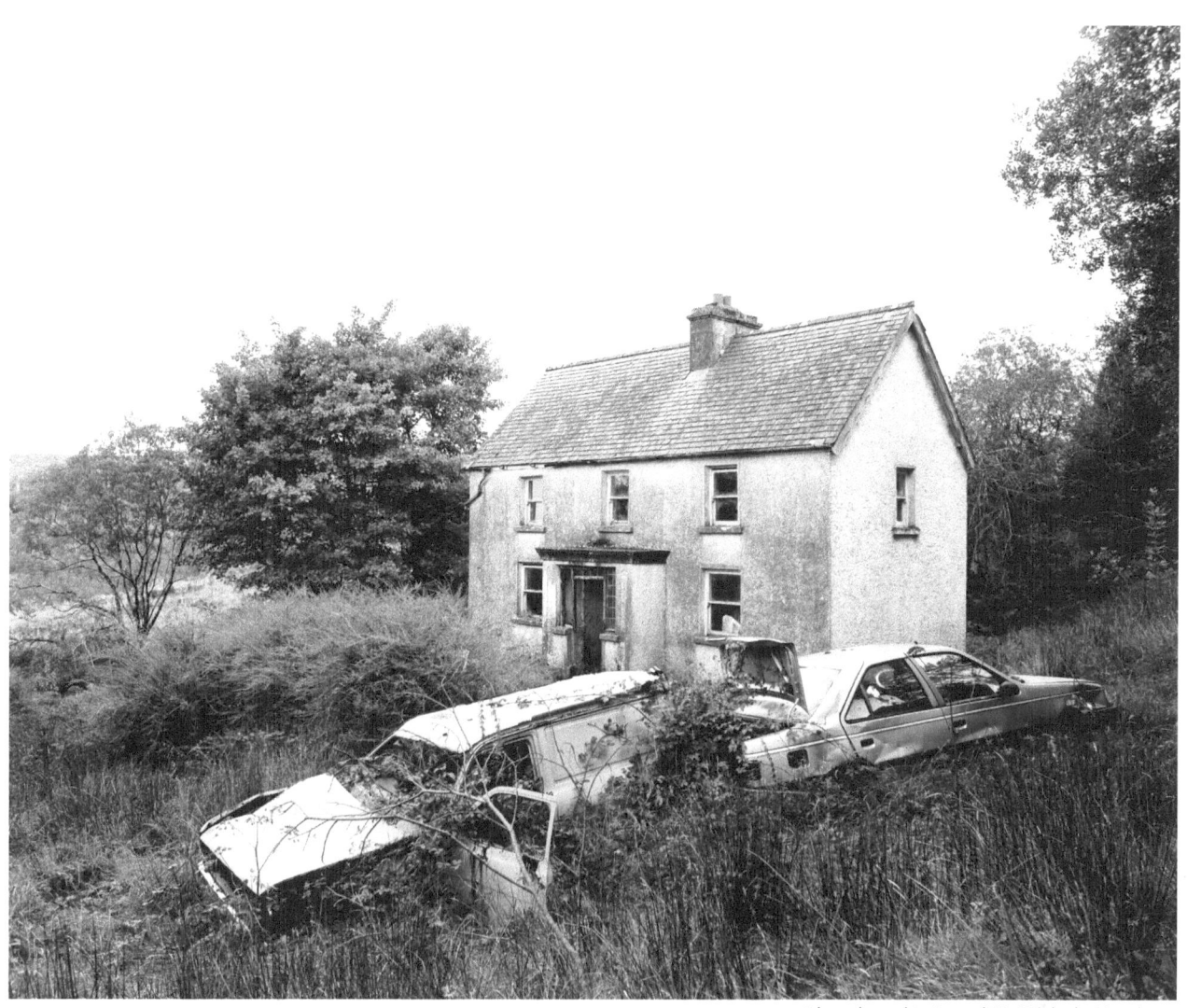

Abandoned I, II, and III, Michele Horrigan

These abandoned, crumbling, forgotten houses in Leitrim, Ireland, still had structure but lacked function. I aimed to "read" the ruin. ... the history and memory that come with an abandoned house ... the ruin as a disused theatre ... the aesthetics of a ruin. "A house that has been experienced is not an inert box." – Gaston Bachelard, *The Poetics of Space*.

—Michele Horrigan

CHAPTER 4

Spinning Quiet Yarns
"The Silent Language of Textiles"

Farah Mébarki

County Donegal in northwest Ireland features a rugged coast with jagged bays and tortured cliffs, peninsulas and small islands. Inland, the scenery displays the uneven beauty of glens, bogs, drumlins, mounds and bald hills, loughs and wild rivers. Here, people have led a tough life for centuries, clinging to their Catholic faith and living on fishing and rearing sheep whose sheared fleece is washed, dyed, carded and spun, providing yarn for knitting garments and weaving fabric and carpets. Small parcels of land are cultivated for household gardens that mainly produce potatoes. When the blight came, the years of famine between 1845 and 1851 were dreadful and many of those who did not die were driven out of the country. Since 1700, 10 million people have emigrated from Ireland, not only due to the Great Hunger, but because of the poverty brought when the English Protestants began colonizing Ireland in 1536.

In 1883, two travelers from London, Alice and Ernest Hart, deeply moved by Donegal's overwhelming distress, decided to revive ancient local crafts like weaving tweed and blankets, knitting (sweaters, shawls, gloves, socks and so on), lace making, embroidery and crochet. The cottage industry improved the standard of living and today, Udaras na Gaeltacha, a government-sponsored rural agency, continues to support the Donegal projects.

The wonderful tapestries of Donegal's women weavers perpetuate a long-standing savoir-faire and age-old memory, "wrought," or written wordlessly, with yarns, creating a silent, but visual, tactile and rural-accented language.

In Palestine, a similar system of women's cooperatives and associations has grown to promote traditional embroidery and help their members economically. The 1948 *Nakba,* or Great Catastrophe – when an estimated 700,000 Palestinians fled or were expelled from their land, and hundreds of Palestinian towns and villages were depopulated and destroyed with the formation of Israel – extinguished the passing on of women's knowledge from one generation to the next. To add insult to profound injury, a later invasion brought ready-to-wear clothes made from printed material,

Exclusively practiced by women, Palestinian embroidery reflects the identity of the maker, her emotions, her tastes, her imagination and what she has borrowed from the past. The embroidery is an expression of – a language for – her faith, her native soil, her village and her Middle Eastern culture. Some non-profit organizations like Sunbulah, "Ear of Wheat," in Jerusalem, have supported the revival of Palestinian embroidery. And visual artists in the Palestinian diaspora have also preserved and enriched – metamorphosed – their heritage through new experiences. Among them are Palestinian-American artist Mary Tuma, whose *Lingering Presence*, exhibited in "*The Map is Not the Territory*," somehow stitches up wounded maps, and Canadian Najat El-Taji El-Khairy, born in Palestine in the year of the Nakba, who delicately entrusts embroidery patterns to ceramic.

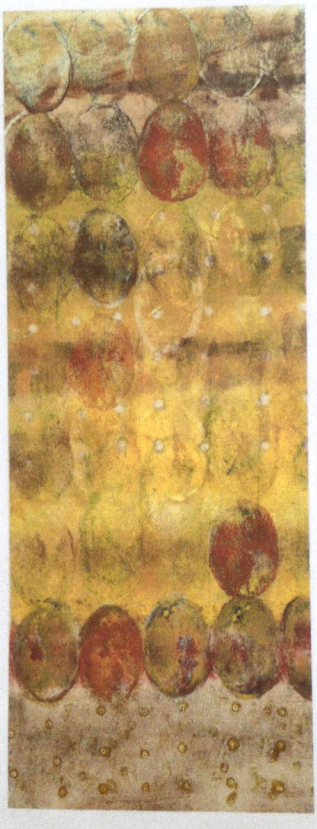

Untitled Potato Print,
Kerry Vander Meer

> While in Ireland, I read and talked to many people about the Great Hunger and the migration of the Irish people. It affected me deeply, and at one point I found myself carving potatoes in the shape of boats. I called them casket ships, a metaphor for the thousands who died making that voyage.
>
> —Kerry Vander Meer

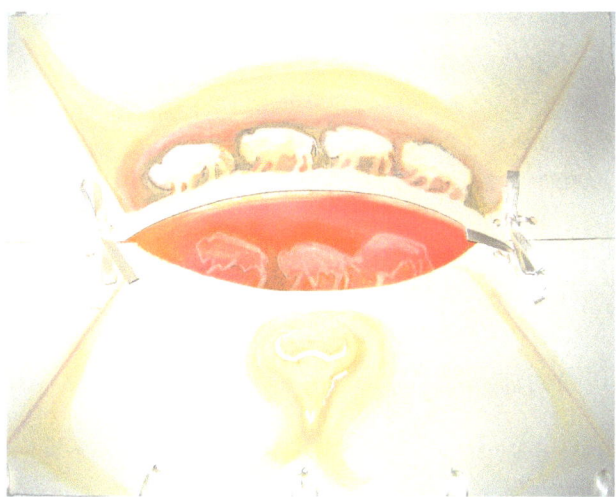
Tatanka Ska Oyate/White Buffalo Nation

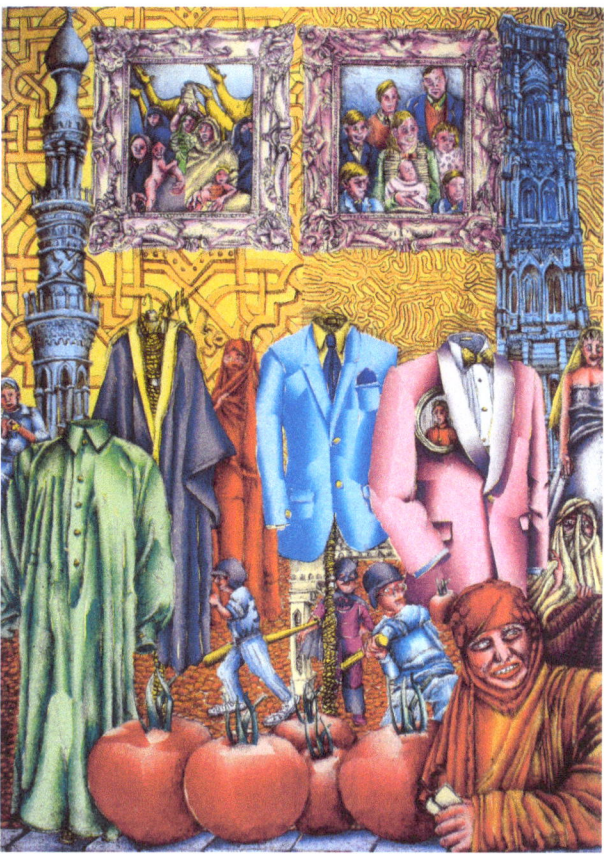
Divergence, Convergence, and Apparel, Matthew Egan

For the Lakota, or Western Sioux, the Buffalo Nation or *Tatanka Oyate* has a special relationship with human beings — as distinguished from four-legged or winged creatures and other life forms of creation. We have a relational concept of nationhood that is not defined by maps but is the territory of the heart, spirit, mind and body of the *Oyate* or The People. It is the landscape of the *Ina Makoce* or Earth Mother represented by the four directions manifested through the forces of nature in the vast oceans of prairie where the *Tatanka* roam, as much a part of her as the land. It is the terrain where our *Mahpiya Ate* or Father Sky is inseparable from *Ina Makoce.* A feminine divine being, The White Buffalo Calf Maiden brought the Sacred Pipe to the Lakota Nation.

—Nadema Agard

Apparel contributes to the material culture and, like architecture, cuisine, geography and visual art, can illustrate the unique qualities of an area or culture. These visual cues can be used to identify a culture or society and/or, more intriguingly, to stereotype. I am mindful of the distinctions between an *abaya, hijab,* or type of *dishdasha,* for example, in terms of fashion, purpose, pride and national identity. I am curious about the parallels and distinctions present in a society that wears suits, tuxedoes, jeans and T-shirts. Do all these garments play similar roles of function, fashion and identity to the societies that wear them? How do they reflect, change, or alter our values, systems of beliefs, family structures or roles in society?

—Matthew Egan

The Palestinian threadwork, the tapestries and knitwork of Donegal, the needlework and weaving of Native Americans all serve to express a powerful connection to roots, the awareness of personal realities and care about the future. The stories they tell are intertwined and in the case of Donegal, as well as among many Native Americans, are still handed down. Some Palestinian embroiderers pass their skills on to younger embroiderers, but, unfortunately, nowadays, girls expect to work at other jobs. Once, all Palestinian daughters learned to embroider at home, even though only a few worked as professionals. However, in refugee camps, some teenagers join groups of widows and older women embroiderers.

(continued)

Tradition is a set of art expressions which develop over the years, are passed on repeatedly with a few inevitable changes, transpositions and personalizations and are supported by evolving technical processes and systems of representation. In Donegal, the repertoire of knitwear patterns is made of designs borrowed from or inspired by the geographical, natural and human environment, such as ocean waves, rocks, brambles, bees, houses, crosses, fishing or basketwork, which have been stylized into traditional zigzags, diamonds, blackberries, honeycombs, plaits, cables, knots, baskets, herringbones and more. Yet, as knitter Mary McNelis illustrates, tradition is never definitely set, but is flexible and growing, feeding on time and the freedom to create. Knitting half diamonds "are just my own idea," she explained. "I don't like doing [the customary full diamond pattern] always the same."[1]

History is remembered, contained, interpreted. The weaver Margaret Cunningham wove a series of tapestries about the Great Hunger, which the Irish call *an Ghorta Mór*. In researching that period she said, she "discovered that American Indians helped the Irish by sending grain. To acknowledge this assistance,"[2] she wove symbols from both cultures: God's helping hands and a whale from the Native American picture repertoire, with red yarn in the margins. Inside, yellow cells are arranged in a coarse circle – like a stone ring – to "represent lives lost and homes burned." In her *Balla An Ghorta* (Famine Wall I) tapestry, "death" is written on a large F in the center of a ring. Celtic Sheela-na-Gig and Native American Kokopelli figures appear in *Balla An Ghorta II*. Cunningham explains that images in this second tapestry were inspired by "a photograph of a house deserted during the famine…The roof was gone, the windows broken and walls were covered with green lichen. Out of this emerged the color and shattered glass imagery for the background." Both tapestries are true icons documenting life, death, hope and love. The ring materializes the Christian rite of circling around a holy place during a pilgrimage. Dancing, flute-playing figures bring music into the scene.

These tapestries are quiet yarn prayers allowing the weaver to narrate and remember the lore and history of her homeland. They offer a memorial to a painful period in Irish history, and may even help in recovering from the trauma.

The same may now be somewhat true for today's Palestinian embroiders, even as they continue to live under occupation. Whether abstract or literal, women's images depict the material to make visible what is immaterial – emotions, thoughts, faith, memory. Maire McGinley puts it clearly: "My roots are intertwined in all of this and I have a strong sense of belonging. Some if it is very spiritual."

This spiritual quality also exists, for instance, in Navajo/Diné weavings. The skill was taught to the ancestors by Spider Woman, *Na'ashjéii Asdzáá,* creator of the world.[3] The first loom was made of sky and earth cords; the tools were sunlight, lightning, white shell and crystal.

Whether Irish, Palestinian or Native American, embroidery, weaving[4] and knitting are always about sharing: diachronic sharing (history passed on from one generation to the next), synchronic sharing (family bonds, women's conversation and advice, contacts with customers, personal emotions and questioning, use of homespun and commercial yard) and cross-cultural sharing. McGinley was, for example "impressed with the Spanish-American weavers at Tierra Wools in New Mexico. Especially the setup of their cooperative – with sheep, dye gardens and a showroom all together. Visitors get an immediate sense of what goes into their weaving."

She was also fascinated by Native American rug patterns. In her famine tapestry, *Cén Fath*, she "borrowed the shapes [she] saw in an image of a [First Nations (Canada)] Chilkat blanket from the 1800s."[5] Other influences include Mayan weavers from Guatemala who spent time in Donegal during an artist exchange. The resulting tapestry "celebrates the resourcefulness of women in both Guatemala and Ireland, fending for food, especially in Ireland during the famine."

Donegal women, like their sisters in the Americas and Palestine, have been extraordinarily creative across centuries. Their lives were and in many cases remain hard, but their subtlety helps them find a way to memorize fleeting things, tell about their experiences and speak to the future. In "*The Map is Not the Territory*," Helen Zughaib's *Woven in Exile,* mimics patterns of textiles from all three groups. The designs, she writes in an artist statement, "carry with them into the succeeding generations, the memories, sadness

The patterns and lace in *Woven in Exile* refer to both the fragility and strength shared by the Native American, Irish and Palestinian peoples.

—Helen Zughaib

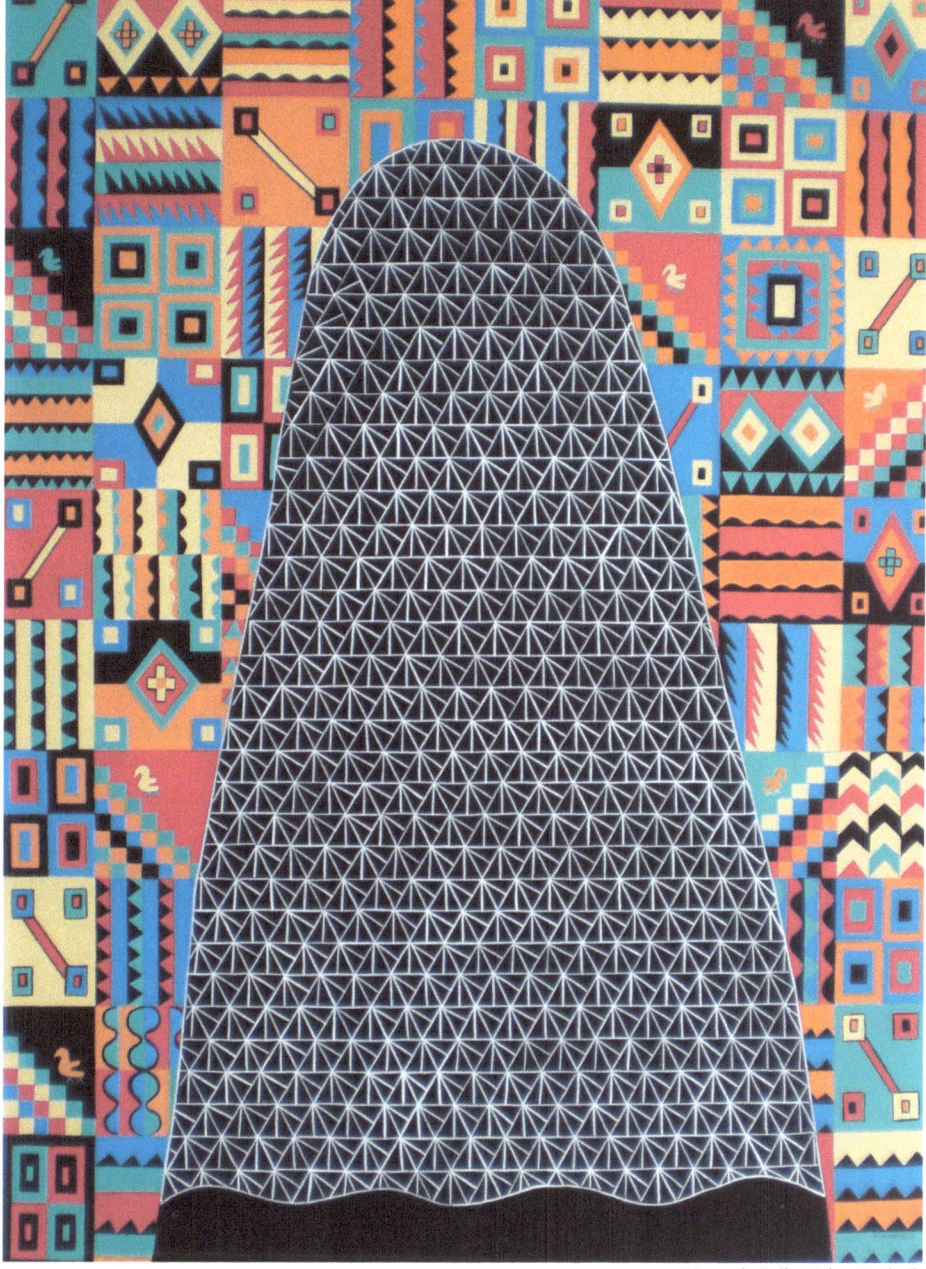

Woven in Exile, Helen Zughaib

We had a lemon tree behind the hedge
Its yellow fruit twinkled in the light
Flowers blew the perfume in our land.
We had behind the hedge a lemon tree, we had!
To beautify our homes
And spread perfume around.
They cut for us our lemon tree
And spring left us behind.

—Mahmoud Darwish

and beauty, of people dispossessed of their land." Yet they are constantly moving forward with creativity and freshness born of history and the land. Like the Greek Chryselaktos Artemis with "a golden distaff," they spin the thread of life.

> My hand is weary with writing;
> my sharp great point is not thick;
> my slender-beaked pen juts forth
> a beetle-hued draught of bright blue ink.
>
> A steady stream of wisdom springs
> from my well-colored neat fair hand;
> on the page it pours its draught of ink
> of the green-skinned holly.
>
> I send my little dripping pen unceasingly
> over an assemblage of books of great beauty,
> to enrich the possessions of men of art—
> whence my hand is weary with writing.[6]

After spinning, knitting or weaving all day, the women of Donegal can claim their hands are "weary with writing." Their "books of great beauty" are not written with "bright blue ink," but with yarn died from the fruits of the land, the *raithneach*, the *fraoch* and the *crotal*.[7]

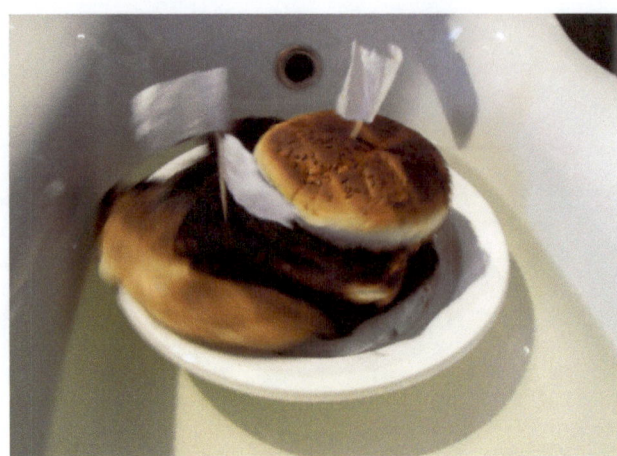

Crumbs of Land: Khobz A Word for Freedom #4, Claudia Borgna

Globalization: a beautiful intention with frightening consequences, a grotesque artifice or simply the natural outcome of human evolution? Where might the line between global interconnectivity trespassing on cosmic consciousness be? Maybe right here, where the illusion of freedom dissolves into blood- soaked imperialism enmeshed in individualism. I – a middle-class, white European woman – travel the fractured land stepping on the crumbs of someone else's bread, someone else's freedom.

—Claudia Borgna

My land follows me wherever I go. The daily suffering of my people is a constant reminder of its existence and struggle. In 2011, on a random stroll with my three-year-old grandson on Sankt Alban-Rheinweg Street along the Rhine in Basel, Switzerland, I encountered a rock formation nestled neatly on the river bank. I was mesmerized by its shape, contouring the borders of my native land. Ironic, isn't it? To discover this little rock, shaped like the map of Palestine right where the First Zionist Congress took place in 1897, the first step in the condemnation of our people to suffering, injustice and oppression.

—Najat El-Taji El-Khairy

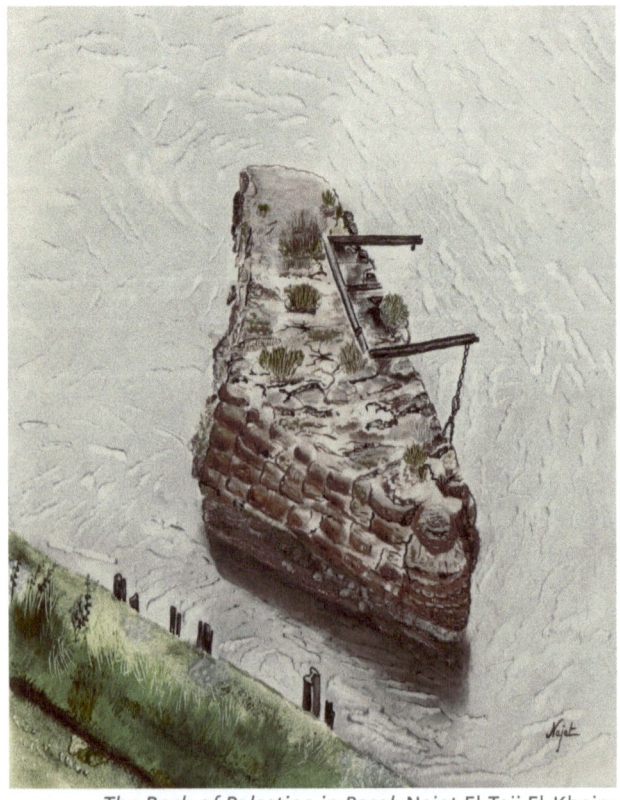

The Rock of Palestine in Basel, Najat El-Taji El-Khairy

CHAPTER 5

Walls and Mirrors
Identity in Art

Germán Gil-Curiel

> " Without Art, the crudeness of reality would make the world unbearable. "
> —George Bernard Shaw

Prelude

Maps are often understood as "guides" to a territory. In fact they act either as devices of political and cultural fragmentation or of unification that pretend to reflect what is. Instead they impose perspectives of "what must be." Therefore, "the map is not the territory."[1]

Widespread concerns have been expressed about the social and cultural impacts experienced by vulnerable populations as a result of invasion and occupation. Notwithstanding the fact that the brutal intrusion of invaders aims at plundering the land, it also targets the annihilation of the local inhabitants' identity.

Michel Foucault's concept of "heterotopia" describes spaces in which the spatiotemporal co-ordinates are broken in a way that maps fail to capture. Foucault distinguishes two categories of spaces, namely the internal and external. While the former concerns our perceptions and intuitions, our dreams and passions, the latter is a heterogeneous space where "… we live, which draws us out of ourselves, in which the erosion of our lives, our time and our history occurs, the space that claws and gnaws at us…"[2] Foucault defines the mirror as a "a sort of mixed, joint experience," an intermediate point between utopia and heterotopia able to reflect both inside and outside spaces. The image we see within the mirror does not exist outside of it, it is simultaneously a faithful reflection in the shape of our own image, hence of our own exterior reality.[3] The arts are such a mirror. Like a mirror, the arts are able to reflect outside and inside realities and may even construct a powerful and meaningful resistance that can liberate us from the ideological constraints imposed by authoritarianism, therefore illuminating the human condition. When the mirror is veiled, the reflection is negated, so that the mirror may as well be a blind wall.

According to Foucault, the mirror is an ambivalent site since it is located between utopias and heterotopias. On the one hand, the mirror is a utopia because it is "… a placeless place. In the mirror, I see myself there where I am not, in an unreal, virtual space that opens up behind the surface; I am over there, there where I am not, a sort of shadow that gives my own visibility to myself, that enables me to see myself there where I am absent…."[4] On the other hand, Foucault contends that the mirror is also a heterotopia because it exists in reality, insofar as it is a place that has, in whatever position we occupy, a sort of returning effect. It is from staring into the mirror, that "I discover my absence from the place where I am since I see myself over there."[5] After this process of reflection, a reconstitution of the self takes place. Looking fixedly at our own countenance reflected in the mirror, "I come back toward myself… there where I am."[6] Foucault concludes that the mirror, as both a utopia and a heterotopia

> makes this place that I occupy at the moment when I look at myself in the glass at once absolutely real, connected with all the space that surrounds it, and absolutely unreal, since in order to be perceived it has to pass through this virtual point which is over there.[7]

The mirror, a mixed instrument between utopia – "an unreal, virtual space that opens up behind the surface" – and heterotopia – the return of an "absolutely real" reflection "connected with all the space that surrounds" the observer, like the trajectory of a boomerang – corresponds to the complex interaction between the identification of a work of art and its spectator. When this identification takes place, what the work of art "reflects," through a subtle alchemy, becomes part of our own personal reality. But when we reconstitute ourselves, the process has just begun, since having returned from the work of art, we are not the same any more. In addition, Foucault points out that utopias and heterotopias have the "curious property of being in relation with all the other sites, but in such a way as to suspect (sic),[8]

(continued)

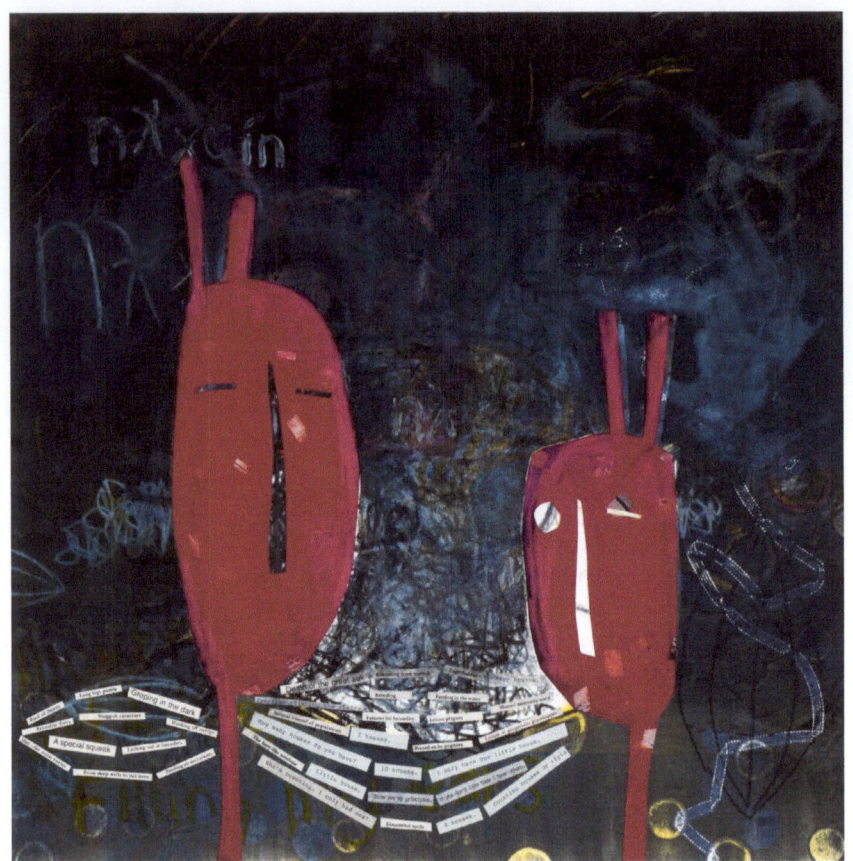

Weight of the Discussion, Neal Ambrose-Smith

My tribe, the Salish, has used Coyote stories for teaching morals and good behavior for thousands of years. Here two animistic masked figures have a heavy conversation about life, so heavy the viewer can see the weight of it. In our stories, there might be an argument between Coyote and Crow over something good to eat, such as a piece of grease. There will be a long discussion before a decision is made and that decision will sometimes be based on who is the cleverest, not the most deserving – very much like life.

—Neal Ambrose Smith

neutralize, or invert the set of relations that they happen to designate, mirror or reflect."[9] Following the metaphor of the mirror as a work of art, the wall – either concrete or abstract – connotes the interruption and neutralization of what the mirror reflects, as we shall see below.

Music and Identity

Brutal invasions, appropriations and exterminations have been practiced by empires (notably Spain, France and England) to establish political control over the territories of North and South American indigenous populations across both continents. Indigenous communities in those countries have been victims of racism, marginalization, poverty and genocide. The ongoing process of colonization continues to have a devastating impact on its victims.[10] Music – conceived as a mirror – sends back the reflection of our own image impregnated by some of the most genuine elements that construct our identities. However, its inverted meaning – as a veiled mirror or even as a solid, concrete blind wall – has undermined indigenous identities through commercialization.

The vast majority of Native communities in North America were exterminated over the centuries. The erosion and exploitation of the cultural-artistic identities of the few survivors has persisted, yielding tremendous profits. This is the case with a series titled *Sacred Spirit*, which comprises about seven albums.[11] Hugely successful from the beginning, this musical project was created by a German team, three accomplished musicians – Claus Zundel, Ralf Hamm and Markus Stabb – calling themselves "The Fearsome Brave" or just "The Brave," who arranged, mixed and produced it.

The second album, *Chants and Dances of the Native Americans*, or *Indians*, released in 1994, was indeed controversial. It has been convincingly argued that the title *Sacred Spirit* was invented to promote a commercial, exotic attraction and does not refer to any genuine Native American principle

(continued)

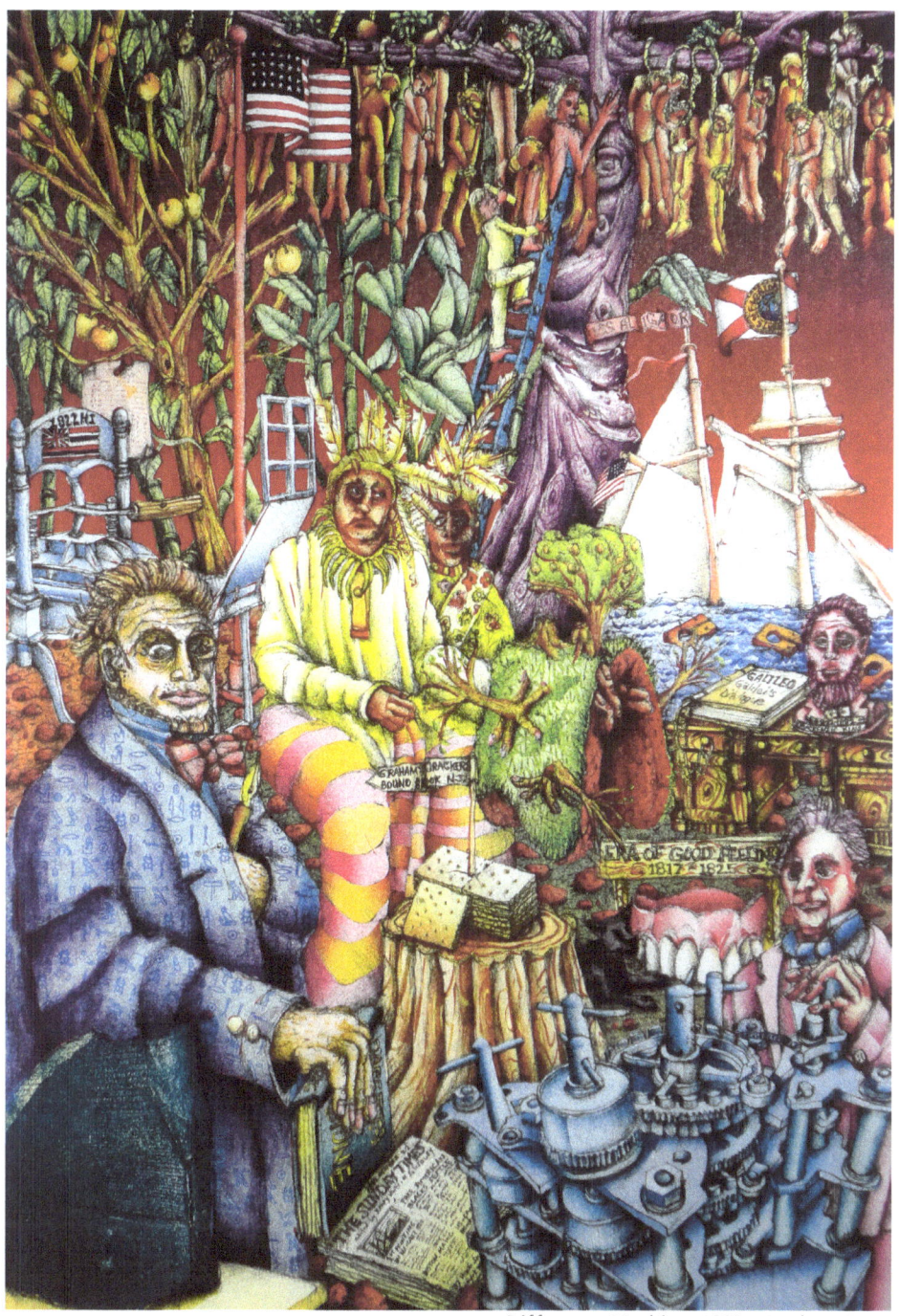

Difference Machine, 1822, Matthew Egan

Difference Machine, 1822 is part of a series of portfolios organized by Brandon Garner about the history of the United States. The notion of contemplating the history of a country during an era of war with Canada, my country of citizenship, prior to my ancestors immigrating to the continent offered both a sense of displacement and thoughts of repatriation. The "difference machine" was invented by Charles Babbage to compute "divided differences." 1822 was marked by several land trades and treaties with Native Americans and the handover of land in New York and Ontario. There are references to Denmark Vesey (whose slave name was Telemaque), who, after buying his freedom, planned a rebellion and was hanged with dozens of fellow conspirators. That year, other events took place, such as the inventions of Graham crackers and dentures, the translation of the Rosetta Stone and the first pages to be printed in Hawai'ian, a speller produced by a Protestant Mission.

—Matthew Egan

or initiative.[12] And although the leaflet identifies two photographs by ethnologist and photographer Edward S. Curtis, it does not credit the picture of a young Indian, taken in 1907 by acclaimed photographer Carl Moon,[13] titled *Navajo Boy*.[14] Moreover, the document *Solsticio de invierno*, cited above, argues that a track in the album, arranged by Peter Kater, called "Ly-O-Lay-Ale Loya" (The Counterclockwise Circle Dance), which claims to be a Native American chant, is not. The vocals instead are authentic Sami *joik* (or *yoik*), one of the longest living music traditions in Europe from the folk music of the Sami people, an indigenous Finno-Ugric people.[15] Although the sounds of yoiking can be heard as comparable to the traditional chanting of some Native American cultures, it is nevertheless not the same.

Once the "The Fearsome Brave" team acquired the Native American recordings, certified in the leaflet as "New World records, recorded anthology of American Music Inc.," they adapted them by adding percussion, wind and stringed instruments, as well as keyboards and digital programs, without acknowledgment of the original Native American material. The final result goes far beyond the American Indian musical traditions. Ultimately, *Sacred Spirit* is a hybrid, music-industry product that draws from but is not authentic to the ancestral ethnic traditions of the American Indian. Adding insult to injury, it also "Indianizes" Sami peoples. As a consequence, representatives of the Native communities involved are said to have denounced the music as "adulterated," an opportunistic, lucrative business deal that did not involve any American Indians. As a result, the production company – to "compensate" Native Americans out of the amazing profits they made selling more than seven million albums worldwide[16] – notes on the back cover of the album claim that the company gives "a donation to the Native American Rights Fund for each CD sold…," although the percentage of the profits is not specified. As has happened repeatedly, the music industry gained enormously from the commercialization of traditional Native American music, while those communities are stripped of their identities. Their music, which should have been, as Foucault notes, an artistic mirror, became instead a blind, confining wall. And as is all too common, these indigenous people were relegated to the familiar role of providers of raw materials, nearly always plundered.

In relation to the capacity of the mirror to suspend or neutralize the meaning of what it reflects, this lucrative product is a kind of mirror that, beyond any of its commercial strategies, has paradoxically had the power to charm and seduce its largely non-Native audience.

A similar case took place in Mexico and involved the commercialization of an excerpt titled "K'in Sventa Ch'ul Me'tik Kwadulupe" (Festival for the Holy Mother Guadalupe), recorded during the festive annual Tzotzil ritual of Chamula, in which the local representation of the Virgin of Guadalupe changes hands from one family to another. These indigenous Tzotzil Maya communities have struggled for generations to preserve two of the last bastions of their identity: their native language and their ancestral music.

In the 1970s, David Lewiston began recording the ritualistic prayers in the town of Chamula, in the state of Chiapas, for an album titled *Fiestas of Chiapas & Oaxaca*.[17] According to music reviewer Adam Greenberg, "Much of the music was recorded during the festival of Guadalupe … Lewiston's recordings … generally attempted to capture as many forms of music as possible to include all on the compilation."[18] Unlike the case of the pseudo-Native American album, *Sacred Spirit*, this is an invaluable collection, which aims at the preservation of disappearing South Mexican indigenous musical and cultural heritage from Chiapas and Oaxaca. This album included "K'in Sventa Ch'ul Me'tik Kwadulupe," a prayer for the Virgin of Guadalupe.[19] As a religious act of worship, the prevailing spirit of this piece is characterized by a sweet, continuous collective praying, with intercalated music between the beginning and the end.[20]

In 2002, the very same recording of "K'in Sventa Ch'ul Me'tik Kwadulupe" was integrated into the Kronos Quartet album titled *Kronos Quartet Nuevo*,[21] arranged by Osvaldo Golijov, adding a marimba and strings, with a very slow tempo on the basis of prolonged notes, glissandos and portamentos, to capture the harmonious atmosphere of worship.[22]

Exoticism and the exploitation of the cultural-artistic identities of indigenous music is common in contemporary Euro-American society. The Tzotzil's syncretic prayers to the Virgin of Guadalupe – conducted in their native language to a

(continued)

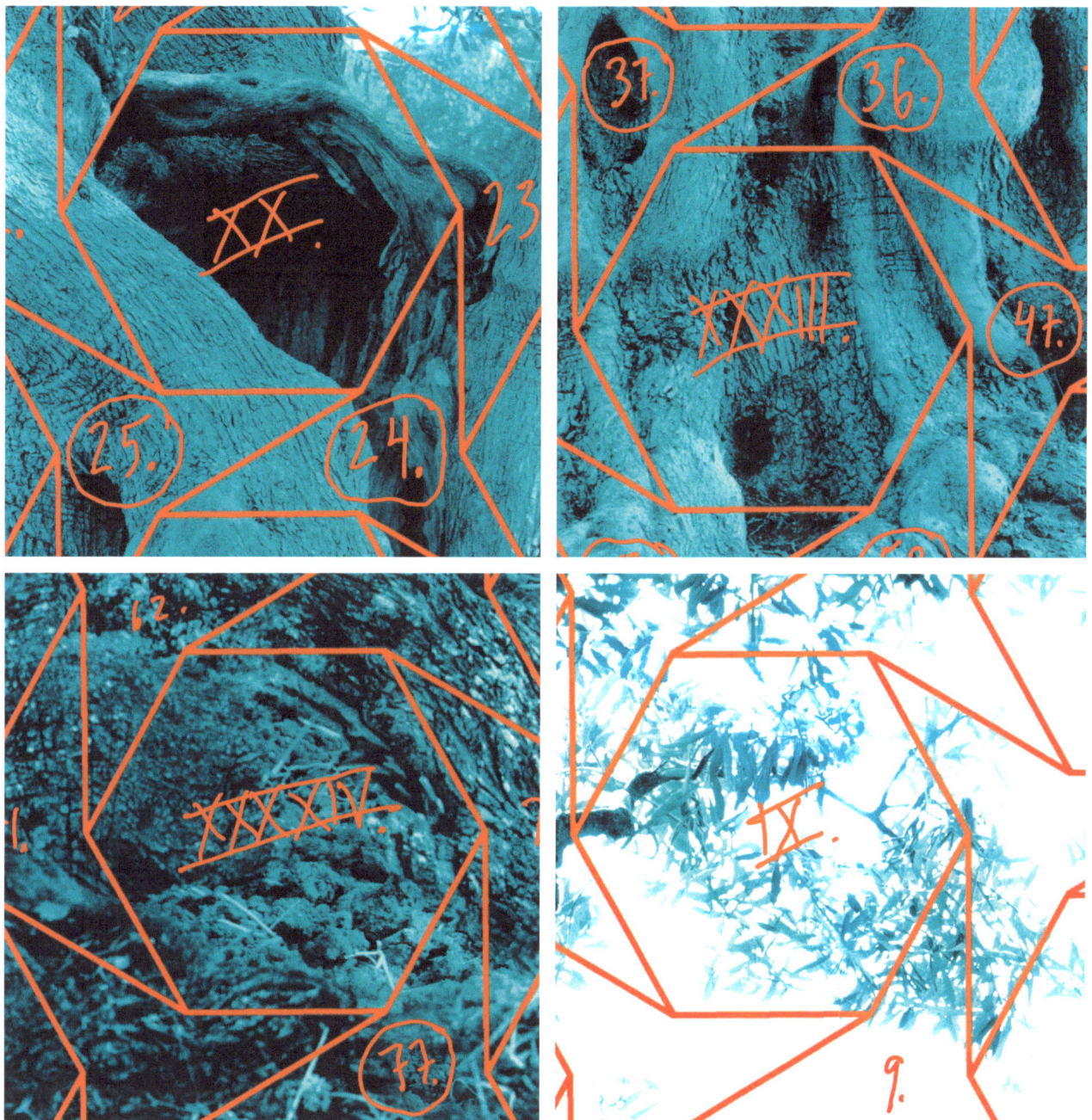

Hex XX, Hex XXXIII, Hex XLIV & Hex IX (details from Pressed), Andrew Ellis Johnson

The Palestinian Minister of Agriculture once stated that "Our agricultural sector has not grown since 1967… In fact, it has diminished." One of his aims was "to plant 10 million trees every year throughout the West Bank for a greener Palestine." The olive orchard, a foundation of economic stability and a symbol of peace in the Middle East, is fragmented in the installation *Pressed: When Words Were Earth*, comprised of photographic murals divided into over 3,000 mirrored tiles. Its fractured sections and the prints that accompany them allude to the deliberate diminishment of agricultural productivity, to the uprooting of livelihoods, to groves demolished or made inaccessible by walls and bypass roads and settlements. Its numbering system speaks to the systematic disruption and disregard for the cultivation of trees that are sometimes over a century old, not to mention the people they sustain.

—Andrew Ellis Johnson

Western icon imposed on them by their conquerors – combined with their ritualistic music, are veiled by the blind mirror of commercialization, which not only distorts their traditional religious ceremonies, along with the music, but absorbs them into no more than an unconventional product, causing them to, for all intents and purposes, disappear. Interestingly, although such a product does not mirror but undermines the indigenous Tzotzil peoples' identity, Golijov's well-crafted arrangements invert this effect, enthralling the consumer.

Walls in Cinema

Walls and mirrors also feature prominently in the film *Lemon Tree* (Ertz Limon),[23] about a Palestinian widow, Salma, whose lemon grove, tended by her family for generations, is threatened with removal by Israeli security forces who consider it a major threat to the Defense Minister and his wife who have just moved next door. The widow sues, but, despite considerable media attention, her case is dismissed. As a result, a concrete wall is built between her property and the Defense Minister's, while the lemon trees are razed almost to the ground.

In *Lemon Tree*, the wall and the mirror as heterotopias amalgamate to create a barrier – initially a barbed-wire fence and later a concrete wall – that veils the image reflected on the mirror, that is to say, the beautiful lemon grove. Indeed, only a few people from the Israeli side are able to see this magnificent reflection: Mira, the Minister's wife, and a young guard posted on the watchtower. Even so, the mirror is veiled and the result is incarceration behind the wall. Not only does the Palestinian widow become a prisoner on her own property, but so does the Minister, surrounded by a wall where the grove used to be. Furthermore, the trees themselves, as a metaphoric reflection in the mirror, acquire the status of people. As one of the characters puts it during a crucial scene

> Day in, day out, Salma and I cultivated the land and the trees. It's not just watering and fertilizing. Trees are like people. They have souls, they have feelings. They need to be talked to, need tender loving care. I don't use a tractor, I only use my own hands.

This identification of the trees and the land with their people is deeply poetic. This reflection on the land-mirror is reiterated by the widow herself when she firmly opposes the destruction of her trees in the Israeli court of law. Interrupting the judge's verdict, she declares

> Your proposal dishonors me, my late father and my late husband. My trees are real. My life is real. You're already building a wall around us. Isn't that enough?

Salma's words clearly allude to the Israeli West Bank barrier, the wall currently being built by Israel to divide Palestine, and her trees metaphorically refer to the Palestinian people, thus providing a further source of reflection. The metaphor of the veiled mirror[24] leads them – both victims and victimizers – to the heterotopia of dehumanisation and devastation, the ultimate void.[25] The closing expeditious sequence of *Lemon Tree* is crucial to the denouement, that is, the Minister's loss of identity and the devastation of Palestine. A final camera shot portrays the Minister, a desolate man, smoking a cigarette alone in the dark living room of his prison-like residence. When he raises the metallic curtains and goes to a window leading into his garden, all he sees is the concrete wall that surrounds the house. As his face is reflected on the windowpane, his distressed countenance is projected for a few seconds onto the wall, a diffused shadowy image about to vanish. On a sudden impulse, he goes into the garden to face the wall, but he finds only the blind hard surface, nothing more. On the other side, the camera allows us to see behind the veiled mirror-wall: the widow walking slowly among her mutilated lemon trees, staring at the wall as well.

Coda

The history of both Palestinians and other colonized, indigenous people has been marked by racism, invasion and extermination. However, behind the concrete walls in Palestine and the metaphorical walls that take place in the dispossession of American and Palestinian indigenous people's cultural and artistic heritage, art inverts the set of relations of heterotopias. Meanings may reverse their original purpose: incarceration generates resistance to violation and oppression, and so-called "protection" becomes vacuity, isolation and disintegration. It is only to be hoped that art can – more disinterestedly and selflessly – continue its restorative work, turning more walls into mirrors. ■

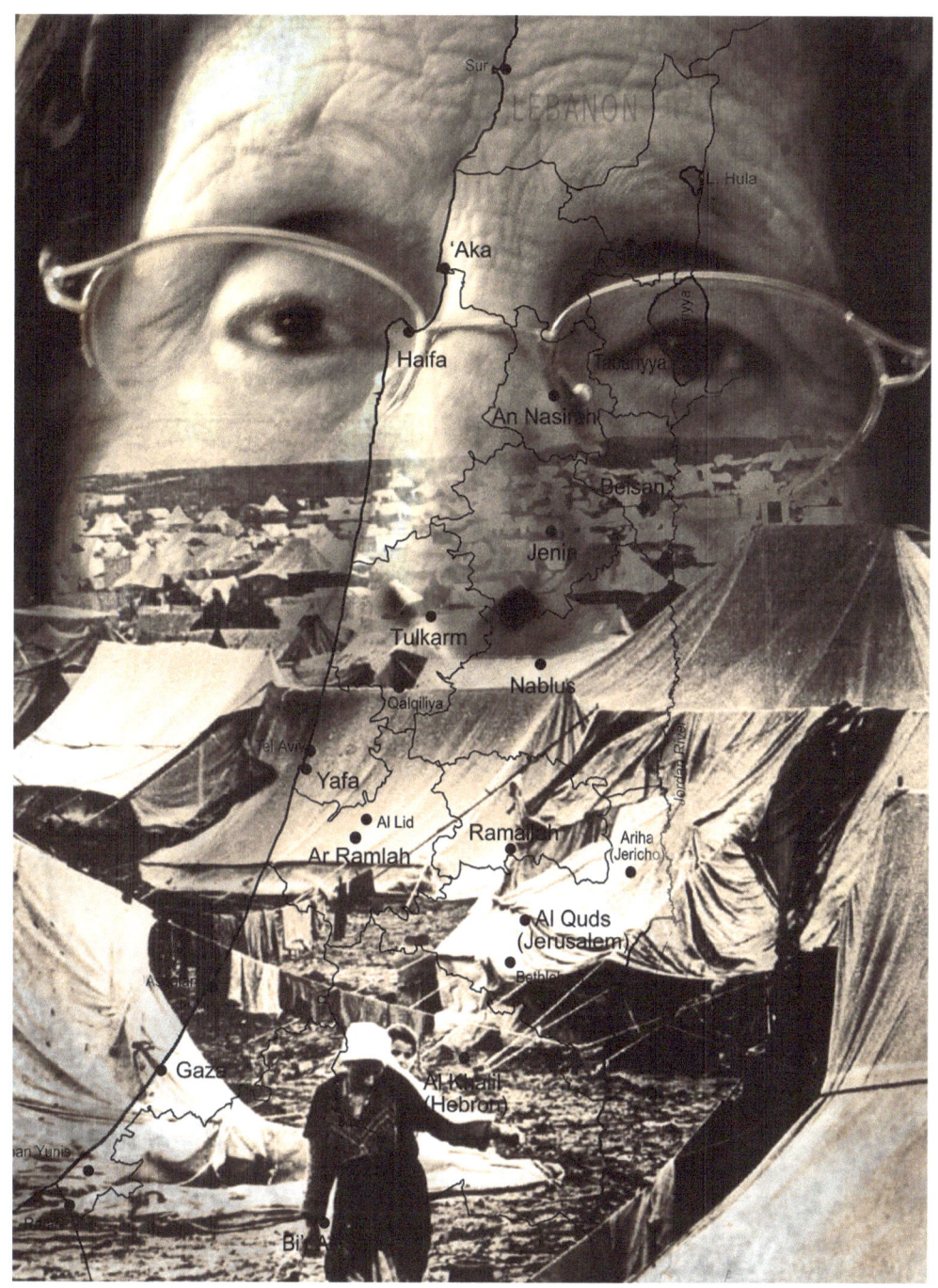

Forgotten Survivors, John Halaka

"We were the masters of the land, then they came and made us their servants."

—Ahmed Essa Brieq

Ahmed Essa Brieq was born in Kweekat, Palestine, in 1924. He became an internally displaced refugee when Israel was established in 1948. He died in the village of Abu Sinan, Isreal/Palestine in 2008.

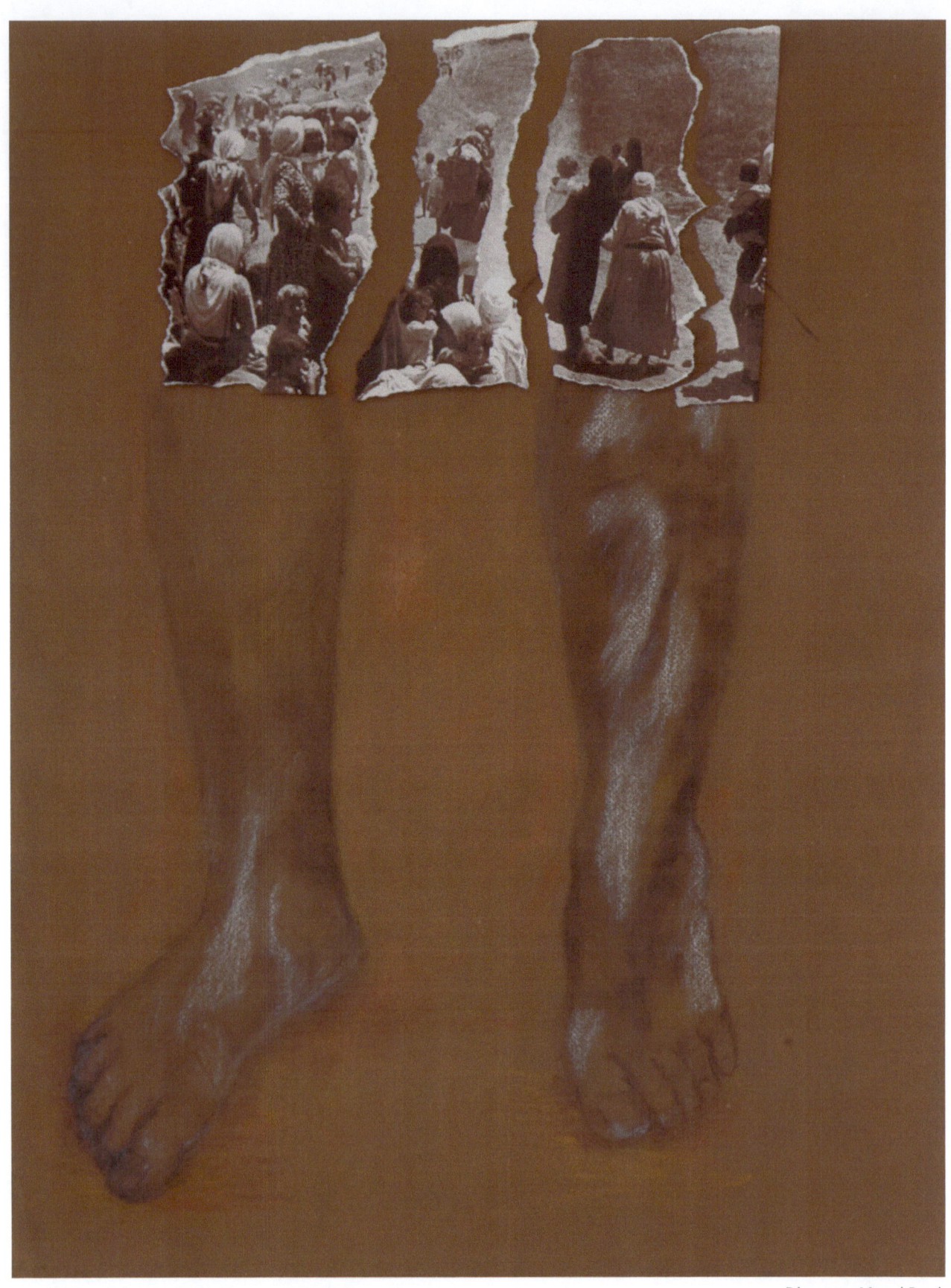

Diaspora, Manal Deeb

CHAPTER 6

Journeys of Survivance

John Halaka

Experiences of forced displacement, exile and genocide have long defined the unbalanced power relationships between colonial settlers and indigenous populations. Although we often say "never again," we have all witnessed and, in many cases, have been party to the destruction of indigenous cultures and the attempted eradication of native people, again and again and again.

"The Map is Not the Territory:" Parallel Paths – Palestinians, Native Americans, Irish[1] bears witness to the long journeys of massive dislocation, attempted annihilation, resistance and persistence of the First People of the Americas, the Irish and the Palestinians. Each of these groups is surviving tragic histories of overwhelming destruction inflicted upon them over extended periods of time. Linking the experiences of indigenous Palestinians, Native Americans and the Irish, are complex connections to European and American imperialism, as well as devastating contacts with invasive movements of settler colonialism. Whether imperial rulers or settler-occupiers, invaders are almost always driven by avaricious desires to dominate and profit from the resources of the lands they colonize. The colonial occupiers of the Americas, Palestine and Ireland were no exception, and were uniformly motivated by contemptuous convictions of their racial and cultural superiority, resulting in a history of unimaginable cruelties. The devastation wreaked by colonial settlers on native populations facilitated their efforts to take the territories they coveted, while forcibly displacing the indigenous inhabitants from their land and tearing them away from the cultural roots that shaped them.

Each of the native cultures featured in the exhibition have experienced what the Palestinians call a *Nakba* (Arabic for *The Great Catastrophe*) that displaced them in huge numbers from their ancestral lands, shattered their cultures, decimated their populations, undermined their historical relationship to their lands and devastated the complex and carefully interwoven threads of family, clan and tribal relationships that defined their societies. Living in the aftermath of an epic history of destruction, the Palestinians, First People of the Americas and the Irish are not simply victims of external domination and manipulation but are first and foremost indigenous survivors who have resisted forced extinction, are creatively rebuilding their shattered societies and are struggling to reclaim their stolen lands. The people of each of those three nations have persevered and continue to rise from the ashes of their respective Nakbas, while gradually reweaving their once vibrant cultural tapestries.

The experiences of Native Americans, Palestinians and the Irish are not unique, but are part of an ongoing global history of land theft through forced displacement, involuntary migration and cultural as well as physical extermination. Focusing the work in this exhibition on those three cultures allows for parts of their untold narratives to be heard and their unseen realities to be witnessed. By stressing these three particular cultures, *"The Map is Not the Territory"* does not in any way diminish the tales of persistence and resistance of other survivors of ethnic cleansing worldwide.

(continued)

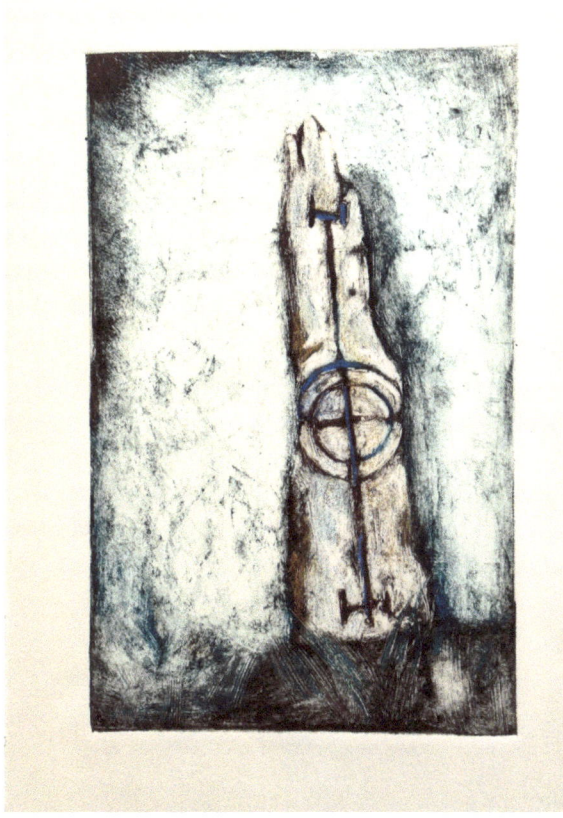

Cross Slabs at Cill Rialaig, Kerry Vander Meer

THE PROVISIONAL GOVERNMENT
of the

ANISHINABE REPUBLIC
TO THE PEOPLE OF TURTLE ISLAND

ANISHINABEININI shigo ANISHINABEKWE In the name of Chi' Manito and of the dead generations from which she receives her old tradition of nationhood. Turtle Island, through us, summons her children to her flag and strikes for her freedoms.

Having organized and trained her people through her secret revolutionary organization, the Anishinabe Republican Brotherhood and through her open military organizations, the Anishinabe Volunteers and the Anishinabe Citizens Army, having patiently perfected her discipline, having resolutely waited for the right moment to reveal itself, she now seizes that moment, and, supported by her exiled children and gallant allies across Mama nan Aki, but relying in the first on her own strength, she strikes in full confidence of victory.

We declare the right of the people of Turtle Island to the ownership of Turtle Island, and to the unfettered control of the Anishinabe Destinies to be sovereign and indefeasible. The long usurpation of that right by a foreign people and government has not extinguished the right, nor the can it ever be extinguished except by the destruction of Anishinabe people. In every generation the Anishinabe people have asserted their right to national freedoms and sovereignty, numerous times during the past 500 years they have asserted in arms. Standing on that fundamental right and again asserting it in arms in the face of the world, we hereby proclaim the Anishinabe Republic as Sovereign Independent State, and we pledge, our laws and the lives of our comrades-in-arms to the cause of it's freedom, of its welfare, and of its exaltation among nations.

The Anishinabe Republic is entitled to and hereby claims allegiance of every Anishinabeinini and Anishinabekwe. the Republic guarantees religious and civil liberty, equal rights and equal opportunities to all its citizens, and declares its resolve to pursue the happiness and prosperity of the whole nation and of all its parts, cherishing all the children of the nation equally and oblivious of differences carefully fostered by and alien government, which have divided and minority from the majority in the past.

Until our arms have brought the opportune moment for the establishment of a permanent National Government, representative of the whole people of Turtle Island and elected by the suffrage's of all her men and women, the Provisional Government, hereby constituted, will administer the civil and military affairs of the Republic in trust for the People.

We place the cause of the Anishinabe Republic under the protection of Chi' Manito, whose blessing we invoke upon our arms, and we pray that no one who serves that cause will dishonour it by cowardice, inhumanity, or rapine. In this supreme hour the Anishinabe nation must, by its valour and discipline and by the readiness of its children to sacrifice themselves for the common good, prove itself worthy of the august destiny to which it is called.

Signed on Behalf of the Provisional Government,

Anishinabe Proclamation, Scott Benesiinaabandan

On the contrary, the exhibit emphasizes the importance of a broad discourse about human rights and the demand for justice for all indigenous populations.

The exhibition raises numerous important questions about the tragic consequences of the unbalanced and violent power relations between indigenous populations and the reckless land hunger of invaders. The art in the exhibit should leave viewers asking how, as people of goodwill, we can avoid repeating these hubristic mistakes. How can we address the rights of those who have suffered unimaginable horrors? How can we relieve the suffering of refugees? And what can we do, not only to remember, but to actively learn from these forgotten survivors?

Survival and resistance are inseparable practices for indigenous populations that have been invaded, occupied, displaced and colonized. The preservation and presentation of their testimonies are critical instruments of "survivance." They are also extremely effective methods of implanting the voices of native people into the cultural imagination of all people. The Native American scholar Gerald Vizenor coined the term "survivance" to describe the creative resilience of the indigenous people of the Americas against cultural and physical extermination.[2] The concept of survivance combines the active processes of "survival" and "resistance," and applies equally to the struggles of the First People of the Americas, the Palestinians and the Irish.

Survivance creatively employs memories, personal and communal stories, as well as tales of ancient customs and evolving traditions, to convey a living culture that refuses to die and disappear. Survivance is the desire and will of a people who reject being swept away, and is an active, indigenous presence against political, physical and psychological absence, whether that absence is from their homeland, from the international discourse on human rights or an internal absence caused by the acceptance of defeat. Survivance highlights the process of active survival shaped by creative and moral resistance to oppression, institutional manipulation, neglect and dehumanization; it underlines the will of the individual while underscoring the power of the collective. Former Israeli prime ministers David Ben-Gurion and Golda Meir,[3] along with many other Zionist leaders and citizens, individuals directly responsible for the Palestinian refugee crisis, have, on numerous occasions, said, "the old will die and the young will forget." The art and literature of survivance are antidotes to forgetting. They help to insure that experiences are preserved and that current and future generations are well informed.

The stories of generations of Palestinians, surviving in exile or under brutal military occupation, remain mostly untold and unknown. The process of collecting, preserving and publically presenting their obscured narratives through art, literature and film, reveals the faces and names of men and women from the Palestinian diaspora, enabling them to emerge from the dark shadows of history, while transforming them from anonymous displaced masses into tangible individuals with unassailable narratives. For Palestinians living in exile, as well as those living under occupation, memory is the engine of their return. Memory allows them to envision and to seek the denied security of their homeland and to design the re-construction of their shattered societies. Memory inspires them to visualize processes with which to re-assemble the hundreds of thousands of families that have been dismembered and globally scattered over the past seven decades of exile. Listening to, recording and displaying the deliberately denied and ignored memories of survivors is a small but critical effort to make the unseen seen, and the unheard heard, so that no one can ever say, "I didn't know."

Memory as survivance requires not only that people of goodwill preserve and present the experience of the indigenous survivors, but demands that we also identify the strategies, methods and consequences of the actions of the colonizers. The indigenous cultures of Palestine – which throughout its millennia-long history included Muslims, Christians and Jews – has, over the past seven decades, been deliberately shattered and its people broadly scattered by a distinctly un-holy, ethno-nationalist colonial movement that openly privileges one cultural/religious group over all others.[4]

Religious pilgrims travel to seek mercy and enlightenment from the sacred stones of Palestine, but most are blind to the experiences and conditions of the "Living Stones"[5] that have struggled for four generations under occupation or been systematically driven out of their homeland. The his-

(continued)

tory of Palestine must not be simply defined by the stories of religious traditions and colonial victors, but should be understood as having been shaped by the lives and experiences of its people. The Palestinians are the living stones, the trees, the fields and the shrines that comprise this diverse, intricate and compelling culture. If anything can be considered holy in the so-called Holy Land, it is the indigenous men and women and their descendants, who maintain evolving historical and spiritual connections to the land. The narrow focus on Palestine's ancient histories and the romantic attachments to its religious sites not only distract from what is truly sacred in the "Land of Sour Milk and Stolen Honey,"[6] but make the pilgrim culpable for the theft of that land and the ongoing ethnic cleansing of its native people.

Many people in the West believe that the sources of the conflict between Palestinians and Israelis are ancient and religious. This deliberate misinformation and oft-repeated propaganda has been used to cover up the ongoing atrocities committed by colonial settlers against the indigenous population. In reality, the conflict between Israelis and Palestinians is recent, completely modern and entirely a product of stated Zionist colonial ambitions to dominate Palestine while ridding it of its indigenous people. By safeguarding and making public the narratives of indigenous Palestinian survivors, we refute the fabrications of the occupiers and shine a bright spotlight of truth on the theft, occupation and domination of Palestinian land.

The single most common experience shared by Palestinian refugees is that of loss. Sudden, total and catastrophic loss. Ordinary domestic life faded into memory for more than 800,000 Palestinians expelled in 1948 and for another 375,000 expelled in 1967. The lives of millions of their descendants, born and still living in exile, are an ongoing nightmare of insecure existence. The massive flood of refugees displaced during the Nakba took shelter in the West Bank, Gaza, Jordan, Lebanon and Syria, believing it was a temporary move to last only a few weeks or a couple of months at the most. But Israel's continuing and systematic

(continued)

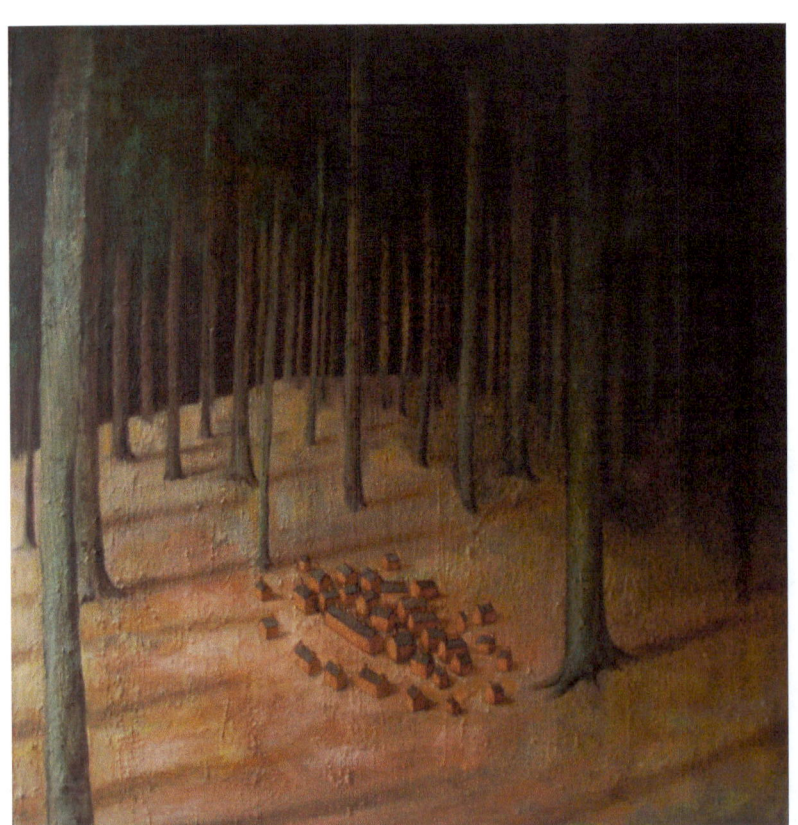

Clearing, Rita Duffy

My work has evolved out of a Belfast, Northern Ireland, context heavily inscribed by the visual components of social, political and national affiliations where meaning is not neutral. I have attempted to renegotiate aspects of language, local narratives and symbols to produce the possibility of new meaning. I have continued to place work in situations where physical and human geographies overlap. This work has been evolved for contexts where space is encountered not only as a physical and economic phenomenon but also as a psychological condition. My art has examined elements of a post-colonial condition intersecting with post-conflict agendas and our society's movement from a war/warrior footing toward civil processes. The suspension of temporary provisions and architectures replaced by civil ideas of future space and reconstruction, have been traced and given form. I have also been interested in the transmission of memorial and public memory through the ancient process of storytelling.

—Rita Duffy

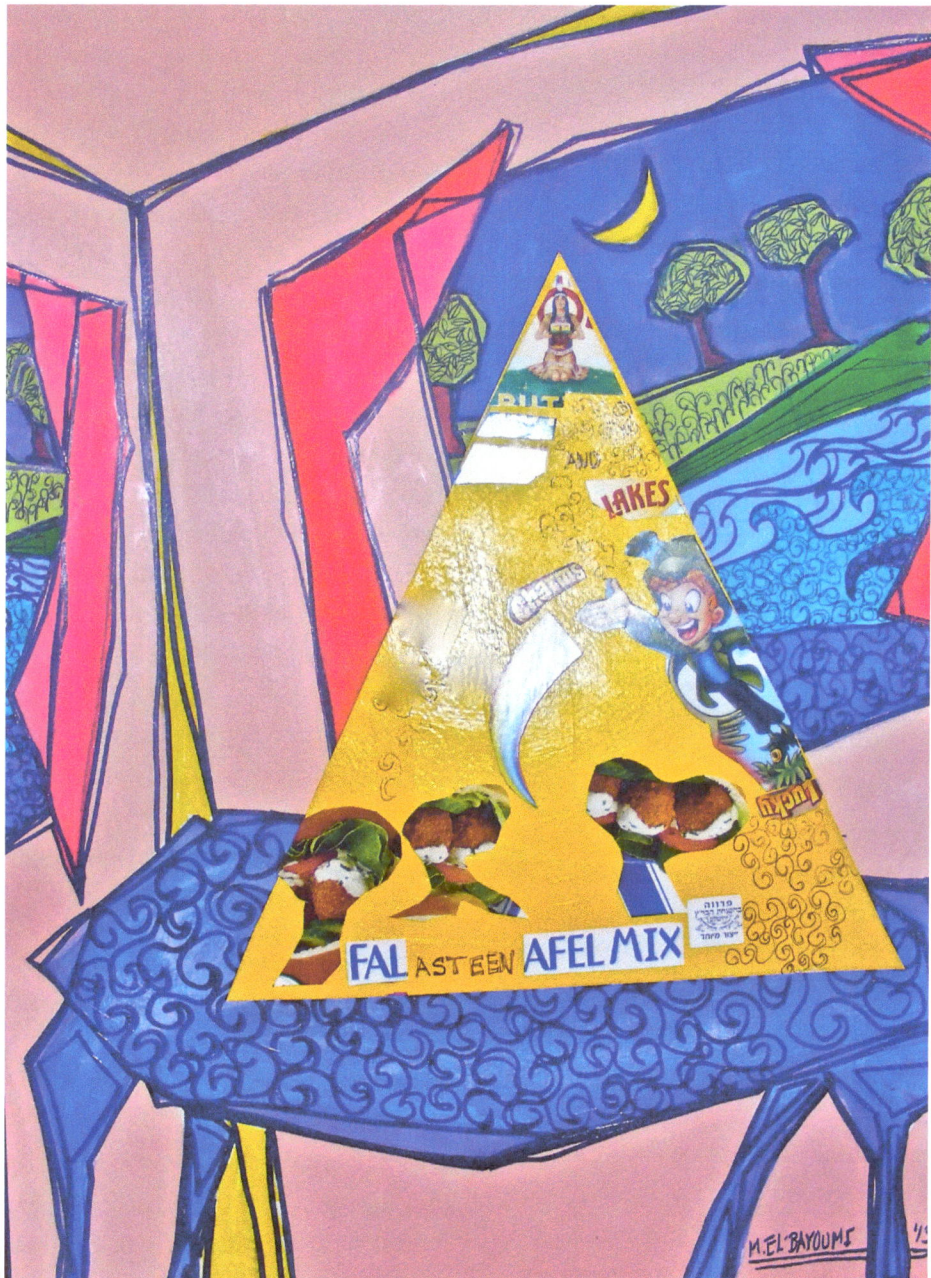

Lucky Can't Find a Piece of Land to Sit and Eat his Falafel Peacefully, Mona El-Bayoumi

While many people around the world and in the U.S. tried to stop the carnage for corporate wealth and imperial expansion, the violent and greedy have unfortunately persevered. Imperial and colonial powers have a number of things in common. Whether it is the United States, Great Britain or Israel, they all share a racist outlook, dehumanize their targeted populations, pursue territorial expansion and appropriate their victims' cultures. In doing so, the aggressors try to redefine and weaken the people they set out to conquer. Not only is land stolen, but so, too, is culture. *Lucky Can't Find a Piece of Land to Sit and Eat his Falafel Peacefully* attempts to express how symbols of an appropriated culture are commodified in the form of advertisement. In the name of good nutrition, advertising rationalizes imperial expansion, whether in relation to the indigenous nations of North America or the peoples of Ireland and Palestine? How can one swallow this?

—Mona El-Bayoumi

expulsion of the indigenous population and its refusal to allow Palestinians to return to their homes has extended the refugee crisis indefinitely.

The total number of refugees in the global Palestinian diaspora is estimated to be between 8 and 9 million. At least 5 million are registered as refugees with the United Nations, while the majority still live in refugee camps, dependent on UN support.[7] Those camps have effectively become reservations, not unlike those of Native Americans who survived extermination in the United States. They have become permanent holding tanks for discarded human beings, forcibly trapping their residents in endless cycles of neglect, poverty and violence. Palestinians have been stripped not only of their land, culture and identity, but, as a stateless and occupied population, they have also been stripped of the "right to have rights."[8]

The ongoing occupation and destruction of Palestine since 1948, has produced the largest and longest refugee crisis in modern history. Even with that dreadful distinction clearly in mind, *"The Map is Not the Territory"* reminds us that the experiences of the First People of the Americas, the Irish and the Palestinians are parts of the global journey of indigenous survival and resistance against colonial strategies of genocide. Their shared experiences of survivance compel us to distinguish between the destructive ideologies of colonial regimes, and the people who have been coerced to implement the policies of such regimes. Although they are still a minority, there is a growing number of Jews, both in Israel and across the globe, who denounce Israel's colonial violence and racist ideologies against the Palestinians, while declaring "Not in My Name!" to militant Zionism's practices of ethnic cleansing, land theft and occupation.[9] While misguided colonial and religious ideologies still shape the mindset of the majority of Israelis and supporters of Israel, it is critical to recognize that for sustainable peace and coexistence to occur, many more people of goodwill need to emancipate themselves from the yoke of racist dogmas, acknowledge their responsibilities to the indigenous Palestinian populations and actively commit themselves to the principles of restorative justice.

Conversely, when it comes to correcting the wrongs of colonial domination and charting sustainable paths toward liberation, Palestinians need to acknowledge the fact that the tragedies of the past can never be changed. Palestinians must remember and learn from the crimes perpetrated on them and their forbearers; they must resist, expose, denounce and bring to justice the executors of those atrocities; they must honor the resilience of their people and the endurance of their culture; and most importantly, they must continue to struggle for the right of return of all Palestinian refugees. But they must also recognize that they can never recreate their shattered past or reset the hands of time. The most effective strategy Palestinians and their supporters can pursue to mitigate ongoing crimes and to stop them from resuming in the future is to continue their personal and collective journeys of survivance. Their moral resistance and persistence will initiate psychological, moral and political conversions in the hearts and minds of people of goodwill in Israel and across the globe. In order for the Palestinians to liberate themselves from occupation, they need to help liberate the colonizing settlers from their bondage to the ideologies of repression. This principled path to liberation would enable the colonized as well as the colonizers, to envision a sustainable journey toward truth, justice, reconciliation, peace and coexistence.

It is crucial to recognize the cyclical nature of massive acts of violence, where victims of genocide can very quickly become perpetrators of crimes against humanity. One of the greatest ironies of the 20th century, and one of the most poignant lessons for Palestinians to consider, is that in the case of Israel, the tragically abused have become the abusers. The primary objective of people of goodwill on either side of the colonial struggle, whether in Palestine, in Ireland, in the Americas or elsewhere, is to help reshape the ethical consciousness of their nations. Fostering individual, as well as collective moral imagination enables the colonized and the colonizers to draw maps of future territories whose psychological topographies would be shaped by the principles of truth, dignity, equality, coexistence and forgiveness.

In the long and uncharted journey of survivance we must seek "Justice and Only Justice,"[10] no matter the injury, and in the struggle for justice we must cultivate the wisdom not to become the monster we wish to destroy. ∎

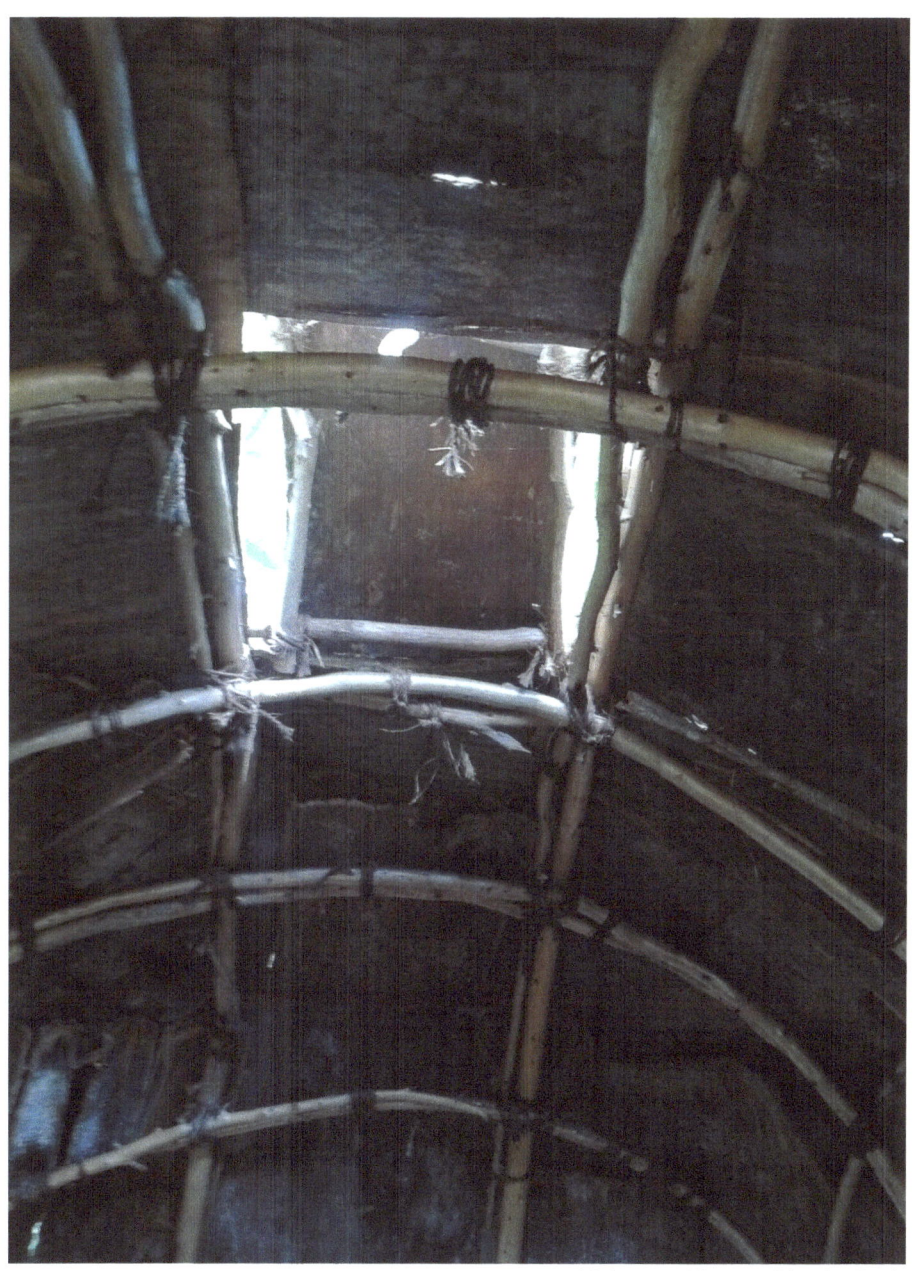
Mohegan Wigwam, Phoebe Farris

ATTAN AKAMIK
RESERVATION TREATY
REPATRIATE BOUNDARY
CLAN DIASPORA TURTLE
ISLAND FIRST NATIONS
INDIAN INDIGENOUS INDIAN
COUNTRY WOODLAND
EARTH TRIBE CLAN
WINGAPO SMUDGE OPENING
ARCHITECTURE NATURAL
ORGANIC LIGHT INTERIOR
ROUND SHELTER ANCIENT
TRADITIONAL WOVEN BARK
WILLOW CREATOR CULTURE
MOTHER EARTH FATHER
SKY SWEAT LODGE LEGACY
AIR MESTIZO HUMAN
BEING DREAM VIRGINIA
DISTRICT OF COLUMBIA
MARYLAND DELAWARE
NEW JERSEY NEW YORK
CONNECTICUT RHODE
ISLAND MASSACHUSSETS
MAINE ABSEGAMI
POWHATAN CONFEDEARACY
RENAPE MATTAPONI
PAMUNKEY CHICKAHOMINY
RAPPAHANNOCK
NANSEMOND NOTTOWAY
LENNI LENAPE NANTICOKE
SHINNECOCK WAMPANOAG
NARRAGANSETT MOHEGAN
PEQUOT MONTAUK RAMAPO
CIRCLE WIGWAM LONG
HOUSE SMOKE SPIRIT
VILLAGE CLAN TOTEM
UPPER WORLD SHAPE
UNFOLD TRIBE FULL BLOOD
HALF BREED KEKEWH
ASASQUETH NITAP CUMAY
BEAUTY CREATE HONOR
BIRTH HEAL POWWOW
GATHERING SHARE NOMAD
HEALER STAR MOON SUN

—Phoebe Farris

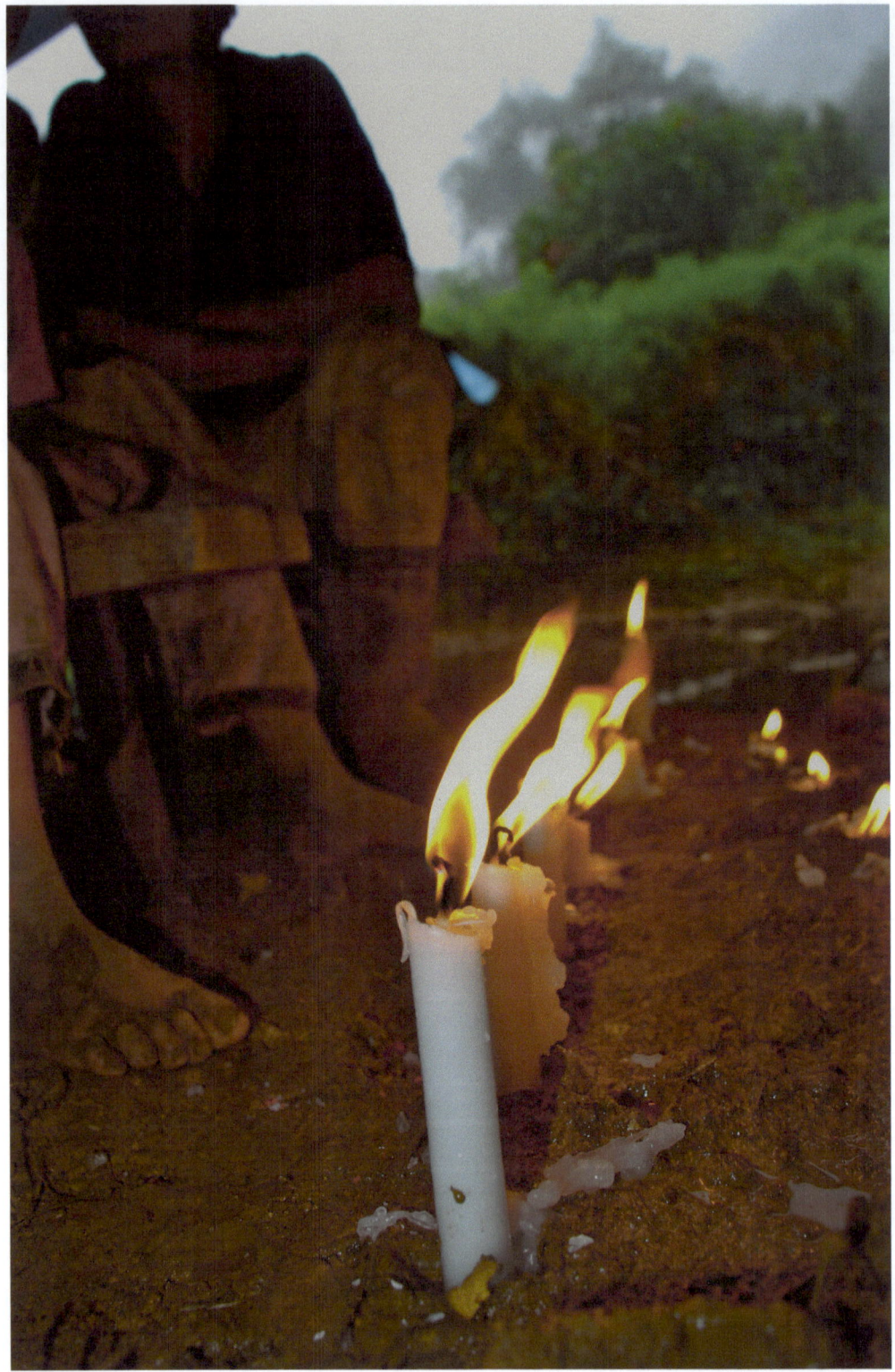

Candles for Water, Vivien Sansour

Women and children of Chiapas gathered with flowers and candles to pray for gratitude and for water. This kind of spiritual practice was present in Palestine until very recent years, when people chanted and prayed for rain with empty pots and colorful flags. Once, human culture everywhere understood the importance of humility toward Nature.

—Vivien Sansour

CHAPTER 7

The Unresolved Grief of a California Indian Tribe

Valentin Lopez

The Amah Mutsun Tribal Band are the documented descendants of the indigenous Mutsun speakers of Mission San Juan Bautista and the Awaswas speakers of Mission Santa Cruz along the central coast of California. The Amah Mutsun are an historic and continuous Tribe, as we have stayed together since the secularization of California missions in 1833. Although we were previously federally recognized, we are today a federally unrecognized Tribe. Because we are federally unrecognized, our Tribe receives no financial assistance from either the state or federal governments. The majority of our Tribal members are very poor and live at or below the poverty line. Consequently, few of our members continue to reside within our traditional territory. Most live in the central valley of California which is much cheaper than the coastal communities.

Our creation story tells us that at Mount Umunhum, which translates to "home of the hummingbird," and is the highest peak in the Santa Cruz Mountains, Creator made our winged, four-legged, finned and plant kin. Creator then made man and woman and very purposefully gave us a higher intelligence so we could figure things out. Then Creator gave us the responsibility to care for the lands of the greater Monterey Bay, which our people know as *Popoloutchum*.

For thousands of years, our ancestors worked to fulfill their obligation. They created many clans including bear, deer, fish and leaf clans, and more, to watch over their namesakes. These clans lived among their namesakes and it is said that our ancestors could talk to the animals and that the animals shared their knowledge. They learned how to use fire as a tool. Our ancestors would divide an open landscape into sections, usually about three to five sections, and then burn one section each year. The fire helped germinate seeds and this increased seed production provided food for both birds and our ancestors. The second- and third-year growth plants provided soft, tender and juicy shoots that were the preferred foods of deer, elk, antelope and other animals.

The high and older brush provided protection for rabbits, squirrels and other small creatures from the birds of prey above. Our ancestors recognized that the plants were gifts from the Creator. They learned to use these gifts as food, medicine, basketry, clothing, housing and much more.

Most importantly, our ancestors were very prayerful. They prayed while harvesting that the food plants would give their people strength, wisdom and love so that their work would please the Creator. They prayed while making arrow heads that the arrow head would swiftly kill the deer and that the deer would not suffer. Our ancestors created ceremonies to call home the salmon and to call home the migrating birds each season. Our ancestors created ceremonies to ask for balance in the four seasons, balance in the four directions and balance within their hearts, minds, bodies and souls. Our ancestors created ceremonies for healing and renewal; they created ceremonies for rites of passage for boys and ceremonies for coming of age for girls.

For thousands of years our ancestors understood their identity and their responsibility. They raised their families with love and passed on the indigenous knowledge that had been learned with each generation.

This period of our history came to an end with the arrival of the Roman Catholic Franciscan friars and the Spanish soldiers in 1769. Spain did not have the people to populate California and they were concerned that Russian fur trappers were entering California's northern territories and quickly moving south. Spain and the Church devised a plan to establish missions throughout California and to populate them with the indigenous people who were already living on these lands. It was Spain's intent to have the priests teach the indigenous people to speak, read and write Spanish so they could become citizens and subjects of Spain. Although Junípero Serra Ferrer, the monk assigned to lead this effort, agreed to this plan, he quickly abandoned it once he arrived in San Diego. Serra felt it was his responsibility to save the souls of the native people rather than make them citizens of Spain.

Serra worked with the Spanish government and military during the conquest of Mexico. He came to believe that Natives had no souls and that they were nothing more that sav-

(continued)

ages and that they would only respond to brutal treatment. California's mission period was devastating to Indians. When an Indian was taken to the mission he or she was given a new name and clothes made of scratchy wool which they were required to wear year round. They were not allowed to speak their own languages, sing their songs or pray as they had learned. Our ancestors could no longer visit their sacred sites, hold their ceremonies, care for the land or gather their traditional resources. They were forced to grow and eat the food of the colonizers. If they tried to run away, the military hunted them down and took them back to the mission, where they were severely whipped as the others were forced to watch.

They were forced to pray to a god they did not know and in a language they did not understand. Their families were separated, and many women and girls were raped by the soldiers. Boys had hernias by the age of ten because of the hard labor. There were tremendous death rates due to disease, malnutrition, depression and beatings. Death rates averaged about 50 percent a year, and, in Mission San Juan Bautista alone, more than 19,421 deaths were reported. During the mission period, it is estimated that over 40 percent of California's Native population died. Father Mariano Payeras, the last Spanish Padre Presidente, admitted, "All we have done to the Indians is consecrate them, baptize them and bury them."

The mission period was followed by the Mexican period in the 1830s. The Mexican government secularized the missions and awarded enormous land grants to men of privilege. The grant holders worked to develop large herds of cattle, sheep and horses. They immediately went to work killing all the bear, deer and elk in the territory. They imported European grazing grasses that effectively eliminated the native grasses and plants. The grant holders also needed a labor force for their immense ranches. Because only Native peoples occupied this territory, land owners forced the Indians to work on their ranches. A few Natives received meager salaries, but most was slave labor. They were severely beaten or killed if they tried to run away, continuing the treatment they received during the mission period.

The Mexican period was followed by the American period. The American period began almost immediately with the discovery of gold in 1846. Thousands of people from around the world rushed to California to seek riches. These miners had no regard for the Indians who lived on these lands and conflict soon erupted. To address the "Indian problem," the governor of California, Peter Burnett, signed an Executive Order to exterminate all Indians. In his 1851 Second Annual Message to the Legislature, Burnett declared, "That a war of extermination will continue to be waged between the two races until the Indian race becomes extinct…"

A bounty of $.25 to $5 was paid for every dead Indian. Military excursions were also sent to find and kill Indians. The State of California spent over $1,500,000 on this effort. To meet these costs, the state issued its first governmental bond to pay for the extermination of Indians. The extermination order was in effect for seven years. This order was followed by laws of indentured servitude, a euphemism for slavery. (Some Indians continued to be indentured into the 1930s.) In the 1860s, the State of California passed a law legalizing the kidnapping of Indian children, who were sold for about $150 and often used as slave labor. At times, even pedophiles bought them. Approximately 10,000 children and adults were kidnapped under this law. Many more laws were passed by the State of California that greatly impacted Indians, so that by the turn of the 20th century, the population had been reduced from nearly one million Natives to between 16,500 to 24,000. California Indian history has never been truthfully told.

The Amah Mutsun believe that the way we love, the way we hate, our bravery, our fear, our optimism, our pessimism, the way we solve problems and the way we deal with difficult issues were all given to us by the seven generations that came before. Likewise, we recognize our responsibility to help the next seven generations.

Today many of our Tribal members suffer from depression, substance abuse, spousal and/or child abuse, suicide, identity issues and poverty. My first five years of life were spent mostly in a tent along the rivers and streams of the Gilroy and Hollister areas with other Tribal members. My grandparents, uncles and aunts, like many other Tribal members, did not read or write. When I started school, every time I left the house, my grandmother or great aunts said, "Remember,

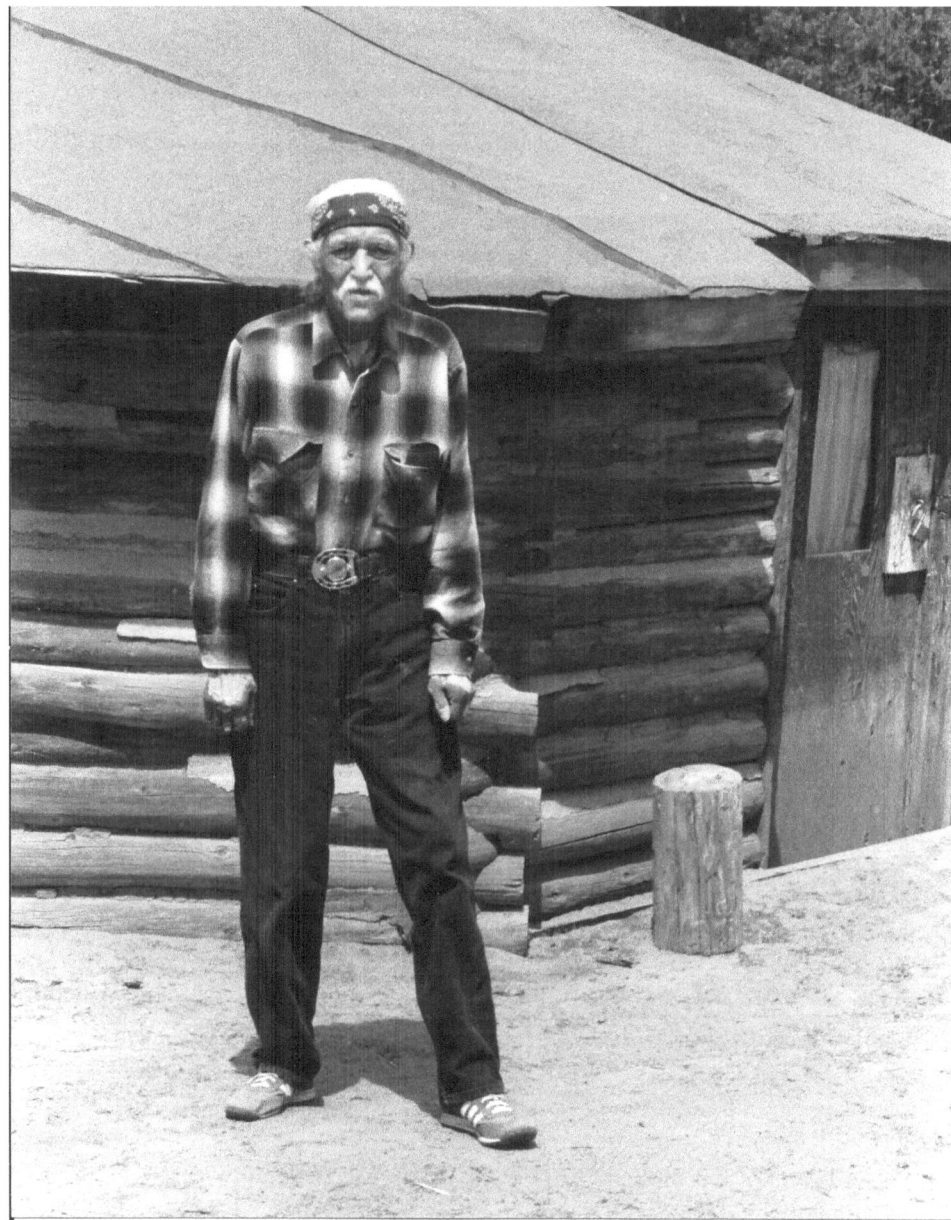

Mr. Bradley – Hozhonahaslii: Stories of Healing the Soul Wound, Donna Schindler

> Hundreds of years of genocide and forced assimilation into a dominant society have left a scar on Native people throughout the world, which some elders refer to as "the soul wound." The unhealed traumas of the past are handed down from generation to generation, resulting in extremely high rates of domestic violence, substance abuse, diabetes and depression.
>
> —Donna Schindler

always say you're Mexican, never say you're Indian." I was not allowed to tell my friends, my classmates, my neighbors or anyone else that I am Indian. I later learned that my grandmother and others of her generation had also been taught to be silent by their grandparents. We have been told that when California became a state, our ancestors gathered in the corner of a room and cried, convinced this meant they were all to be annihilated. During the American period, though our primary language was English, our ancestors claimed they were Mexicans and not Indians hoping they would not be killed for bounty money or that their children would not be stolen.

In the 20th century, our members did their best to maintain

(continued)

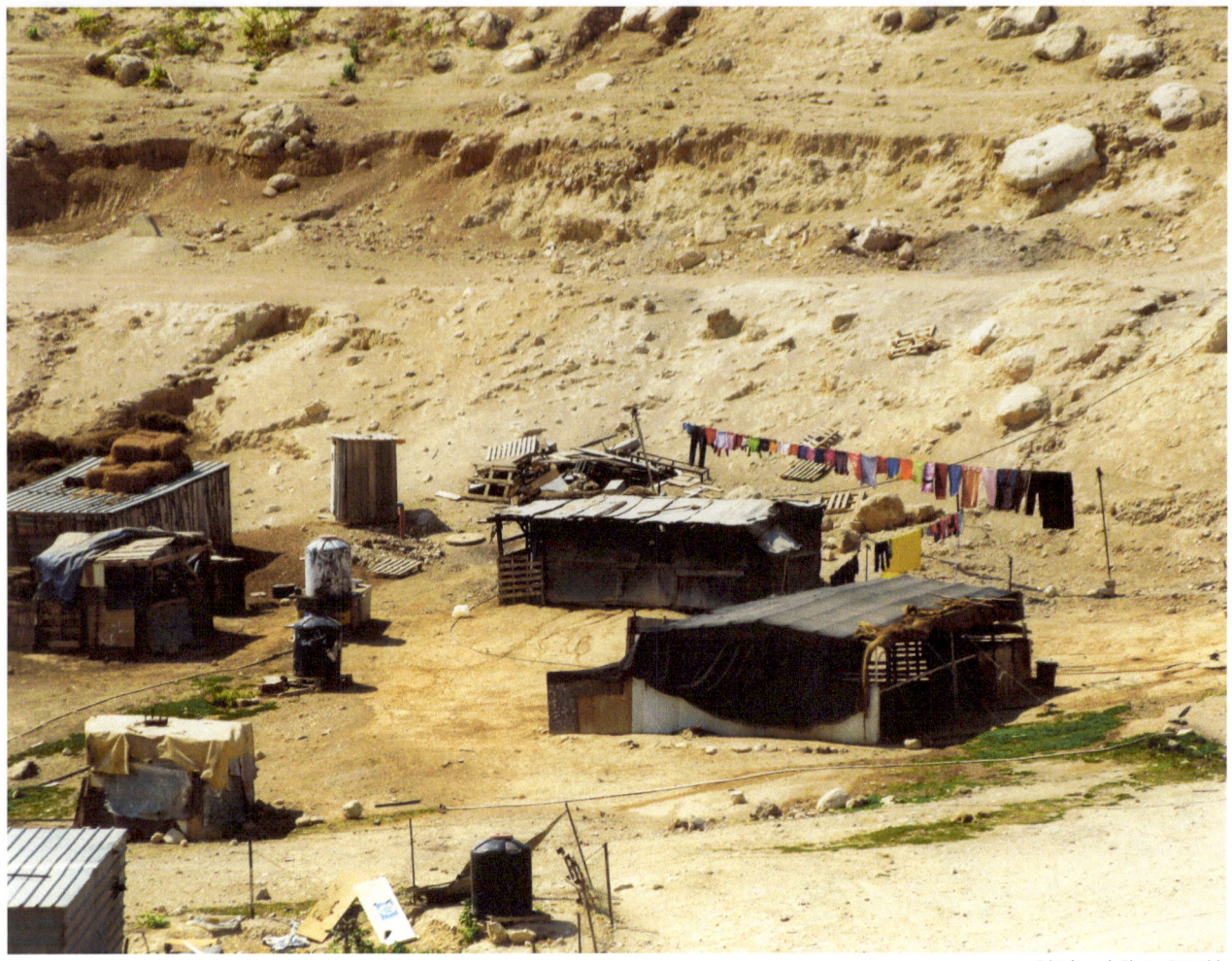

Displaced, Elena Farsakh

Bedouins are known to roam. The notion of supreme freedom is poignantly romantic. In Palestine and in Israel, the right of Palestinians to move freely through their own country has been walled and fenced physically, politically and emotionally. The beautiful expanse of Bedouin and Palestinian territory is cut off – limited by the frame of this photograph. The view of a proud and historic people is caged.

—Elena Farsakh

low profiles. They worked on farms or sheep ranches far from any town. They were afraid to speak up when they were cheated on their wages and were often given a bottle of whisky in lieu of wages.

As Tribal Chairman I recognize that most of our members suffer from historic trauma. Historic trauma occurs when there is unresolved grief that has resulted from cumulative emotional and psychological wounding over a lifespan and across generations. How could our ancestors teach their children to love, be secure, care for and protect Mother Earth and all living things or hold ceremonies to balance their lives when, for nearly one hundred years they were enslaved, beaten and raped, knowing that only death would set them free? (I've read that at one mission a mother cupped her hands over her newborn child's mouth and suffocated the baby so that it would not have to grow up in that place.)

How, during the Mexican period, could a father teach his son to hunt and fish in the traditional way? How could our ancestors pass on the knowledge of food and medicinal plants, when these plants could no longer be found? How could parents protect their children from being violated by land owners? It did not take long before our knowledge of sacred and traditional sites, places of power, language, customs and ways of daily life were lost.

Our federal recognition status was illegally terminated around 1930 by the Indian Field Services (now Bureau of Indian Affairs) of the Department of the Interior. Superintendent L.A. Dorrington was asked to determine the needs of California Tribes so each tribe could be given land. Dorrington is on record as saying, "No tribe deserves land," and reported that over 180 California tribes had no need of it. Shortly afterward, our federal recognition status was terminated without notice. "In San Juan Baptista," Dorrington wrote, "we find the San Juan Baptista band, which resides in the vicinity of the Mission San Juan Baptista, which is located near the town of Hollister. These Indians have been well cared for by the Catholic priests and no land is required." This was the extent of Dorrington's report on our Tribe. He provided no substantiating documents. It seems that the federal government attempted to delegate responsibility for our Tribe to the Catholic priests. Recent letters from the Church and Diocese Archivist refute this claim; they report that the Church had no program for or contact with Indians.

As Tribal Chairman, I look back seven generations and ask myself, how our ancestors could have taught their children to love, to understand their obligation to Creator, to learn and pass on their language, songs, ceremonies, spiritual beliefs and knowledge of the universe, when, since the Spanish conquest, survival was their only goal. Since the time of the missions and into the present, many individuals, government workers and religions have tried to tell us how to live, requiring us to abandon the ways of our ancestors and our directive from Creator.

In 2005, several Tribal Elders attended a Tribal Council meeting to tell us that Creator has never rescinded his directive that we take care of Mother Earth and all living things. They then added, "We must find a way to do this." I left the meeting worried and confused. We are an extremely poor tribe, we own no land, we have few members living in Popo-

loutchum. How can we ever fulfill our obligation to Creator?

It was shortly after this that I received a phone call from the Superintendent of Pinnacles National Park asking to meet with us. This meeting resulted in our Tribe working with Pinnacles to reintroduce traditional Mutsun land stewardship to the park. In 2009, much to our disbelief, we conducted a cultural burn at the park. When we scheduled a landscape-tending day at Pinnacles, it was not unusual to have more than fifty members volunteer. In 2012, our Tribe was named Outstanding Volunteer of the Year for the United States National Park Service and our Vice-Chair and I were presented the award by the park's director in Washington, D.C.

Since our first meeting with Pinnacles, our Tribe has established relationships with California State Parks, local County Parks, and several land conservation organizations to bring indigenous land stewardship to these lands. We have also worked to restore and practice our traditional ceremonies at several sites. In 2012, we developed the Amah Mutsun Land Trust to protect our sacred and traditional sites and to continue our work to restore native plants and stewardship.

In addition to our stewardship work, in 2012 we began holding bi-monthly wellness meetings for Tribal members. In 2013, psychiatrist Dr. Donna Schindler, who specializes in historic trauma – and whose film, *Hozhonahaslii: Stories of Healing the Soul Wound* is featured in the exhibition "*The Map is Not the Territory*": *Parallel Paths-Palestinians, Native Americans, Irish* – began working with our Tribe. At our wellness meetings, we have discussed topics such Tribal history, historic trauma, culture, traditions, addiction, abuse, grieving, relationships and more. Donna has helped many of our Elders be able to "tell their story." This has been important not only for their peace of mind, but for our youth, who hear these stories and can pass them on to future generations.

Traditionally, our ancestors never owned land; the land belongs to Creator. Our ancestors understood this and understood that it was their responsibility to care for Mother Earth and all living things. This is the path the Amah Mutsun Tribal Band will return to. This is the path that Creator has asked us to follow and it is the path that will allow our members to heal from our historic trauma.

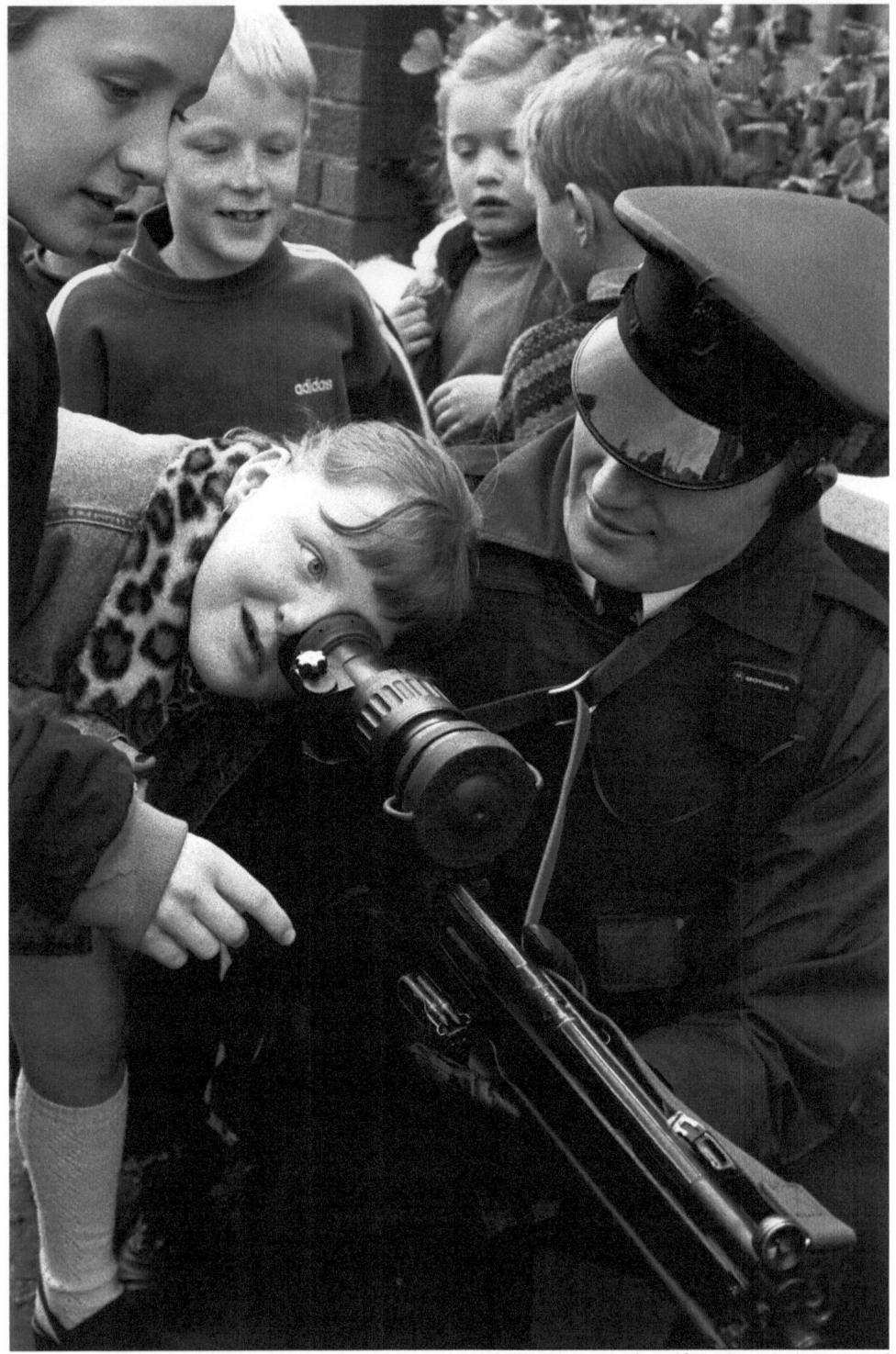

Child's Play, North Belfast, Tom Quinn Kumpf

My fascination with the Irish began while working in Northern Ireland as a photojournalist during the Troubles (late 1960s to 1998). I asked a man in Catholic West Belfast if he knew where his ancestors were from originally. Assertively and proudly, he pointed to the ground at his feet and said, "From this very bit of turf right here. It was my people who fought over it, who bled for it and the ancient mounds, stones and that dolmen on the hill above the city prove it."

—Tom Quinn Kumpf

CHAPTER 8

Sharing the Burden
Solidarity Through a Recognition of Injustice

Rawan Arar

I am Palestinian. This fact surfaces most often when I exclaim my Palestinianess in personal statements for scholarships or other formalized platforms that fish for neatly packaged individuality. Otherwise, I don't proclaim my Palestinianness in line at the grocery store or in the changing room at the gym – but when was the last time I actually made it to a gym anyway? To the untrained eye, I'm just a woman with long curly dark hair and stark eyebrows. My bubbliness makes up for my lapses in eloquence and I like to think I am just self-deprecating enough to be approachable while preserving a semblance of confidence. I've grown up with many of the privileges allotted to the children of loving, middle-class, educated parents in the United States.

It wasn't until a few years ago, while working on an MA in women's studies, that I began "coming out" as Palestinian to strangers even before I could evaluate any potential prejudice that might linger between spoken words. In 2015, Palestinians live all over the world and their experiences reflect the places in which they reside. I am not one of the five million Palestinians who rely on UNRWA (United Nations Relief and Work Agency), created in 1949 and tasked with providing protection and assistance to Palestinian refugees, most of whom live in Gaza, the West Bank, Syria, Lebanon or Jordan. I am not stateless, systematically discriminated against as a second-class citizen, unemployed, caged-in, facing imprisonment without cause, in fear of imminent violence, suffering from Post-Traumatic Stress Disorder, hungry, on hunger strike, in need of shelter or in need of re-building a demolished home. Instead, I am armed with a shiny U.S. passport, a liberal education and all the right words that make my indignation articulate if not appropriate.

I suppose my Palestinianness has witnessed hypocrisy and ignorance far more than cruelty. I have a lot of "huh" moments – like noticing that a certain airline now offers a hummus and pita bread lunchbox option while simultaneously selecting Arab passengers for "random screenings"; or, traveling northbound down Interstate 5, between San Diego and Los Angeles, and passing a neighborhood on a hill that starkly resembles an Israeli settlement in the West Bank; or, navigating the occasional, but still frequent, terrorist / Palestinian / Arab /Muslim joke that eerily reveals something unpleasant about the person who said it. I observe, take notes and comment upon poetic injustice or the ways in which culture can detach itself from history. I bite my teeth, rationalize, practice compassion, inform, suggest, learn and, to echo Gloria Steinem's sentiment, unlearn. I spend a good amount of time thinking about how fear, the threat of scarcity and the birthright entitlement associated with citizenship status has nested itself so comfortably in our consciousness that we justify the most horrendous acts against one another. I'm a scholar-in-the-making as a sociology Ph.D. student and I'm learning how to make human rights issues relevant to wider audiences.

In 2011, I spent half the year in both pro-British and pro-Irish parts of Belfast, Northern Ireland. My stay in Northern Ireland was preceded by chance encounters in Dublin several months prior in the summer of 2010. At the time, I was writing about Iraqi refugees in Jordan. The moment I mentioned refugees, my new Irish friends would tell me all about the Palestinians. As a Texan-Palestinian, I'd never seen such enthusiasm for the Palestinian cause come leaping toward me from non-Arab lips. This happened again and again.

In Killarney, a cab driver spent twenty-five minutes explaining the Israeli-Palestinian conflict to me. "What are you? Italian?" he asked as he loaded my suitcase into the back of the van. Before I had a chance to respond, he continued, "Are you Israeli? Are you Spanish?" I said "no" to all the above before he cut me off to share his experiences as a United Nations peacekeeper in Lebanon in the 1980s. I sat in stunned silence listening to the driver elaborate about the details of the conflict, taking mental notes so that I could recap the story to my friends and family. I didn't agree with everything he said, but I was amazed at how much he had to say and how eagerly he said it. As our journey came to an end, I revealed with a laissez-faire cool, fizzing with anticipation on the inside, that I am Palestinian. He laughed. "You could have said something sooner."

(continued)

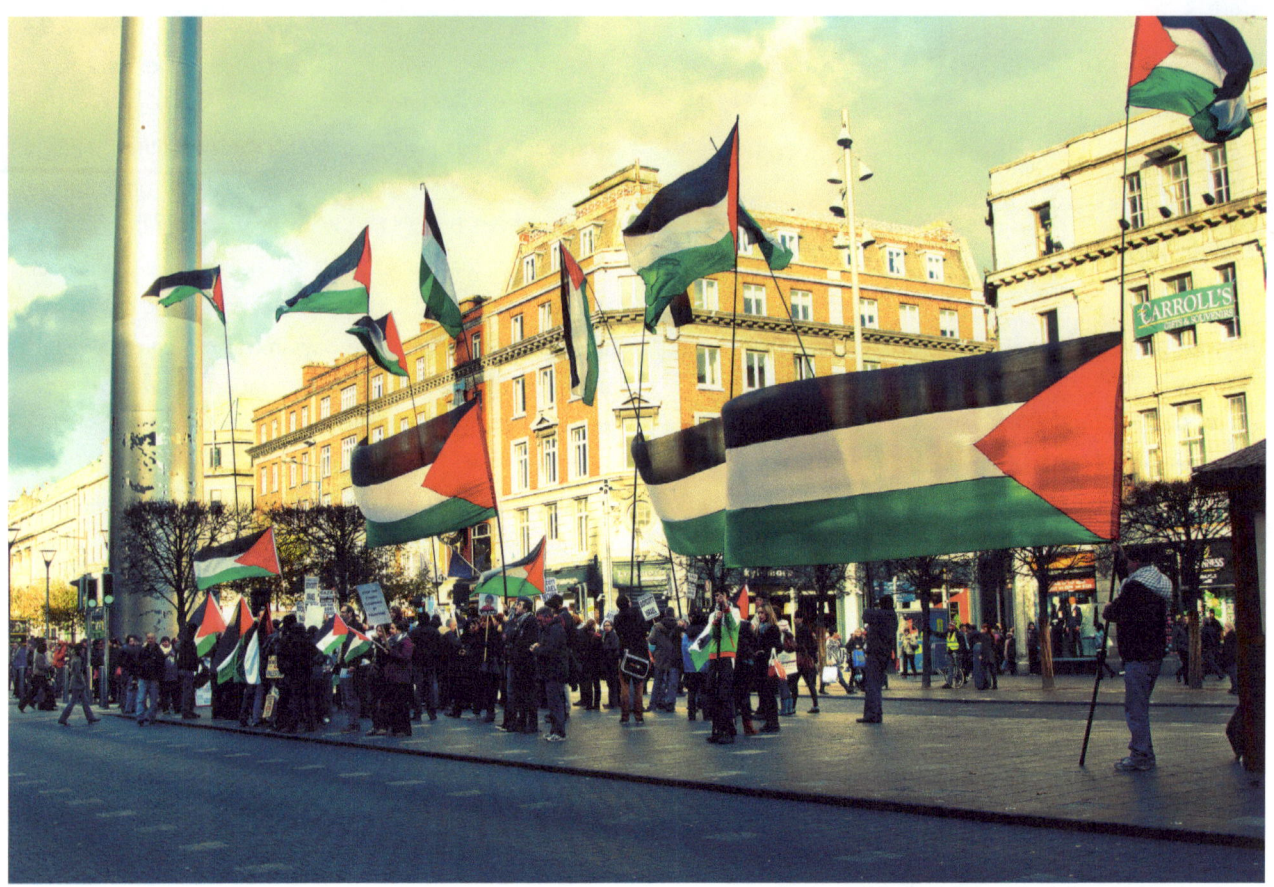

Palestine Dublin, 2012, Fatin al-Tamimi and LisaMarie Johnson

The protest in solidarity with Gaza, during an Israeli attack, took place on O' Connell Street, in front of the General Post Office, which served as the headquarters of Irish rebellion leaders during the Easter Rising in 1916. The 800-year British occupation of what at last became the Republic of Ireland in 1922 closely resembles today's occupation of Palestine.

After a week in Ireland, I was determined to explore this Irish-Palestinian affinity. After all, I'd traveled throughout the Middle East and never witnessed so much unbridled support. I'd spent my whole life, it seemed, stepping on eggshells as I cautiously revealed my stereotyped and misunderstood ethnic identity. Back home in the U.S., I sat at my computer and sent emails to universities throughout Northern Ireland and the Irish Republic: "Will research for place to stay." Somehow, things worked out, and, in 2011, I ended up as a visiting scholar at the Irish School of Ecumenics in Belfast, Northern Ireland.

The pro-British and pro-Irish demarcation is an overgeneralization, but these are the terms that I will use to refer to sectarianism in Northern Ireland so as not to conflate religious and political beliefs. Others may refer to a Protestant / Catholic or Unionist / Nationalist divide. Despite the multiple identifiers, each of which is uniquely nuanced and consequential, there exists a discernible division in Northern Ireland rooted in a settler-colonial history that laid the foundation for systematic and institutionalized privileges and prejudices.

I believe that the use of symbols and rhetoric, including those adopted from the Israeli-Palestinian conflict, has assumed a more salient role for both pro-British and pro-Irish communities since the signing of the Good Friday Agreement in 1998. The peace accord garnered 71.12 percent of votes, which were in favor of ending the violence. However, this consensus did not apply to the subsequent power-sharing initiatives nor did it broker a mutually accepted retelling of

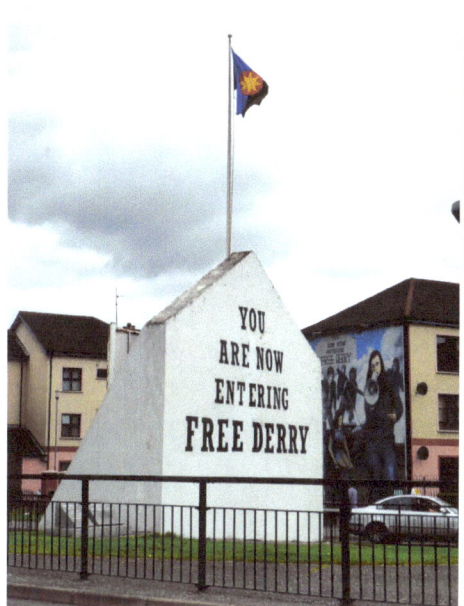
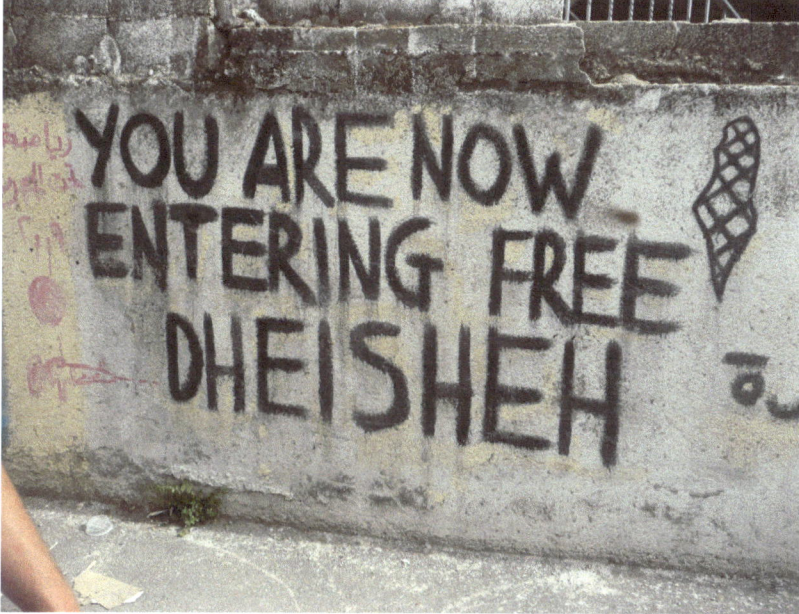

Solidarity Flag Derry, Scott Benesiinaabandan *Free D*, Rawan Arar

the Troubles. Without a truth commission, there remains no agreement as to who are the victims, perpetrators and beneficiaries of the Troubles. The term beneficiaries is important because it acknowledges that some of the people who did not commit maleficent acts continued to benefit from the spoils of injustice which are allocated across ethnic lines.

Seventeen years after the signing of the Good Friday Agreement, the legacy of difference separates pro-British and pro-Irish communities in almost every aspect of daily life. More than 90 percent of schools segregate Protestant and Catholic children.[1] Belfast is home to ninety-nine "peace lines," barriers constructed from iron, brick and steel that barricade one community from another, sometimes reaching a height of 25 feet. A recent survey found that while 27 percent of the general population of Northern Ireland "would like Peace Line(s) to come down now," 49 percent of the general population would like the barriers to come down at some time in the future, *but not now.*[2] It is within this divided context that I observed the pervasive incorporation of the Israeli-Palestinian conflict in Northern Ireland.

British-Israeli and Irish-Palestinian allegiances have a long and politicized past uniquely tailored to engage the conflict in Northern Ireland. As early as 1937, and before the establishment of the state of Israel in 1948, the first governor of Jerusalem, Sir Ronald Storrs, claimed in his memoirs that a "Jewish homeland … will form for England 'a little loyal Jewish Ulster' in a sea of potentially hostile Arabism."[3] The term Ulster refers to the counties of Northern Ireland and exudes pro-British sentiments. Commenting on the Irish-Palestinian connection, Trinity College Dublin lecturer Owen Sheehy Skeffington stated in 1936 that "the Arabs are fighting for their liberty against British Imperialism which is using the Zionist movement as a willing instrument."[4] The Irish-Palestinian comparisons thrived throughout the Troubles when members of the Provisional IRA (Irish Republican Army) created ties with the PLO (Palestinian Liberation Organization).[5] According to Andrew Hill and Andrew White, pro-British affinity for the Israeli cause became widespread in response to pro-Irish solidarity during the second Palestinian *Intifada* or uprising in 2002.[6]

In contemporary times, political actors plant Israeli and Palestinian flags that wave throughout sectarian neighborhoods. Political murals, posters and graffiti proclaim allegiances. Support for either Israel or Palestine can be found in political speeches on the floor of the Northern Ireland Assembly, in songs and other forms of media. Notably, Irish support for Palestinians is more vocal and widespread. In

(continued)

2012, former Irish hunger striker Tommy McKearney and Sinn Féin Member of Parliament Michelle Gildernew voiced their support for Palestinian hunger striker Khader Adnan via Youtube calling upon the world to take notice.[7] Self-identifying members of the Irish diaspora have also chimed in to express solidarity with the Palestinians. David Rovics wrote and performed a song titled *Khader Adnan, Bobby Sands*, drawing explicit comparisons between the Irish and Palestinian struggles and resistance.[8] Declan de Barra performs *Curfew*, in which he sings from the perspective of a Palestinian child.[9]

The Irish-Palestinian connection is prevalent, if not well-documented. I was surprised, however, to stumble upon Palestinians who relied on Irish symbols of resistance to proclaim their rights, although this practice does not seem widespread. It was after my time in Northern Ireland that I discovered the image that appears in "*The Map is Not the Territory*," titled *Free D*. The photograph was taken haphazardly in 2010 in Dheisheh, a Palestinian refugee camp outside of Bethlehem. I was visiting the West Bank for the first time and was photographing almost every other moment. Before I left to Palestine from Jordan, my aunt hugged me and instructed, "Take pictures of everything. We want to see everything. You are going on behalf of all of us." I was able to enter Israel and the West Bank as an American citizen. My aunt, like much of my extended family, holds Jordanian citizenship. Although parts of the West Bank are accessible to my aunt, her citizenship status makes it difficult for her to travel throughout Israel.

The phrase "You are now entering Free Dheisheh," scrawled on the camp wall, is a direct adaptation from the emblematic sign that appears in Derry / Londonderry, a Northern Irish city where even the name of the town is controversial because it signifies sectarian allegiances. The "Free Derry" mural commemorates the Irish civil rights movement with the words "You are now entering Free Derry." The sign has been recreated several times and expressions of Palestinian solidarity usually coincide with Israeli bombardments of Gaza. In 2005, the white background of the "Free Derry" mural was replaced with a Palestinian flag but the writing remained the same, visually invoking both the Irish and Palestinian struggles. In 2009, the "Free Derry" mural included a drawing of an Israeli jet dropping bombs on a baby carriage to represent the killing of children in the densely populated area of Gaza. The mural read, "You are now Entering Free Gaza." In the summer of 2014, the "Free Derry" mural exclaimed, "End Genocide in Gaza," with a partial drawing of a Palestinian face crying bloody tears.

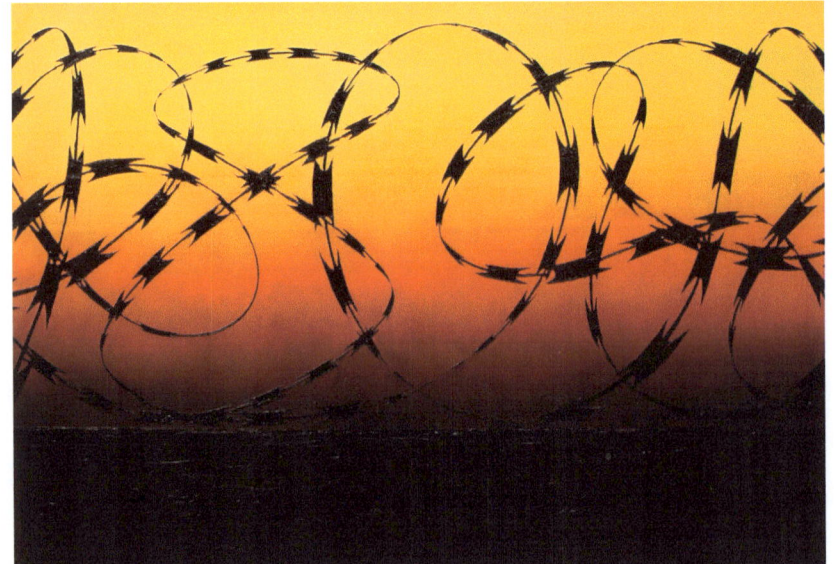

The Second Intifada, Michael Elizondo, Jr.

As a descendant of nations with an on-going list of clashing socio-political histories, much of my overall subject matter reflects a dichotomy of positive and negative perspectives. Gaining much influence from my Southern Cheyenne and Chumash backgrounds, I find myself at peace with the beautiful history and culture my ancestors left behind but often find that history clouded by a number of grim topics and events. While creating my artwork, I alternate these perspectives, which ultimately brings forth a balance of how I interpret our contemporary state and the relationship my people have with the mainstream society.

—Michael Elizondo, Jr.

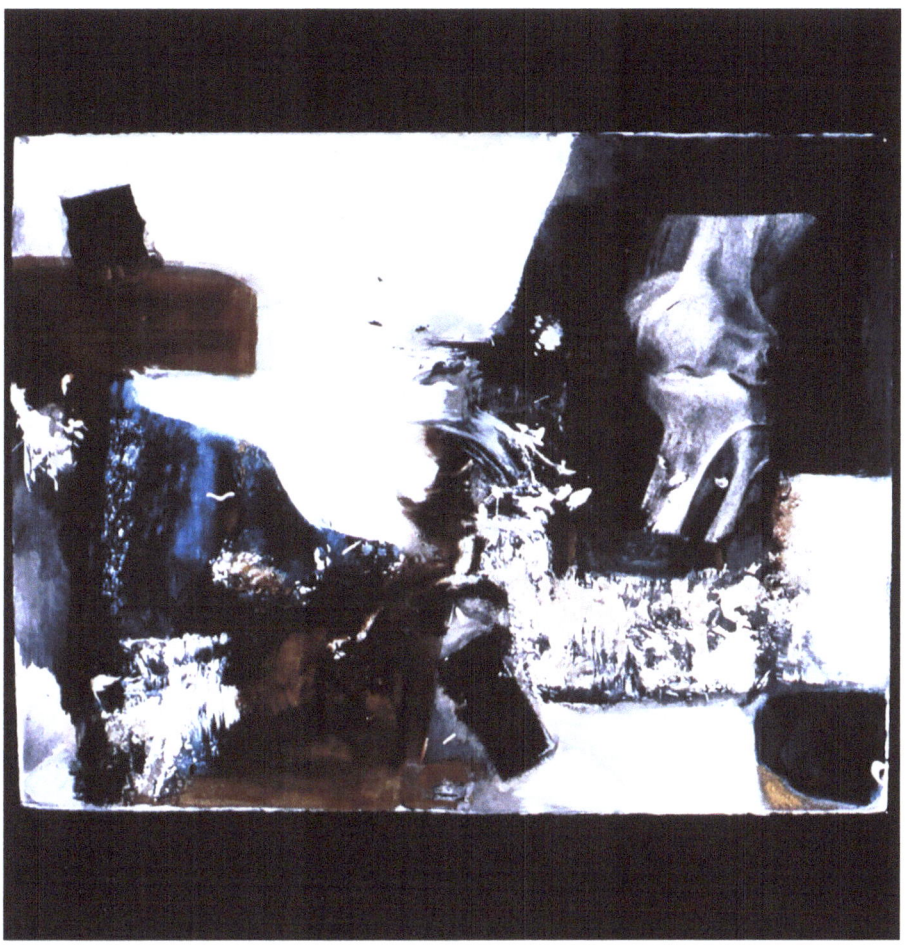

Irish History Lesson #1, Alan Montgomery

The summer of 2014 was a particularly ugly episode in the Israeli-Palestinian saga. According to the UN Office of Coordination of Humanitarian Affairs, the military action which Israel called "Operation Protective Edge" claimed the lives of 2,104 Gazans in just under two months: including 495 children and 253 women. The Palestinian Ministry of Health records a higher number and accounts for 102 elderly people who died. The violence also yielded a ghastly count of Gazans injured in the attack – 11,100 people. Israel also suffered casualties with sixty-six military personnel and six civilians killed.[10] Needless to say – although on second thought maybe it should be reiterated with every breath – each life is valuable, should be accounted for and deserves to be mourned.

In Ernest Renan's words, "…indeed, suffering in common unifies more than joy does."[11] Renan was referring to the creation of a nation, presumably enclosed by borders. Solidarity, however, often includes the recognition of suffering across borders – an evocative initiative that unites through a shared burden. Solidarity can take many forms, not the least of which can be a simple recognition of past injustice practiced through mourning. With "*The Map is Not the Territory*," we make the time, and create a space, to mourn the losses experienced of Native American, Irish and Palestinian people. Mourning is not a zero-sum game because humanity is also not a zero-sum game. I believe that it is only through truth, through an acknowledgment of historical injustice and the legacies that follow, that we can move toward reconciliation, despite whatever that should entail. In the case of Irish-Palestinian solidarity, the recognition of shared suffering has become a platform to criticize imperialism and the legacies of colonialism on a global scale. Through solidarity and coalition building, new tools to interpret injustice and construct resistance emerge in the nation building and remembering process.

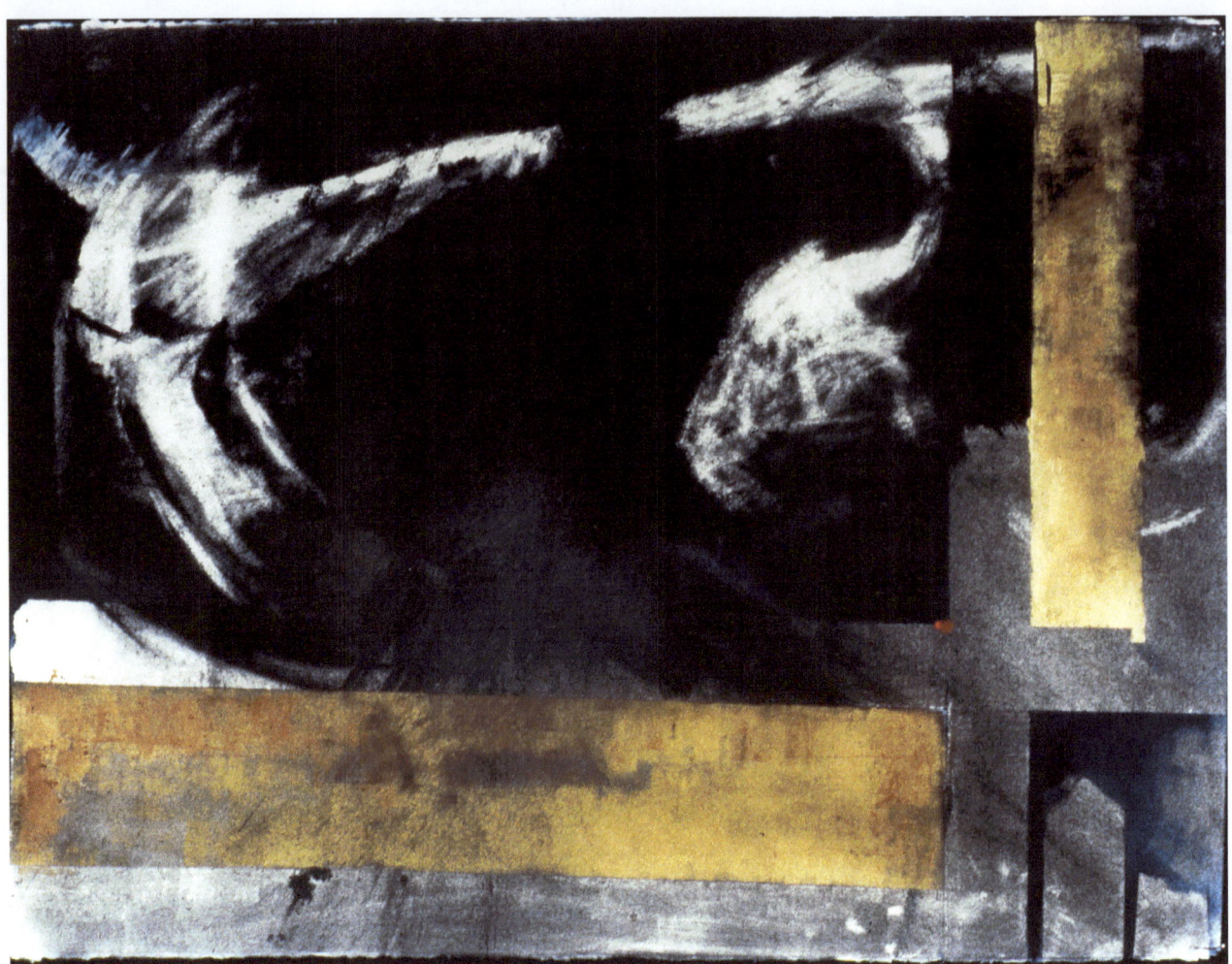

Irish History Lesson #2, Alan Montgomery

The rupture between figuration and abstraction is where I find associations that are both personal and universal. There are no prescriptions, canons or rules for making images in this territory. Thematic transitions accompany relocations in working spaces, geography and cultural community. I am from Northern Ireland and I am keenly aware of how place, community and physical space affect my work. The Troubles in Northern Ireland left a definite impact on so many lives. The drawings are suspended in time, open to interpretation. Marks and factures create a ground against which figurative elements are embedded, smashed and squeezed until I sense they are nearing boiling point. The physical and the spiritual are folded into a pictorial space that is sensuous, provocative, alive. *Irish History Lessons* embodies the Irish Troubles and events at Wounded Knee, South Dakota, in 1973, which occurred during the height of the turmoil in Belfast. I tried to align the histories of our two cultures (Lakota and Irish). In 1973, so-called "knee cappings," by both the loyalist Ulster Volunteer Force and the nationalist IRA, signaled a new era of torture and brutality. Knee capping was so commonplace that the Royal Victoria Hospital became world renowned for the development of prosthetics and treatments for the injury. Now, years later, Wounded Knee and the events surrounding the Troubles, have come full circle for me.

—Alan Montgomery

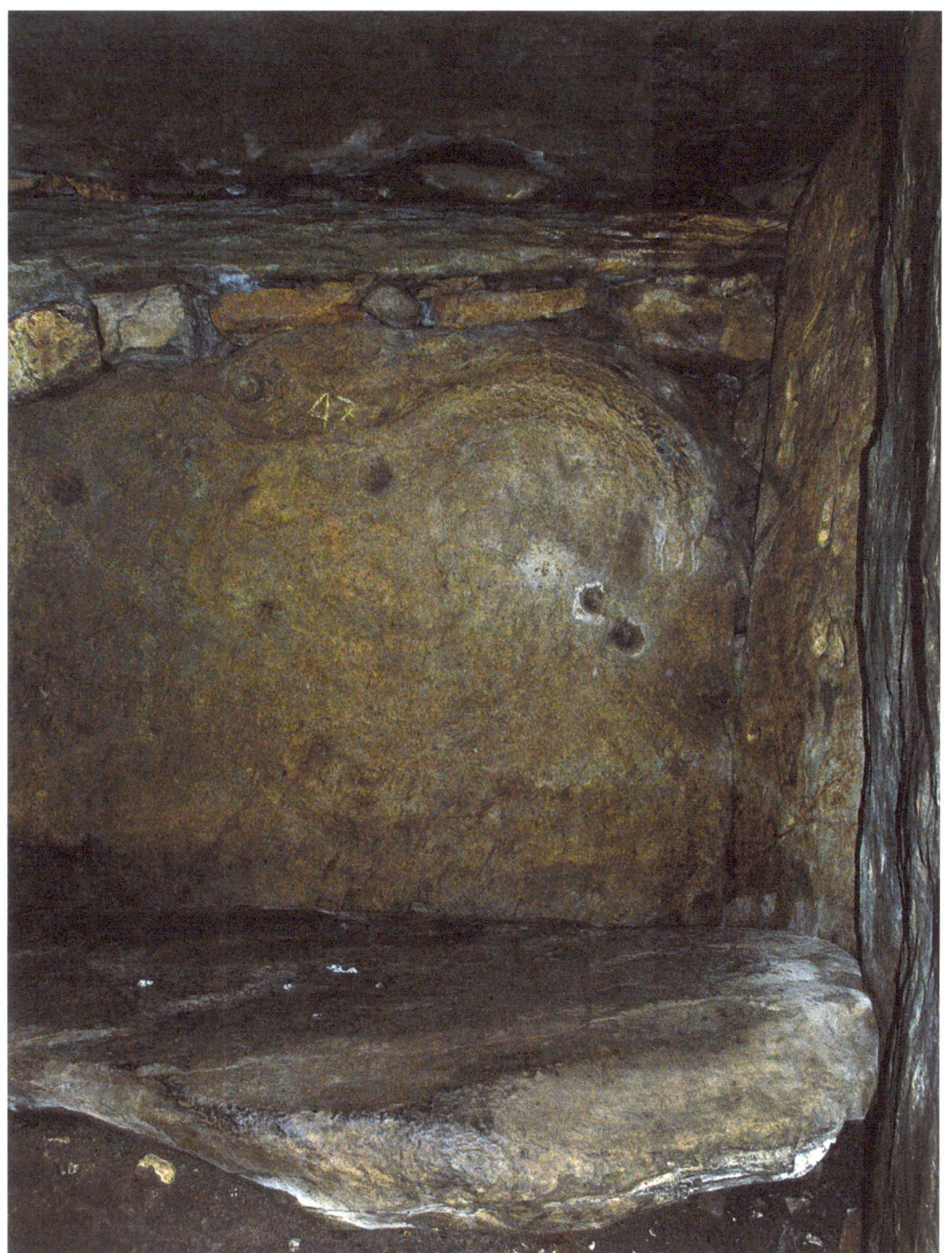

Moonstone, 3200 BC East Chamber Knowth, Co. Meath, Tom Quinn Kumpf

Uninfluenced by the Romans, Irish mythology is pure and unique; their legends and tales are still passed on through generations. They depend on the four seasons, the cycles of sun and moon, and have great reverence for the more than 200,000 ancient monuments dotting the landscape. While so many countries are losing their sacred sites to "progress," the Irish preserve and protect places like New Grange, Knocknarea and Knowth, a chambered cairn that not only contains two-thirds of all the megalithic art in Europe, it also shelters the oldest map of the moon, carved from a huge stone more than 5,000 years ago.

—Tom Quinn Kumpf

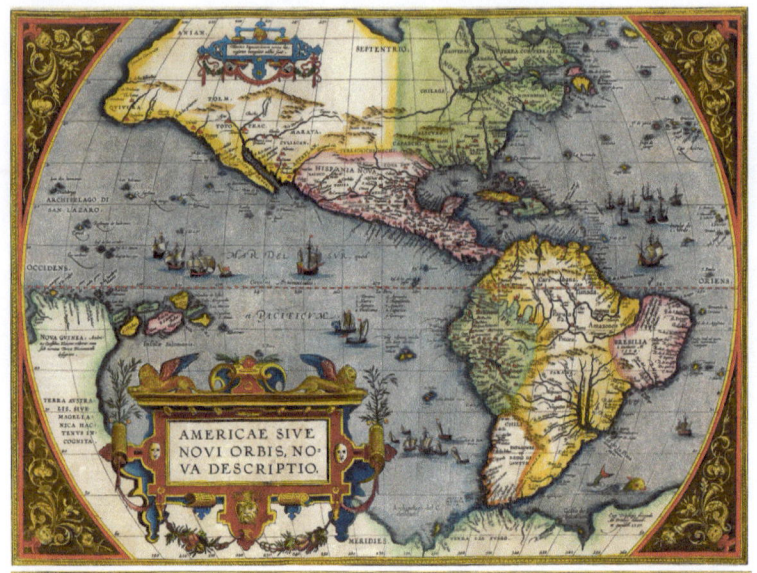
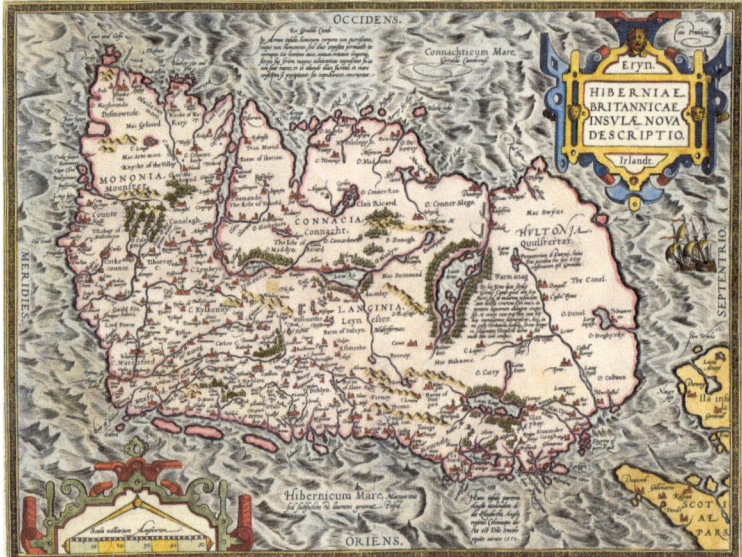
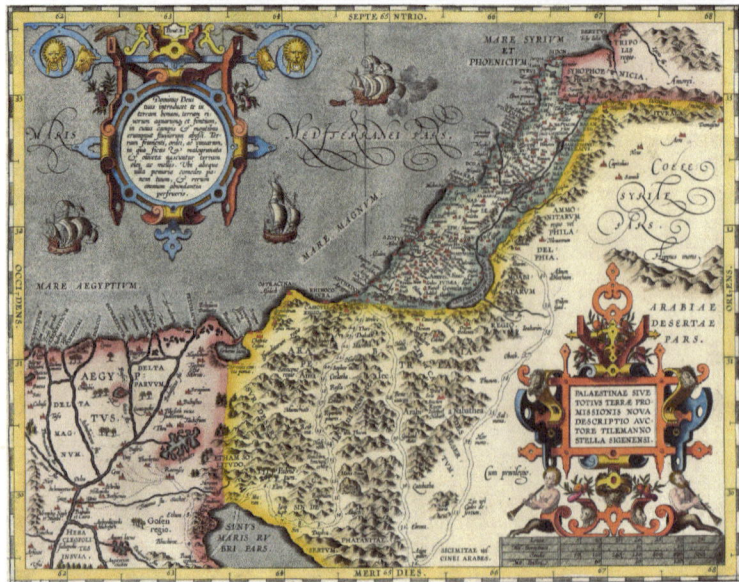

The Americas; Ireland; Palestine, reproductions from Dutch cartographer/geographer, Abraham Ortelius, 1570

CHAPTER 9

Place-making

Mapping Territories, Landscapes, Lives

Nessa Cronin

The framed space of any map encloses a space that speaks to a spatial understanding of the human world. It frames possibilities that have been opened up and displayed for all to view on the map itself, and possibilities that have been closed off with the silencing of other ways of viewing the same territory. Maps then operate on two levels: as artefacts of a given material culture and as cultural and ideological expressions of the map-producing and map-consuming society. The map is therefore a visual iteration not just of places plotted and marked out across lines of longitude and latitude, but a spatial register of intersecting social, cultural and political relations that have marked the history of places and cultural heritages – it is a spatial register that can in many ways also determine the shape of their future.

The History of the European Map

In the European tradition of historical cartography, the development of what is known as map literacy is often associated with the rise of the nation-state, the processes of positivist science and modernity and the expansion of the colonial world, during the so-called Age of Exploration. In such a context, knowledge codified by the map is an "official" knowledge marked, regulated and legitimized by a given authority (for example, the nation-state), whereas "unofficial" knowledge (such as "picture books," illustrated manuscripts, oral literatures, local place-making practices) does not gain a visual or material presence in the final map imprint. Such "knowledges" offer a competing narrative of history and geography, and demonstrate other ways of knowing place often by foregrounding local, regional and indigenous ways of being in the world

(continued)

WE CHANGE THE MAP

This new map, unrolled, smoothed,
seems innocent as the one we have discarded,
impersonal as the clocks in rows
along the upper border, showing time-zones.

The colours are pale and clear, the contours
crisp, decisive, keeping order.
The new names, lettered firmly, lie quite still
within the boundaries that the wars spill over.

It is the times.

I have been always one for paths myself.
The mole's view. Paths and small roads and the next bend.
Arched trees tunnelling into a coin of light.
No overview, no sense of what lies where.

Pinning up maps now, pinning my attention,
I cannot hold whole countries in my mind,
nor recognise their borders.

These days I want to trace
the shape of every townland in this valley;
name families; count trees, walls, cattle, gable-ends,
smoke-soft and tender in the near blue distance.

—Kerry Hardie
from *A Furious Place*

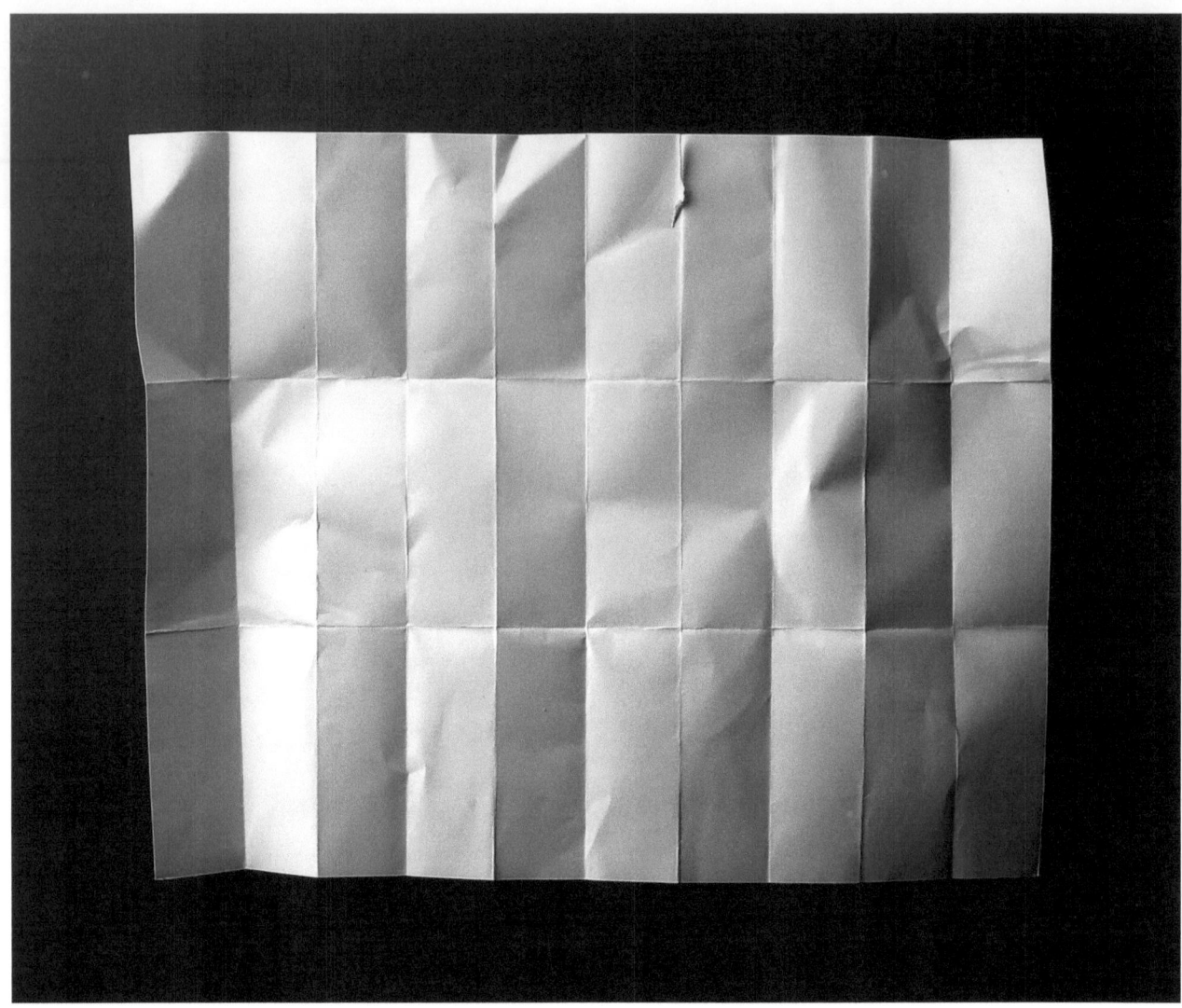

Epitaph for a Roadmap, Rajie Cook

In April 2002, President George W. Bush unveiled his Middle East peace plan: "A performance-based roadmap to a permanent two-state solution to the Israeli-Palestinian conflict." Diplomats and journalists referred to it as "the roadmap to peace." Devised by the United States, the European Union, the United Nations and Russia, the roadmap was a three-phase blueprint designed to reach a peaceful settlement between the Israelis and Palestinians by 2005. The plan contained a step-by-step process calling for both parties to take certain actions to reach its eventual objective: the creation of a sovereign, independent Palestinian state, peaceably existing side-by-side with the entity of Israel. Bush's roadmap for peace proved to be nothing more than a blank folded white sheet of paper. As a cartographer, his map led to nowhere.

—Rajie Cook

and knowledge formations that are particular to place. In *Mapping the New Spain: Indigenous Cartography and the Maps of the Relaciones Geograficas,* Barbara E. Mundy highlights the point that "The colonizers were not the only ones to map their surrounding worlds, making it visible through maps; the colonized also did this," the issue being that "they shared few of the same formal and conceptual constructs."[1] The maps she examines from colonial Mexico show us "the indigenous world – how its inhabitants, still reeling, no doubt, from the blows of conquest, reshaped their once insular maps to keep pace with the rapid changes in their understanding of the surrounding world."[2]

Such "alternative" histories, viewpoints and perspectives may challenge and contest the dominant rhetoric and are often written in another code or language that needs translation and interpretation. Such mappings often operate at a spatial level "below" that of the nation, and often are focused on particular places or regions that have significance and meaning for their audiences and communities. Issues then of history and memory, tradition and heritage, become intertwined with knowledge-making and map-making, and contestation over the meaning and significance of the places marked on any map are necessarily a part of any cartographic practice. Staking a claim to the land often means staking a claim to a certain mode of language and, more importantly perhaps, to history as well.

Culture and Value: De-coding the Colonial Map

As a visual statement of space, the map can be defined as a symbolic image of geographical "reality" as briefly described by the International Cartographic Association.[3] In Western Europe, traditional geographic thought has foregrounded the positivist belief that land and territory can be properly mapped, and that progress toward increased accuracy is a feature of advanced cartographic technologies and cognitive development. In this context, the map is an accurate representation of the territory, demonstrating a point-for-point likeness between the geographic "reality" of the land and its material re-presentation on the map. A map in this sense is a scientific abstraction of reality that is visually represented in material (manuscript/print/digital) form.

Recent work in historical cartography and cultural geography has, however, opened up critical discussions as to how politics, culture and history have shaped not only what is included in maps, but how such cultural processes shape the very way maps are created in the first instance. Scholars such as J.B. Harley, Matthew H. Edney and John Pickles use critical social theory to closely analyze the processes involved in map-making, and argue that as an enterprise embedded within a Eurocentric model of time and space, it is very much embedded within the context of colonial expansion and the rise of the European nation-state as a discrete geopolitical entity.[4] In "The Idea of the Map," cultural geographer Anne Godlewska argues that maps represent a simplified form of reality, which has been given a particular ordering and hierarchical coding in the western tradition.[5] Maps are not neutral zones of communicating spatial realities, but are by definition intrinsically subjective (connected to the cultural code of the cartographer and the map-producing society), and construct a particular geopolitical knowledge that is then "refracted" back into the space of the map. It is the guise of scientific accuracy that lends maps their cloak of objective reality. For Godlewska, maps are geographic visual representations of specific cultural values and are as much about particular cultural values as they are about "universal" geographical "facts." For such scholars, colonial maps are the "tools of empire" supported by monarchs and ministers and have a use that is both symbolic and functional in terms of the appropriation, exploitation and consolidation of territory, resources and populations. The content of what is contained within the map, in addition to the acknowledgement of their origins and subsequent uses, therefore opens up the question as to the objectivity of maps, and their claim to being a neutral representation of a geographical "reality," Maps simultaneously reflect the world *and* create it.

In the Americas, in the early colonial period, the visual and verbal rhetoric of the colonial map reflected the context of land possession and ownership and this cartographic rhetoric was as much an expression of an Old World view of space as it was about the American continent itself. It can also be argued that the map *preceded* the territory, in that colonial maps were produced that enabled the expansion

(continued)

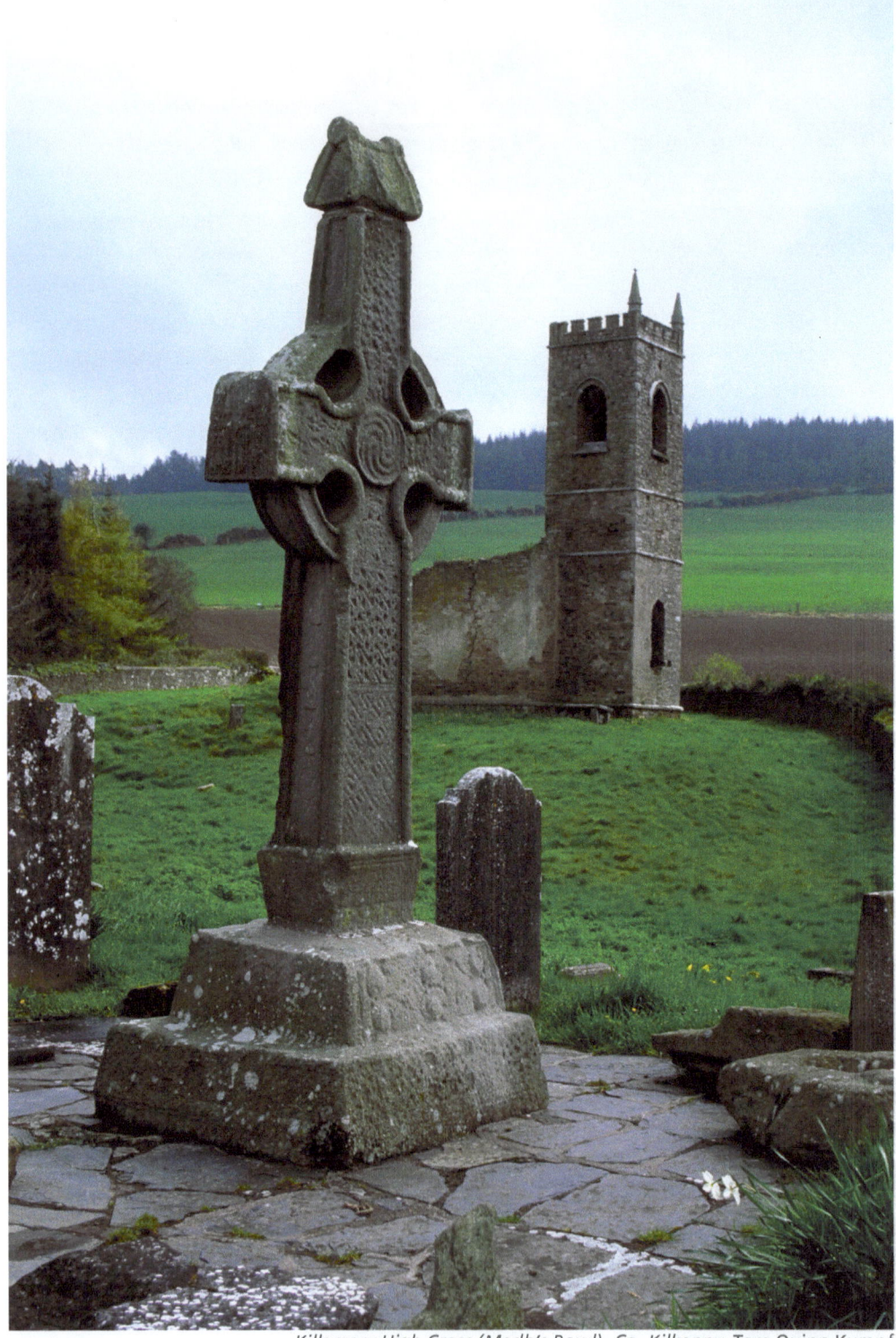

Killamery High Cross (Medb's Bowl), Co. Kilkenny, Tom Quinn Kumpf

Clearly more Celtic than Christian, Killamery High Cross took two monks thirty-five years to complete and has, as I have found at so many similar Irish sites, a hollowed-out slab of stone at its base said to be a watering bowl for wrens, the birds believed to be the earthly attendants of Medb, Queen of the Tuatha dé Danann.

—Tom Quinn Kumpf

of colonial power to enter further into, and take control of, indigenous space. An idea of what that space, and what those places looked like, was already in the mind's eye. The processes of military incursion and land dispossession were rendered silent or invisible, and what was foregrounded (in historical and geographical narratives alike) was the possession of this new territory, this *terra nullius* as empty, virgin territory, land passively waiting for inscription, plantation and colonization. This is described by the environmental historian William Cronon in his work, *Changes in the Land*, which investigates the dynamics of colonial ecologies and biopower in early modern New England.[6] Maps were then not only tools of conquest (useful for explicit military purposes, as well as for more low-key paths of individual way-finding), but also served to *legitimize* conquest of the land, its people and natural resources. The map, then, *was* the territory.

Place – Landscape – Territory

As displayed throughout the artworks in "*The Map is Not the Territory*," maps and imagined cartographies show how maps are in many ways less about the representation of a given reality, and more about the *contested terrain* of competing historical and political narratives. The artworks displayed here are an expression of the cultural practices and processes through which places are created, made and rendered as being meaningful at a particular time and for particular viewers, audiences and communities. The works take on a different resonance and character in turn according to the site of the exhibition, where it travels and, according to the various constituencies that engage with, read and interpret the artworks involved.

The legacies of invasion, occupation and colonization have been part of the stories of the Americas, Ireland and Palestine, and such legacies are evidenced in various ways throughout the exhibition. One challenge is with the idea of "original" or "originary" inhabitants, as such a formulation seeks to rightly recognise the role of indigenous populations, but can also (within a different register of meaning) privilege a narrative of "origins" and "authenticity," that can easily slip into an ethnocentric narrative of race, purity and ethnic exclusivity. Yet, a balance must be struck between a place maintaining a distinct cultural identity and the need to recognise the interlocking histories of places and the peoples that have inhabited them for millennia. This often entails balancing an acknowledgement of a difficult and often deeply traumatic past, with the ever-pressing and urgent needs of the present. Between the pull of history and politics is also the need to recognize the primary human need for place- and home-making, and this is particularly felt in communities that have been displaced, and un-homed, for whom a sense of place and belonging is a vitally important part of their cultural, political and spiritual identity. As ethnographer Keith Basso noted in the introduction to *Wisdom Sits in Places: Landscape and Language Among the Western Apache*, a sense of place only becomes particularly important to us when we lose it and become deprived of our attachment to that place.[7]

With this in mind, there are three distinct ways of thinking about mapping (whether "real" or "imaginary") that have a resonance for this exhibition. The first is the importance of place and of a sense of place; how place comes to hold specific meanings for communities that are attached to, or associated with, a certain space. This entails thinking about place in terms of physically, emotionally, spiritually and intellectually "being in" or "attached to" place, which foregrounds the primacy of the lived experience. Place, for cultural geographer Tim Cresswell, is both conceptual and real; it is both "a way of understanding the world" and "a meaningful location."[8]

The second concept is that of "landscape," which has been traditionally defined as "A portion of the Earth's surface that can be comprehended at a glance."[9] W.G. Hoskins, one of the key thinkers on English landscapes in the last century, described the landscape as being "the richest historical record we possess," for those who knew how to read it "correctly."[10] The concept of landscape has of course a particular aesthetic register and genealogy in that it emerged from a mercantile capitalist sensibility in the Low Countries during the Renaissance, and was used to refer to the vision/view/perspective of a particular portion of land. It was adapted for use in terms of landscape painting and architecture, and as the cultural historian Simon Schama has noted, the term also implies the role of the human hand on the land. Reading and

(continued)

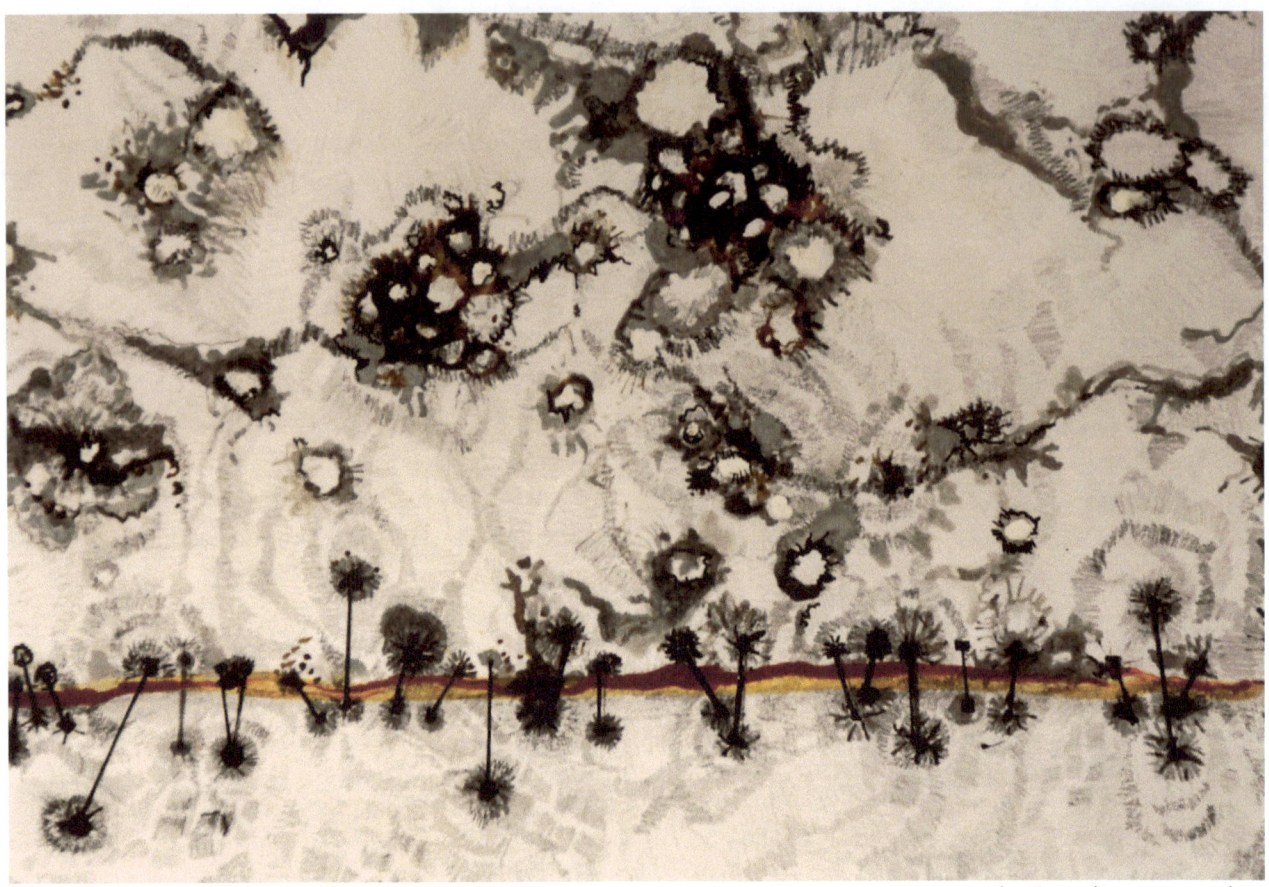

Border Tunnels, Jane McMahan

I try to find the moment when the open system becomes closed, when the construction stops and the deconstruction begins – or when both are battling it out. Like a cracked rock through which a weed is growing. Cells stop dividing and begin to die. When do ecosystems change? When do cultures stop being what they were and begin to be the new culture? When does a border change the topography?

—Jane McMahan

interpreting landscapes involves in many ways an acknowledgement that often we have a preconceived image of that landscape at play in our minds, before the encounter with "the real." As Schama explains, "Before it can ever be the repose for the senses, landscape is the work of the mind. Its scenery is built up as much from strata of memory as from layers of rock."[11] Landscapes are therefore culturally constructed, and are not merely "natural" phenomena to be viewed at a distance. Finally, places and landscapes differ as to the concept of territory, in that "territory" is often primarily associated with a political context. William Connolly notes the etymological traces of the word "territory," where the Latin noun *terra* refers to "land," and the verb *terrere* is "to frighten," "to terrorize." "Territory" holds the dual resonance of sustenance and terror in being largely defined by Connolly as "land occupied by violence."[12]

A Colonial Geopolitics: Roots or Routes?

The conquest and occupation of land by violent means, through the creation of colonial territories, was largely justified by the concept of *terra nullius* (a concept shaped by this dual resonance of sustenance and terror), while the expropriation of land also served to detach or dispossess indigenous populations from their complex social and cultural landscapes and histories. The question of what this loss entailed (and still entails in many instances) when the vital connection between people and place was/is forcibly severed, is what is at stake in many formerly colonized countries today. And it has a particular resonance for populations that have endured forced migration and relocation to different homes, reservations, territories, nations, for a myriad of reasons.

The question of retrieving, authenticating and legitimizing a previously silenced history is an important project of cultural memory and recovery, and it can be an enabling narrative through which progressive and alternative futures can be imagined. However, there is a dangerous slippage between cultural retrieval and cultural ossification, when certain narratives become privileged over others, and so a hierarchical process of memory and active forgetting can also take place within such operations of cultural retrieval and recuperation. This is particularly evident in the Irish case with the re-creation of foundation myths of a nation-state undergoing decolonization, as noted by the literary scholar Declan Kiberd in his postcolonial reading of modern Irish nationalism and the cultural revival at the turn of the last century.

Marxist geographer Doreen Massey has also noted this problem of the privileging of roots over routes in her discussion of what she terms "a progressive sense of place." For Massey, a focus on the idea of "roots" for a given locale or culture necessarily entails an exclusionary politics of "insider/outsider" dialectic, which can become very problematic in that it does not allow for the movement of people and ideas, and for the processes of cultural exchange and traditions that happen in societies in different ways at different times. Massey allows that "there is the need to face up to – rather than simply deny – people's need for attachment of some sort, whether through place or anywhere else." The question is "how to maintain to that geographical notion of difference, of uniqueness, even of rootedness if people want that, without it being reactionary."[13] If people have multiple identities, it is argued, then so can places. The problem for Massey is when enabling discourses of resistance and affirmation become reactionary and exclusive narratives of place, people and belonging. The balance to be struck then is one that simultaneously recognizes the need for many people to have an attachment to place and for that attachment to be legitimized, while also allowing for an open, progressive sense of place that also welcomes mobility, diversity and difference as strands that add to the web of place-making.

Deep Mappings and Socially Engaged Art Practices

Cresswell's formulation of place as "a way of understanding the world" is important as it puts the emphasis on the processes of understanding and knowledge and our subjective relationship to the world, as well as our place in it. In recent years, different ways of mapping different and often contested relationships to places have been rendered visible particularly in the realm of the visual arts. The close connection between the art and science of cartography and socially engaged art practices has been a fruitful ground for many artists, academics and writers in Ireland and Britain in particular. The engagement with the idea of "deep maps" and "deep mapping," stemming from the writings of William Least Heat-Moon (and more recently through the performance/archaeology works of Michael Shanks and Mike Pearson within a Welsh context), has also had a particular resonance and influence in terms of exploring different ways and forms of mapping the lived experience of distinct places and landscapes. Such deep mappings operate with an almost transversal movement into place that is then registered in various interconnected forms and platforms, be they visual, oral, textual, digital or embodied. Artist and scholar Iain Biggs argues that "deep mapping aims, broadly speaking, to engage with, narrate and evoke 'place' in temporal depth by bringing together a multiplicity of voices, information, impressions and perspectives as a basis for a new connectivity."[14] The new connectivities that such "deep maps" exhibit open new ways of viewing old spaces, of legitimizing counter-cartographies, of foregrounding mapping as a collaborative process, and, most of all perhaps, to question the authority of any map of any time and of any place.

What can be easily forgotten in an increasingly homogenized and seemingly globalized world is that *places are different*, and that we live with such differences in the spaces

(continued)

we create and move through every day. And so maps of those places must be different too, and in this way the map is most certainly not the territory but can display an approximate view of that space and of that experience. As Clifford Geertz remarks, "Like Love or Imagination, Place makes a poor abstraction. Separated from its materialization, it has little meaning."[15] Specificities of vocabulary and color, sound and touch, are necessary to understand the contour, range and register of a place and the people who create it. What can be perceived as a difficulty in documenting what these places mean to people, and how that experience can be accurately and sensitively represented, is testament to the plurality of lives, experiences, histories and personal memories associated with such places. The representations of such cartographic imaginings on display in the exhibition *"The Map is Not the Territory"* speak to all of these issues – the importance of place and place-making, the distinctions between landscape and territory, the ethics and politics of recovering a colonial past – and serve as a collective reminder that our way of imagining our relationship to place also entails a consideration how places have shaped the people, the communities and the nations that we are today. ■

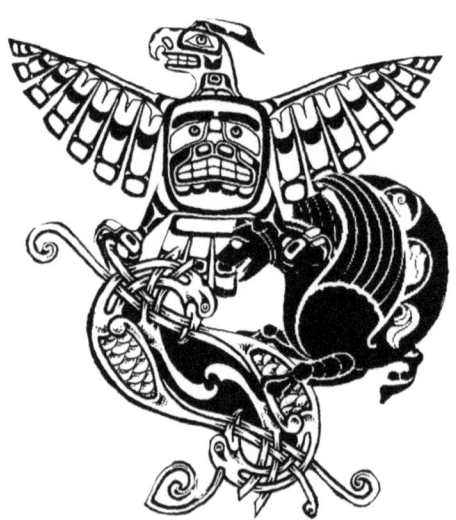

Notes

Chapter 1, "The map is not the answer," pages 25 to 32

[1] M. Kendig, ed., *Alfred Korzybski: Collected Writings, 1920-1950* (Englewood, N.J: Institute of General Semantics, 1990), 229.

[2] Korzybski, 299.

[3] Ibid, 568.

[4] Ibid, 299-300.

[5] Ibid, 300.

[6] Mahmoud Darwish, trans., Ibrahim Muhawi, *Journey of an Ordinary Grief* (Brooklyn: Archipelago Books, 2010), 25.

[7] Ibid..

[8] Ibid.

[9] Ibid, 19.

[10] Ibid, 30.

[11] Ibid, 43.

[12] Mahmoud Darwish, trans. Omnia Amin and Rick London, "And we have countries…," *Now, as You Awaken*, (San Francisco: Sardines P, 2006), 7.

[13] Ibid.

[14] Ibid.

[15] Ibid.

[16] Edward W. Said, *Culture and Imperialism* (London: Vintage, 1994), 402-03.

[17] Shane Connaghton, *The Run of the Country* (Harmondsworth, UK: Penguin, 1995), 4.

[18] Patrick Quigley, *Borderland* (Dingle, Ireland: Brandon, 1994), 213.

[19] Patrick McCabe, *Breakfast on Pluto* (New York: Harper Collins, 1998), xii.

[20] Paul Muldoon, "The Boundary Commission," *Poems, 1968-1998* (New York: Farrar, Straus, Giroux, 2001), 80.

[21] Ibid.; *italicized in original*

[22] Eugene McCabe, "Borderlands," Malcolm Anderson and Eberhard Bort, eds., *The Irish Border: History, Politics, Culture,* (Liverpool: Liverpool University Press, 1999), 1.

[23] Paul Muldoon, "Rita Duffy: Watchtower II," *One Thousand Things Worth Knowing* (New York: Farrar, Straus, Giroux2015), 30.

[24] Ibid.; 30.

[25] Ibid, 31.

[26] Jon Calame and Esther Charlesworth, *Divided Cities: Belfast, Beirut, Jerusalem, Mostar, and Nicosia* (Philadelphia: University of Pennsylvania Press, 2009), 62.

[27] Seamus Heaney, "Act of Union," *Opened Ground: Selected Poems, 1966-1996* (New York: Farrar, Straus, Giroux, 1998), 120.

[28] Ibid.

[29] Ibid.

[30] Ibid.

[31] Gloria Anzaldúa, *Borderlands/La Frontera: The New Mestiza* (San Francisco: Aunt Lute Books, 2012).

[32] Anzaldúa, *Borderlands/La Frontera*, 95.

[33] Ibid,102.

[34] Ibid, 111-12.

[35] Darwish, *Journey,* 26.

[36] Anzaldúa, *Borderlands/La Frontera*, 92.

[37] The original narratives are in Arabic and have been translated by Rawan Gedeon, Dalia Deareyyah, Aref Nammari, and Ala' Younis.

Chapter 2, "Spaces of Memory," pages 33 to 41

[1] "The map is not the territory" was coined by philosopher/scientist Alfred Korzybski.

[2] Boullata, observing the same phenomenon for young artists working in Ramallah, writes, "One of the most striking aspects of the works on display in the 2002 exhibition, all of which were created against a background of extraordinary violence, destruction, and death, was the fact that these themes were evoked only obliquely, if at all. And because Palestinian society is under siege and engaged in a ferocious political and military struggle, the outsider could easily expect more overtly politicized works." Kamal Boullata, "Art Under Siege," *Journal of Palestine Studies,* 33(2004): 74.

[3] Joan Gibbons, *Contemporary Art and Memory: Images of Recollection and Remembrance* (London: I.B. Tauris, 2008).

[4] It should be noted, however, that the debate about whether personal narrative and memory possess effective counter-hegemonic political agency remains beyond the scope of this essay, although the question of why it figures in Halaka's, Zurob's and Tuma's work is not.

[5] Jessica Winegar, "The Humanity Game: Art, Islam and the War on Terror," *Anthropological Quarterly* 81(2008): 675.

[6] Winegar, "Humanity," 675.
The first venues for *"The Map is Not the Territory"* were institutions that specialize exclusively in Middle Eastern Art. But despite the additional focus on Native Americans and the Irish, which might have been thought to ease the difficulty, co-curator Jennifer Heath reports that as of this writing, 468 venues have turned down or ignored her attempts to place the exhibit.

[7] Lisa Isam Haddad, "Palestine US Exhibit Stirs Controversy," *aljazeera.com,* April 20, 2005. http://www.aljazeera.com/archive/2005/04/2008410135347730135.html.

[8] Remi Kenazi, "The Art of Politics," *ZNet,* March 4, 2006. https://zcomm.org/znetarticle/the-art-of-politics-by-remi-kanazi/

[9] Winegar, *"Humanity,"* 675.

[10] Rob Eshelman, "Made in Palestine," *Counterpunch,* April 8, 2005. www.counterpunch.org/eshelman04082005.html.

[11] Delinda C. Hanley, "Palestinian Costumes Vanish at Los Angeles Airport," *Washington Report on Middle East Affairs,* March 2004. http://www.wrmea.org/2004-march/palestinian=costumes-vanish-at-los-angeles-airport.html.

[12] This phrase is commonly first attributed to Christian Zionists of the 19th century.

[13] Lila Abu-Lughod and Ahmad H. Saidi, *Nakba: Palestine, 1948 and the Claims of Memory,* New York: Columbia University Press, 2007), 6.

[14] Halaka has begun in recent years to make documentary films and has founded his own production company, Sitting Crow Productions. http://www.sittingcrowproductions.com/.

[15] *Passport.Palestine,* by Manal Deeb in *"The Map is Not the Territory"* presents the actual passport of the artist's grandfather, Atta Ahmed Musleh, who passed away in 1975. As shown in the passport, he was born in Deir Tarif (the suburbs of the city of Lud, which no longer exists, around Tel Aviv) and was an orange grower, with the clear nationality status of Palestinian Citizen. The passport was issued on the 28th day of August 1947 just a few months before the 1948 Nakba.

[16] In a 2014 personal communication, Halaka informed me that when he met Rif'a AbedAllah El Kurd, she was living in the Sheikh Jarrah neighborhood of East Jerusalem, but had just received an expulsion notice from the Israelis. He did not recall the village from which she was expelled in 1948.

[17] Kaja Silverman, *Male Subjectivity at the Margins,* (New York: Routledge, 1992), 135.

[18] Personal communication with the artist, 2015.

[19] Hani Zurob, artist statement for at beginning of *"The Map is Not the Territory": Parallel Paths-Palestinians, Native Americans, Irish,* 2013, curated by Jennifer Heath and Dagmar Painter. Zurob goes on to movingly describe his son's working through the separation with his father via his toys: "Like all other children, Qoudsi is selective about which toys he wants to play with. He subconsciously uses them to express his thoughts and concerns. I notice that he increasingly chooses to play with transportation toys, in his belief that there must be a vehicle that can get us together at his grandfather's house in Jerusalem. Once, he suggested that we should take his small car. Another time, he wanted to put me in his travelling suitcase. And he suggested that I could go with him on his bicycle after he learned how to ride it. His search is relentless, but every time he travels to Jerusalem, I feel he has matured and his thoughts become more developed. His selection of toys that will provide a solution changes as he grows."

[20] Halaka's series discussed here does this through documentation and its focus on others, while Zurob does so by producing art based on self-expression, leaving much unstated. To this I would add the contemporarily defined formal beauty of Zurob's painting, although some might disagree with me on the operative agency of the aesthetic.

[21] Frank Trentmann, "Materiality in the Future of History: Things, Practices, and Politics." *Journal of British Studies* 48 (2009): 300. Trentmann is here discussing Martin Heidegger and Maurice Merleau-Ponty in a passage on the political dimension of things: "Things appear at once more integral to political processes and sensibilities and more fragile, precarious, and politicized than in conventional accounts. Instead of starting with political actors who then appropriate objects for symbolic effects … Things, in other words, recruit us into politics as much as we recruit them."

[22] *Homes for the Disembodied* was originally shown at the now closed al-Wasiti Gallery, then became part of the tragically short-lived 2003 Made in Palestine exhibition, and later traveled for five years (2008-2012) with Jennifer Heath's *The Veil:*

(continued)

Visible & Invisible Spaces.

²³ Personal communication, 2014.

²⁴ Mary Tuma, artist statement for *"The Map is Not the Territory": Parallel Paths: Palestinians, Native Americans, Irish.*

²⁵ Hakim, for example, has recently launched his own "memory project," *Home Away from Home: Little Palestine by the Bay,* which opened at the Rayko Photo Centre in October 2014 in San Francisco and will tour.

²⁶ Immanuel Wallerstein, "Culture as the Ideological Battleground of the Modern World-system," Immanuel Wallerstein, in *Geopolitics and Geoculture,* ed. Immanuel Wallerstein (Cambridge: Cambridge University Press, 1991), 158-83.

²⁷ There are also many things to criticize within the complex and sometimes violent arena of Palestinian politics, but they remain beyond the scope of this essay, especially as they are over- reported.

²⁸ John Berger, The *Sense of Sight* (New York: Vantage Books, 1985), 8.

Chapter 3, "Art and Activism," pages 43-50

¹ "The map is not the territory" was coined by Alfred Korzybski.

² Lucy R. Lippard, *Mixed Blessings: New Art in a Multicultural America,* New York: Pantheon Books, 1990, 26.

³ I collaborated with *"Map Is Not the Territory"* artists Nadema Agard, Norman Akers and Jaune Quick-to-See Smith in the traveling exhibition, *Visual Power: 21st Century Native American Artists/Intellectuals* (2005-2010), curated by me for the U.S. Department of State. It is inspiring to see their work in this venue where indigeneity from two other cultures is explored.

⁴ For more about historic trauma, please see chapter 7 in this volume, "The Unresolved Grief of a California Indian Tribe," by Valentin Lopez.

⁵ Chicano or Chicana (also spelled Xicano or Xicana) is a chosen identity of some Mexican-Americans in the United States. The term "Chicano" is sometimes used interchangeably with Mexican-American. Both names are chosen identities within the Mexican-American community in the United States. However, these terms have a wide range of meanings in various parts of the Southwest. The term became widely used during the Chicano Movement of the 1970s … to express an identity of cultural, ethnic and community pride. http://en.wikipedia.org/wiki/Chicano.

⁶ Malaquias Montoya, artist statement, *"The Map is Not the Territory": Parallel Paths-Palestinians, Native Americans, Irish.*

⁷ A *parfleche* rawhide bag was typically used for holding dried meats and pemmican. The word was originally used by French fur traders (it was not a word used by the Native Americans).

⁸ Nadema Agard, artist statement, *"The Map is Not the Territory": Parallel Paths-Palestinians, Native Americans, Irish.*

⁹ Coyote is a trickster, a character that can take many shapes and is used in a humorous way to teach lessons about ethical behavior. Many tribes use Coyote stories to educate children about correct behavior and tribal norms.

¹⁰ The Canadian Indian Act of 1876 has been amended many times and has been an ongoing source of controversy. The Act is wide-ranging, covering governance, land use, healthcare, education and more on Indian reserves. It sets out rules for governing Indian reserves, defines how bands can be created and spells out the powers of "band councils." In addition, it defines who may be recognized as an "Indian" and allowed to be "registered" with membership in bands. http://en.wikipedia.org/wiki/Indian_Act.

¹¹ In a personal correspondence, December 11, 2013.

Chapter 4, "Spinning Quiet Yarns," pages 54 to 58

¹ All weavers' and knitters' words quoted here appear in Meghan Nuttall Sayres, *Weaving Tapestry in Rural Ireland. Taipéis Gael, Donegal,* (Cork: Atrium Cork University Press, 2006).

² In 1847, members of the Native American Choctaw Nation – themselves brutally dispossessed of their lands in 1831 – collected $170 from their meagre means to donate to the starving Irish. The money was sent to Ireland through a United States famine relief agency. Meanwhile, Charles Trevelyan, a British colonial administrator, notoriously closed the food depots and refused to distribute the Indian corn to prevent the desperately hungry Irish from becoming "habitually dependent" on the British government, rather, he stated, "Irish property should support Irish poverty."

³ Spider Woman is also called Spider Grandmother, and is an important figure in the religions, mythology and folklore of many Native American cultures. In some mythologies she spun a web, laced it with dew, threw it into the sky and the dew became the stars. In Navajo/Diné tradition, men, as well as women, are the weavers. Before the Europeans arrived, weaving was almost the exclusive province of Navajo/Diné men, while women did the herding and farming.

⁴ The word for "loom" in Palestinian Arabic is *nôl*, with a long o, *nawl* in classical Arabic, from a verb, *nâla*, meaning "to give, to offer." The ground loom, or fixed-heddle loom, was used by the *fellahin* (Egyptian peasants) in villages and by the Bedouin, generally women. The treadle loom or horizontal frame loom was used by men in weaving shops in towns and large villages.

⁵ Chilkat weaving is practiced by Tlingit, Haida, Tsimshian, and other Northwest Coast peoples of Alaska and British Columbia. It is considered one of the most difficult forms of weaving in the world; one blanket can take up to a year to make. They are worn by high-ranking tribal members on civic or ceremonial occasions, including dances. In the 1990s only an estimated six people still practiced true Chilkat weaving, but today the technique is enjoying a revival.

⁶ From a poem in honor of the Irish St. Colmcille, aka St. Colomba (521-597 CE), born in Donegal and who founded the abbey on Iona. The poem was likely written during the 11ᵗʰ or 12ᵗʰ century.

⁷ *Raithneach* is bracken, which gives yellow-orange dye; *fraoch* is heather, which gives a yellow color and crotal are tree lichens from oaks and maples, which yield a russet dye.

Chapter 5, "Walls and Mirrors," pages 59 to 64

¹ "The map is not the territory" was first coined by scientist/philosopher Alfred Korzybski, in 1931 in a paper he presented at a meeting of the American Association for the Advancement of Science, titled "Science and Sanity."

² Michel Foucault, Jay Miskowiec, trans., *Of Other Spaces, Diacritics,* Vol. 16, No. 1 (Spring, 1986), 23.

³ Ibid, 24.

⁴ Ibid.

⁵ Ibid.

⁶ Ibid.

⁷ Ibid. My emphasis.

⁸ In Of *Other Spaces,* Miskowiec translated the French term *suspendent* (from the verb *suspendre*) into English as "suspect." As this verb only connotes the meaning of "suspicion" or "mistrust," I would instead propose the verb "suspend," which perfectly matches the meaning in French of "interruption" or "suspension" of an action or a meaning.

⁹ Foucault, *Of Other Spaces,* 24.

¹⁰ This has been the case with the genocides perpetrated against the Mayan indigenous populations and Ladino peasants of Guatemala during the Guatemalan Civil War, from 1960 to 1996. These atrocities were denounced by the 1983 documentary, *When The Mountains Tremble,* directed by Pamela Yates (Brooklyn, NY: Skylight Pictures), which focuses on Rigoberta Menchú, herself a Quiché indigenous woman, who received the Nobel Peace Prize in 1992.

¹¹ *Sacred Spirit. Chants and Dances of the Native Americans,* Virgin Records Ltd., 1994.

¹² For this and other claims in this article about the second album from the series Sacred Spirit, see the website: Solsticio de invierno, "Sacred Spirit: Cantos y danzas de los indios americanos." (2012 1-October). http://solsticiodeinvierno.blogspot.ie/2012/10/sacred-spirit-cantos-y-danzas-de-los.html.

¹³ Photographs of Carl Moon, 1903-1915, MS285 Arizona University Libraries, http://speccoll.library.arizona.edu/collections/photographs-carl-moon.

¹⁴ Karen Wentworth, "Taking an academic sabbatical to sleuth: Kelly to spend next six months on a hot trail," *Inside UNM,* University of New Mexico, January 7, 2015. http://news.unm.edu/news/taking-an-academic-sabbatical-to-sleuth.

¹⁵ The Sami people, known erroneously in English as Lapps or Laplanders, inhabit the Arctic area of Sápmi, which today encompasses parts of far northern Norway, Sweden, Finland, the Kola Peninsula of Russia and the border area between south and middle Sweden and Norway. The Sami are the only indigenous people of Scandinavia recognized and protected under the international conventions of indigenous peoples.

¹⁶ "audio-music dot info," *Sacred Spirit,* http://www.audio-music.info/htm/s/Sacred_Spirit.htm.

¹⁷ David Lewiston. *Fiestas of Chiapas and Oaxaca,* H72070 Nonesuch Records, 1976.

¹⁸ Adam Greenberg, "All Music," http://www.allmusic.com/album/fiestas-of-chiapas-oaxaca-mw0000039022.

[19] *K'in Sventa Ch'ul Me'tik Kwadalupe.* (2008 5-February). YouTube, https://www.youtube.com/watch?v=oospWucgxac.

[20] Ibid.

[21] Kronos Quartet, *Kronos Quartet Nuevo,* Nonesuch, 2002.

[22] Ibid, track 7.

[23] Eran Riklis (director), *Lemon Tree* (original title, Ertz Limon), Israel: Heimat Films, et al, 2008.

[24] Interestingly, a sign of mourning in a Jewish household is to cover the mirrors with black veils. I am grateful to Jennifer Heath for this insight.

[25] The storyline of *Lemon Tree* was based on a real incident between Israeli Defense Minister Shaul Mofaz and his neighbors, a Palestinian family, who, although they sued the minister, lost the case and their trees were cut down. Andre Soares, "LEMON TREE: Q&A with Eran Riklis." *Alt Film Guide.* http://www.altfg.com/blog/film-interviews/lemon-tree-eran-riklis-interview.

Chapter 6, "Journeys of Survivance," pages 67 to 72

[1] "The map is not the territory" was coined by Alfred Korzybski.

[2] Gerald Vizenor is a well-known scholar and author. He is an Anishinabe native and a member of the Minnesota Chippewa Tribe. Among several academic posts, Vizenor was the director of Native American Studies at the University of California, Berkeley, and is currently professor of American Studies at the University of New Mexico. He is the author of numerous scholarly publications, including *Manifest Manners: Narratives of Post-Indian Survivance* (University of Nebraska Press, 1999) and *Survivance: Narratives of Native Presence* (University of Nebraska Press, 2008).

[3] David Ben Gurion (1886-1973) was the founding prime minister of the State of Israel, serving from 1948 to 1954 and from 1955 to 1963. He was born David Grun, in Plonsk, Poland, which was then part of the Russian Empire, and first moved to Palestine in 1906. Golda Meir (1898–1978) was Israel's fourth prime minister, serving from 1969 to 1974. She was born Golda Mabovitch in Kiev, Ukraine, then part of the Russian Empire. She moved to Palestine in 1921.

[4] Zionism is a political movement founded in Europe at the end of the 19th century. (The first Zionist congress was held in Basel, Switzerland, in 1897.) Zionism has its roots in Jewish history in Palestine and the desire to establish a national home where Jews could escape the brutal cycles of anti-Semitic persecution in Europe. Zionism also has its political origins in 19th-century European nationalist movements.

[5] The term "Living Stones" has been used by artist Rajie Cook in reference to the families of people of Palestine.

[6] "The Land of Sour Milk and Stolen Honey" is the title of an installation about the Nakba by the artist Gadi Gofberg.

[7] United Nations Relief and Works Agency for Palestine Refugees in the Near East (UNRWA) currently administers eight camps for Palestinian refugees in the Gaza strip, nineteen in the West Bank, twelve in Lebanon, ten in Jordan and nine in Syria, for a total of 5 million registered Palestinian refugees in those regions alone.

[8] "The right to have rights" is Hannah Arendt's conceptualization of the individual's rights within national and political structures. Stateless individuals are denied the right of nationality and the rights and protections provided by the nation.

[9] For example: Zochrot is an Israeli organization committed to restorative justice. Its goals focus on informing the public of its responsibilities to exiled Palestinians and to the return of refugees. Their educational and documentary projects investigate Israel's history of ethnic cleansing, the unearthing and reclaiming of the 531 Palestinian villages eradicated and renamed since the establishment of Israel; and the right of return for Palestinian refugees. Zochrot has also been developing structures that would eventually lead to truth and reconciliation committees in Israel/Palestine. http://www.zochrot.org.
The Jewish Voice for Peace is an international organization founded by non-Zionist and anti-Zionist Jews whose educational and activist work is committed to exposing the destructive colonial structures of the Zionist state. http://jewishvoiceforpeace.org.

[10] Naim Ateek, *Justice and Only Justice: A Palestinian Theology of Liberation* (Maryknoll, NY: Orbis Books, 1989).

Chapter 8, "Sharing the Burden," pages 81 to 85

[1] "Northern Ireland Peace Monitoring Report: Community Relations Council Briefing," *Hansard Official Report* (Northern Ireland Assembly, 2012), http://www.niassembly.gov.uk/Assembly-Business/Official-Report/Committee-Minutes-of-Evidence/Session-2011-2012/June-2012/Northern-Ireland-Peace-Monitoring-Report--Community-Relations-Council-Briefing/.

[2] Jonny Byrne, Cathy Gormley Heenan and Gillian Robinson, "Attitudes to Peace Walls," *Research Report to the Office of the First Minister and Deputy First Minister* (Northern Ireland: University of Ulster, 2012), 20.

[3] Sir Ronald Storrs, *Orientations* (London: Nicholson & Watson, 1937), 364.

[4] Rory Miller, *Ireland and the Palestine Question: 1948-2004,* (Co. Kildare: Irish Academic Press, 2005), 8.

[5] Bill Rolston, "'The Brothers on the Walls' International Solidarity and Irish Political Murals" (*Journal of Black Studies* 39(3), 2009), 446-70.

[6] Andrew Hill and Andrew White. "The Flying of Israeli Flags in Northern Ireland" (*Identities: Global Studies in Culture and Power* 15(1), 2008), 31-50.

[7] Tommy McKearney, "Khader Adnan receives message of support from former Hunger Striker Tommy McKearney," February 8, 2012, https://www.youtube.com/watch?v=G1iwWZJPl_k.

[8] Gildernew, Michelle, "Khader Adnan receives message of support from Michelle Gildernew M.P," February 20, 2012, https://www.youtube.com/watch?v=bnSKHJ3Qejo.

[9] David Rovics, *Khader Adnan, Bobby Sands,* February 19, 2012, https://www.youtube.com/watch?v=UoEPftesWyA.

[10] Declan de Barra, *Curfew,* August 30, 2013, https://www.youtube/watch?v=XHdsMCdpqRo.

[11] BBC News Middle East. "Gaza crisis: Toll of operations in Gaza," September 1, 2014, http://www.bbc.com/news/world-middle-east-28439404.

[12] Ernest Renan, "What Is a Nation?" *Nation and Narration,* H. Bhabha, ed. (New York: Routledge, 1990), 8-22.

Chapter 9, "Place-Making," pages 89 to 96

[1] Barbara E. Mundy, *Mapping the New Spain: Indigenous Cartography and the Maps of the Relaciones Geograficas* (Chicago and London: Chicago University Press, 1996), xi-xii.

[2] Ibid, xix.

[3] As noted on the ICA website, cartography "is a symbolized representation of geographical reality, representing selected features or characteristics, resulting from the creative effort of its author's execution of choices, and is designed for use when spatial relationships are of primary relevance." It is also "the discipline dealing with the art, science and technology of making and using maps." As cited from, http://icaci.org/mission/

[4] See J.B. Harley, in Paul Laxton, ed., *The New Nature of Maps: Essays in the History of Cartography,* (Baltimore: Johns Hopkins Press, 2001); Matthew H. Edney, *Mapping an Empire: The Geographical Construction of British India, 1765-1843* (Chicago: University of Chicago Press, 1990); John Pickles, *A History of Spaces: Cartographic Reason, Mapping, and the Geo-coded World* (London: Routledge, 2004).

[5] Anne Godlewska, "The Idea of the Map," in S. Hanson, ed., *10 Geographic Ideas That Changed the World* (New Jersey: Rutgers Press, 1997), 29.

[6] William Cronon, Changes in the Land: *Indians, Colonists, and the Ecology of New England* (New York: Hill & Wang, 1983).

[7] Keith Basso, *Wisdom Sits in Places: Landscape and Language Among the Western Apache* (Albuquerque: University of New Mexico Press, 1996), xiii.

[8] Tim Cresswell, Place: *A Short Introduction* (London: Blackwell, 2004), 7, 11.

[9] J. B. Jackson, *Discovering the Vernacular Landscape* (New Haven: Yale University Press, 1984), 8.

[10] W.G. Hoskins, *The Making of the English Landscape,* (London: Hodder and Stoughton, 1995), 14.

[11] Simon Schama, *Landscape and Memory* (London: Harper Collins, 1995), 6-7.

[12] William Connolly, "Tocqueville, Territory and Violence," in M. Shapiro and H. Alkers, eds., *Challenging Boundaries: Global Flows, Territorial Identities* (Minneapolis: University of Minnesota Press, 1996), 144.

[13] Declan Kiberd, *Inventing Ireland* (London: Jonathan Cape, 1995).

[14] Doreen Massey, "A Global Sense of Place," as cited in Cresswell, 66-67.

[15] Iain Biggs, "The spaces of 'Deep Mapping': A partial account," *Journal of Arts and Communities,* Vol. 2, No. 1. (July 2011), p. 5.

[16] Clifford Geertz, "Afterword," in Keith Basso and Stephen Feld, eds., *Senses of Place* (Santa Fe, New Mexico: School of American Research, 1996), p. 259.

SELECTED BIBLIOGRAPHY

Abu-Lughod, Lila and Ahmad H. Saidi. *Nakba: Palestine, 1948 and the Claims of Memory*. New York: Columbia University Press, 2007.

Alfred, Taiaiake. *Peace, Power, Righteousness: An Indigenous Manifesto*. Oxford, UK: Oxford University Press, 1999.

Allen, Paula Gunn. *The Woman Who Owned the Shadows*. San Francisco: Aunt Lute Books, 1984.

_____. *The Sacred Hoop: Recovering the Feminine in American Indian Traditions*. Boston: Beacon Press, 1992.

Ankori, Gannit. *Palestinian Art*. London : Reaktion Books.

Anzaldúa, Gloria. *Borderlands/La Frontera: The New Mestiza*. San Francisco: Aunt Lute Books, 2012.

Aruri, Naseer. *Occupation: Israel Over Palestine*. Washington, D.C.: Association of Arab-American University Graduates, 1989.

_____, ed. *Palestinian Refugees: The Right of Return*. London: Oxford University Press, 1992.

Ashrawi, Hanan. *This Side of Peace*. New York: Touchstone, 1995.

Ateek, Naim Stifan. *Justice, and Only Justice: A Palestinian Theology of Liberation*. Maryknoll, N.Y.: Orbis Press, 1989.

Bartelt, Dana, Sliman Mansour, Yossi Lemel and Fawzy El Emrany. *Both Sides of Peace: Israeli and Palestinian Poster Art*. Raleigh, North Carolina: Contemporary Art Museum, 1996.

Basso, Keith. *Wisdom Sits in Places: Landscape and Language Among the Western Apache*. Albuquerque: University of New Mexico Press, 1996.

Berger, John, *The Sense of Sight*. New York: Vantage Books, 1985.

Berkhofer, Robert F., Jr. *The White Man's Indian*. New York: Vintage, 1979.

Boullata, Kamal, and John Berger. P*alestinian Art: From 1850 to the Present*. London: Saqi, 2009.

Boyden, Joseph, ed. *Kwe: Standing With Our Sisters*. Toronto: Penguin Canada, 2014.

Braithwaite, Niki. *Poetic Land – Political Territory*. Sunderland, UK: Northern Centre for Contemporary Art, 1995.

Calame, Jon and Esther Charlesworth. *Divided Cities: Belfast, Beirut, Jerusalem, Mostar, and Nicosia*. Philadelphia: University of Pennsylvania Press, 2009.

Castanha, Tony. *The Myth of Indigenous Caribbean Extinction: Continuity and Reclamation in Boriken (Puerto Rico)*. Hampshire, UK: Palgrave Macmillan, 2013.

Churchill, Ward. *A Little Matter of Genocide: Holocaust and Denial in the Americas 1492 to the Present*. San Francisco: City Lights, 1997.

Connaughton, Shane. *The Run of the Country*. Harmonsworth, UK: Penguin, 1995.

Cresswell, Tim. Place: *A Short Introduction*. London: Blackwell, 2004.

Cronon, William, *Changes in the Land: Indians, Colonists, and the Ecology of New England*. New York: Hill & Wang, 1983.

Curtis, L. Perry. *Apes and Angels: The Irishman in Victorian Caricature*. Washington, D.C.: Smithsonian Institution Press, 1971.

Darwish, Mahmoud. Munir Akash and Daniel Moore, eds. *The Adam of Two Edens*. Syracuse: Syracuse University Press, 2000.

_____. Ibrahim Muhawi, trans. *Journey of an Ordinary Grief*. Brooklyn: Archipelago Books, 2010.

_____. Omnia Amin and Rick London, trans. *Now, as You Awaken*. San Francisco: Sardines Press, 2007.

Deloria, Vine, Jr. *Custer Died for Your Sins: An Indian Manifesto*. Norman: University of Oklahoma Press, 1988.

_____. *Behind the Trail of Broken Treaties: An Indian Declaration of Independence*. Austin: University of Texas Press, 1985.

Farris-Dufrene, Phoebe M. *Voices of Color: Art and Society in the Americas*. Atlantic Highlands, N.J.: Open Humanities Press, 1997.

Fanon, Frantz. Haakon Chevalier, trans. *A Dying Colonialism*. New York: Grove Press, 1965.

_____. *Women Artists of Color: A Bio-critical Sourcebook to 20th Century Artists in the Americas*. Westport, Connecticut: Greenwood Publishing Group, 1999.

Forbes, Jack D. *The American Discovery of Europe*. Chicago: University of Illinois Press, 2007.

_____. *Africans and Native Americans: The Language of Race and the Evolution of Red-Black Peoples*. Chicago: University of Illinois Press, 1993.

_____. *Columbus and other Cannibals*. New York and London: Seven Stories Press, 1979

Gibbons, Joan, *Contemporary Art and Memory: Images of Recollection and Remembrance*. London: I.B. Tauris, 2008.

Grinnell, Jennifer and Austin Conley, eds. *Re/Dressing Cathleen: Contemporary Works from Irish Women Artists*. Cork, Ireland: Cork University Press, 1998.

Grounds, Richard, George E. Tinker and David Wilkins, eds. *Native Voices: American Indian Identity and Resistance*. Lawrence: University of Kansas Press, 2003.

Halaby, Samia A. *Liberation Art of Palestine: Palestinian Painting and Sculpture in the Second Half of the 20th Century*. Ramallah and New York: H.T.T.B. Publications, 2001

Harithas, James, Gabriel Delgado and Tex Kerschen. *Made in Palestine*. Houston: Ineri Publishing, 2004.

Heath, Jennifer and Kristine Smock, illustrator. *SuperColón: Admiral of the Ocean Sea*. Boulder, Colorado: Baksun Books, 1992.

_____. *On the Edge of Dream: The Women of Celtic Myth and Legend*. New York: Penguin, 1998.

_____. *The Scimitar and the Veil: Extraordinary Women of Islam,* New York: Paulist Press, 2004.

Heaney, Seamus. *Opened Ground: Selected Poems, 1966-1996*. New York: Farrar, Straus, Giroux, 1998.

Jackson, J.B. *Discovering the Vernacular Landscape*. New Haven: Yale University Press, 1984.

Jayyusi, Salma Khadra, ed. *Anthology of Modern Palestinian Literature*. New York: Columbia University Press, 1992.

Kanafani, Ghassan. Hilary Kirkpatrick, trans. *Men in the Sun*. Boulder, Colorado: Lynne Rienner Publishers, 1999.

Kendig, M., ed. *Alfred Korzybski: Collected Writings, 1920-1950*. Englewood, New Jersey: Institute of General Semantics, 1990.

Kiberd, Declan. *Inventing Ireland*. London: Jonathan Cape, 1995.

Kidwell, Clara Sue, Homer Noley and George E. Tinker. *A Native American Theology*. Maryknoll, New York: Orbis Books, 2001.

Kumpf, Tom Quinn. *Children of Belfast: Reclaiming Their Place among the Stones*. Lafayette: Devenish, 2000.

_____. *Two Sides: Haiku and Other Words*. Boulder, Colorado: Devenish, 2007.

_____. *Ireland: Standing Stones to Stormont*. Boulder, Colorado: Devenish, 2004.

Laxton, Paul, ed., *The New Nature of Maps: Essays in the History of Cartography*. Baltimore: Johns Hopkins Press, 2001.

Lassieru, Allison. *Before the Storm: American Indians Before the Europeans*. New York: Facts on File, Inc. 1998.

Lippard, Lucy R., ed. *Partial Recall: Photographs of Native North Americans*. New York: The New Press, 1992.

Lippard, Lucy R. *Mixed Blessings: New Art in a Multicultural America*. New York: Pantheon Books, 1990.

_____. *Overlay: Contemporary Art and the Art of Prehistory*. New York: The New Press, 1983.

Makhoul, Bashir and Gordon Hon. *The Origins of Palestinian Art*. Liverpool: Liverpool University Press, 2013.

McBreen, Joan, ed., *The White Page/An Bhileog Bhán: Twentieth-Century Irish Women Poets*. Cliffs of Moher, Co. Clare: Salmon Poetry, 2007.

McCabe, Patrick. *Breakfast on Pluto*. New York: Harper Collins, 1998.

Miller, Rory. *Ireland and the Palestine Question: 1948-2004*. Sallins, Co. Kildare, Ireland: Irish Academic Press, 2005.

Mohawk, John C. *Utopian Legacies: A History of Conquest and Oppression the Western World*. Santa Fe, N.M.: Clear Light Books, 1999.

Muldoon, Paul. *Poems, 1968-1998*. New York: Farrar, Straus, Giroux, 2001.

Mundy, Barbara E. *Mapping the New Spain: Indigenous Cartography and the Maps of the Relaciones Geograficas*. Chicago and London: University of Chicago Press, 1996.

Niatum, Duane, ed. *Harper's Anthology of 20th Century Native American Poetry*. New York: Harper & Row, 1988.

Olson, Pamela J. *Fast Times in Palestine: A Love Affair with a Homeless Homeland*. Berkeley, California: Seal Press, 2013.

Palmer, Kathleen. *Women War Artists*. London: Tate Publishing, 2011.

Pickles, John. *A History of Spaces: Cartographic Reason, Mapping, and the Geo-coded World*. London: Routledge, 2004.

Prashad, Vijay. *The Darker Nations: A People's History of the Third World*. New York: The New Press, 2007.

Quigley, Patrick. *Borderland*. Dingle, Ireland: Brandon Books, 1994.

Said, Edward W. *Culture and Imperialism*. London: Vintage, 1994.

_____. *The Question of Palestine*. New York: Vintage, 1994.

Salaita, Steven. *The Holy Land in Transit: Colonialism and the Quest*. Syracuse, New York: Syracuse University Press, 2006.

Sayres, Meghan Nuttall. *Weaving Tapestry in Rural Ireland: Taipéis Gael, Donegal*. Cork, Ireland: Atrium Cork University Press, 2006.

Shehadeh, Raja. *Palestinian Walks: Forays into a Vanishing Landscape*. New York: Scribner's, 2008.

Silko, Leslie Marmon. *Ceremony*. New York: Penguin, 1986.

Storrs, Sir Ronald. *Orientations*. London: Nicholson & Watson, 1937.

Schama, Simon. *Landscape and Memory*. London: Harper Collins, 1995.

Smith, Paul Chaat and Robert Allen Warrior. *Like a Hurricane: The Indian Movement from Alcatraz to Wounded Knee*. New York: Free Press, 1996.

Vizenor, Gerald. *Survivance: Narratives of Native Presence*. Lincoln, Nebraska: University of Nebraska Press, 2008.

_____. *Manifest Manners: Narrative of Post-Indian Survivance*. Lincoln, Nebraska: University of Nebraska Press, 1999.

Weaver, Jace. *Other Words: American Indian Literature, Law and Culture*. Norman: University of Oklahoma Press, 2001.

Whitelam, Keith W. *The Invention of Ancient Israel: the Silencing of Palestinian History*. New York: Routledge, 1996.

Tayac, Gabrielle, ed. *African-Native American Lives in the Americas*. Washington, D.C.: Smithsonian Institution Press, 2009

Yeats, W. B. Michael *Robartes and the Dancer*. Whitefish, Montana: Kessinger, 2003.

Zinn, Howard. *A People's History of the United States*. New York: Harper Perennial Modern Classics, 2005.

Artists' and Contributors' Biographies

ARTISTS' BIOGRAPHIES

6+: A WOMEN'S ART COLLECTIVE
Daughters of Palestine: Personal Narratives from the Young Women of the Dheisheh Refugee Camp (Page 31)

6+: a women's art collective is a group of women artists based in the United States, who seek to develop a supportive, creative network of women artists through a practice of direct engagement – including exhibitions, publications and community collaborations. The collective has focused on several projects in the West Bank in the Occupied Territories of Palestine. 6+ initiated the exhibition *Secrets* with eight Palestinian women artists, which premiered in Bethlehem before traveling to Ramallah and Jerusalem, then on to Boulder, Colorado, and Chicago. The *Secrets* exhibition catalogue features essays by Lucy R. Lippard and Maymanah Farhat. The collective has also facilitated several workshops with young women in the Dheisheh Refugee Camp in the West Bank. The art works that have resulted from these workshops – the video *Turning Our Tongues* and the web-based project *Daughters of Palestine* – have shown throughout the U.S. and internationally.

NADEMA AGARD
Tatanka Ska Oyate/White Buffalo Nation (Page55)

Nadema Agard (*Winyan Luta*/Red Woman) is an artist, illustrator, curator, educator, lecturer, storyteller, writer, poet, published author, museum professional and consultant in Repatriation and Multicultural/Native American arts and cultures. She has a BS in Art Education from New York University and an MA in Art and Education from Teacher's College, Columbia University. As a New York City-born Cherokee/Lakota/Powhatan, who has been educated and travels internationally, she is a bridge between urban and traditional cultures. She is currently the Director of New York's RED EARTH STUDIO CONSULTING/PRODUCTIONS, where she advocates for contemporary Native arts and cultures as a former consultant and NGO to the United Nations Permanent Forum on Indigenous Issues. In recognition of this work, she received the INGRID WASHINAWATOK AWARD FOR COMMUNITY ACTIVISM. Her artwork is often dedicated to the Divine Feminine, reflecting her immersion into the world of feminine empowerment and spirituality with a global vision from an Indigenous core.

NORMAN AKERS
Crowded (Page 47)

Norman Akers was born in Fairfax, Oklahoma, and is a member of the Osage Nation. He has a BFA in Painting from the Kansas City Art Institute, a Certificate in Museum Studies from the Institute of American Indian Arts and an MFA from the University of Illinois, Urbana-Champaign. He has had solo exhibitions at the Lawrence Arts Center, Jan Cicero Gallery and the Gardner Art Gallery and participated in numerous group exhibitions at, among others, the Katonah Museum, the Albuquerque Museum and the National Museum of the American Indian. His paintings are held in several collections, including the Gilcrease, Rockwell, Heard and Eiteljorg museums, as well as the National Museum of the American Indian and the Santa Fe Museum of Fine Arts. In 2007, he was selected to participate in the *We Are All Knots* print project, sponsored by the National Museum of the American Indian and ART in the Embassies Program Print Series. He received the Joan Mitchell Painters and Sculptors Grant in 1999. He is an Associate Professor of Painting and Drawing at the University of Kansas and taught previously at the Institute of American Indian Art.

FATIN AL-TAMIMI & LISAMARIE JOHNSON
Palestine Dublin, 2012 (Page 82)

Fatin Al-Tamimi is a freelance Palestinian photographer, who has lived in Ireland for 25 years. Her family lives in Hebron, Gaza and Tulkarem. In 2009, she graduated with a diploma in Photographic Media from Griffith College-Dublin. Her passions are portraiture and documentary photography. She is a member of the Network of Photographers for Palestine and frequently photographs solidarity actions that take place in Dublin and shares them around the world through Facebook and Flickr. She has exhibited her work at the Cowshed Theatre and Temple Bar in Dublin and has had work written up in Deinblick magazine.

Lisa Marie Johnson is a visual artist working primarily in performance. She has performed and shown her work at the Banff Center Canada, the Augusta Gallery in Finland, the Lab Gallery, Koza Museum of Visual Art Turkey, Brazilian World Social Forum, Jameson Film Festival, Temple Bar Galleries, The Project Arts Centre, EV+A, Eigse, Tulca, Excursions 08; Live @ 8, Live Zonz Holland, Item Slovenia, Liverpool Biennial, Shunt Gallery London, Crane Arts Festival, Burgundy, The Olympic Café Rue De Lyon, Paris, Flugraben Gallery Berlin, the Dark Light film festival Ireland and the Phibsboro Art Festival. She is a recipient of the Kunstwerk 2010 scholarship to Essen Germany, artist-in-residence for Common Ground in Rialto Dublin and her film work was shortlisted for Guggenheim Graduates. She has collaborated with First Nations in Canada and is currently making a film about her time with them. She holds an MFA from the National College of Art and Design in Dublin.

NEAL AMBROSE-SMITH
Weight of the Discussion, Baby Bird Brain, Stealing a Ride on the White Man's Bus, & Going Where No Man Has Gone Before (Pages 60, 23, 43 & 32)

Neal Ambrose-Smith has worked in the arts for twenty years as a studio assistant, goldsmith, graphic designer and freelance photographer for artists. He has traveled extensively in the United States, Mexico and Europe, where he did a year's independent study in Spain. His work is in numerous collections, including the Beach, Missoula, Boise, Eiteljorg, Springfield and Denver art museums; the Smithsonian Institution; the Galerie D'Art Contemporain, Chamalieres, France; the New York Public Library Print Collection; Hong-ik University, Seoul, Korea; Cork Printmakers, Ireland; and Australia's Monash University. He is a consultant to the Joan Mitchell Foundation and a working artist.

RAWAN ARAR
Free D (Page 83)

Rawan Arar currently lives in San Diego where she pursues her Ph.D. in sociology. Her parents met in Jordan after both their families were forced to leave Palestine. They moved to San Antonio, Texas, when Arar was three years old. "Being Palestinian," she says, "was my introduction to human rights, but that is not where my education stopped." She holds a BA in sociology with minors in women's studies and legal studies from the University of Texas and an MA in a Women's and Gender Studies MA from the University of Texas

(continued)

at Austin. In 2010, she conducted fieldwork in Jordan with Iraqi refugees as a Rotary Ambassadorial Scholar. She lived in Belfast, Northern Ireland, in 2011 as a visiting scholar at the Irish School of Ecumenics. Her current research interests span international immigration, refugees, conflict and reconciliation, feminism, and the body.

SCOTT BENESIINAABANDAN
Flags of Our Fathers, A Small Note from the North of Ireland, Anishinabe Proclamation, Solidarity Flag Derry & God Save the Queen (Pages 17, 11, 68, 83 & 46)

Scott Benesiinaabandan is an Anishinabe mixed-media artist who works primarily in photography, printmaking, and video. He has completed international residencies at Parramatta Artist Studios in Australia, Context Gallery in Derry, North of Ireland and in Oklahoma with photographer Rita Leistner, along with international collaborative projects in both the United Kingdom and Ireland. He is currently in Montreal, working on a Canada Council New Media Production grant through OBx Labs/Ab-tech and Concordia, one of multiple grants he has been awarded in the past four years from the Canada Council for the Arts, Manitoba Arts Council and Winnipeg Arts Council. Benesiinaabandan has taken part in several group exhibitions across Canada and the United States, most notably Harbourfront's *Flatter the Land/Bigger the Ruckus* and the Winnipeg Art Gallery's *Subconscious City.* His recent solo exhibitions include, *unSacred*, at Gallery 1C03 and *Mii Omaa Ayaad/Oshiki Inendemowin* in Sydney, Australia.

CLAUDIA BORGNA
Crumbs of Land: Khobz A Word for Freedom #4 (Page 58)

Claudia Borgna graduated from Genoa University (Italy) in Foreign Literature, then received a BFA from London Metropolitan University (UK). She leads a nomadic life, exhibiting nationally and internationally and attending fellowship residency programs. She is a recipient of a Joan Mitchell Foundation grant, a Pollock-Krasner Grant and the Royal British Society of Sculptors Bursary Award, as well as the Pritzker Foundation Endowed Fellowship Award. In 2010, she was voted the "Public Speaks" winner of the Broomhill National Sculpture Prize (UK), short-listed for the BBC2 documentary, "School of Saatchi" and for the British Women Artists Prize. Borgna's artificial landscapes are the materialization of an ongoing observation and questioning of how "plastic" and natural realms interact with one another and thereby come to create new ephemeral orders. Her flimsy constructions are only intended for the moment: apt to collapse and subject to change.

RAJIE COOK
Birth of a Nation & Epitaph for a Roadmap (Pages 50 & 90)

Rajie Cook is an internationally known graphic designer, photographer and artist who lives in Washington Crossing, Pennsylvania, and is the son of Najeeb and Jaleela Cook from Ramallah, Palestine. He was the founder (1967) and President of Cook and Shanosky Associates, Inc., a graphic design firm, which produced all forms of corporate communications including: Corporate Identity, Advertising, Signage, Annual Reports and Brochures. Among the major international corporations which have used his graphic design and photography are IBM, Container Corporation of America, Montgomery Ward, Squibb Corporation, Black & Decker, Volvo, Subaru, AT&T, New York Times, Bell Atlantic, BASF, and Lenox. President Ronald Reagan and Elizabeth Dole presented Cook with a 1984 Federal Design Achievement Award for the Arts in the Indian Treaty Room of the Old Executive Office Building in Washington, D.C. In 2003, "Symbols Signs," a project he and his firm designed for the U.S. Department of Transportation was accepted by the Acquisitions Committee to the collections of Cooper Hewitt, National Design Museum, Smithsonian Institution. In 1997, Cook was selected as Pratt Institute Alumni of the year, and has served on the Pratt Advisory Board. He has been a member of the American Institute of Graphic Arts.

WAHSONTIIO CROSS
Uncharted Territory (Page 16)

Wahsontiio Cross is an artist, historian and arts educator from Kahnawake Mohawk Territory, Quebec. She is a member of the Kanien'kehá:ka (Mohawk) Nation, Bear clan. She holds an MA in Art History and a BFA in Art History and Studio Art, both from Concordia University in Montreal. Her group exhibitions include *The Jean Berger Project* (FoFA Gallery, Montreal), the *Fall Art Show* at the Kanien'kehá:ka Onkwewenna Raotitiohkhwa Language and Cultural Centre (Kahnawake) and *Izhizkawe: To Leave Tracks to a Certain Place* (FoFA). Collections include a mural at Step by Step Child and Family Centre and Sequoia Bath and Body, both located in Kahnawake. Her essays have appeared in various publications, among them *Fuse* magazine and *Craft Journal,* as well as online publications, including essays and digital artwork as part of the Virtual Museum of Canada's *Canada's Got Treasures!* Online Exhibition. She has also participated in curatorial projects and recently completed an internship at the Canadian Museum of Civilization in Gatineau, Québec. She currently teaches art to children in Kahnawake as part of a community arts organization.

MANAL DEEB
Passport.Palestine & Diaspora (Pages 21 & 66)

Manal Deeb is a Palestinian-American artist born in Ramallah, who moved to the United States in 1986. She studied Studio Arts at the University of Illinois and received her BA in Interdisciplinary Studies (BIS), with a concentration in Psychology of Art from George Mason University. Her work is adapted from the history and eternal presence of Palestine, reflecting profoundly pertinent issues of identity and memory. Textured surfaces convey memory's persistence and perseverance. In 2012, thirty pieces of her artwork were displayed at the United Nations visitor center in New York as a celebration of the UN's Palestinian solidarity day. In March 2013, Deeb received a recognition award from the Arab-American Anti-Discrimination Committee for her contribution to Arab-American society, as part of the celebration of International Women's Day. She has exhibited at The Jerusalem Fund Gallery, The International Women's Museum, George Mason University and ARC Gallery, Chicago. Deeb's artwork and achievements have been featured in articles and interviews nationally and internationally.

RITA DUFFY
Police Station, Clearing & Territory (excerpt from Act of Union, by Seamus Heaney) (Pages 28, 70 & 29)

Rita Duffy is one of Ireland's leading artists. She has maintained an art practice in Belfast for twenty-seven years. Over this time she devised works for galleries and the built environment, gaining a broad range of experience and awards for her collaborative projects. Duffy's work addresses issues of Irish identity, history and politics, and is often autobiographical. Symbolism, and a strong connection to the figurative/narrative tradition, characterizes her art stylistically. Her work has examined elements of a post-colonial condition and her socially engaged practice continues to explore particular local and international issues. Her work is featured in *Women War Artists,* a major publication and joint project between the Tate Modern and the Imperial War Museum London. She was granted a Leverhulme Fellowship in 2010 in conjunction with the Transitional Justice Institute at the University of Ulster. She has recently relocated her studio practice to the border area between the north and south of Ireland, and in 2013, created a new project for Derry, *The Shirt Factory,* with her usual energy and enthusiasm.

MATTHEW EGAN
Divergence, Convergence, and Apparel & Difference Machine, 1822 (Pages 55 & 61)

Matthew Egan is currently a visiting academic at the University of Sharjah in the United Arab Emirates, coming from teaching and practicing printmaking as an Associate Professor in the School of Art and Design at East Carolina University. Egan was born in Newmarket, Ontario, Canada to an Irish–Catholic family and earned a BFA in printmaking with a minor in multi-media art at the University of Windsor. He received an MFA in printmaking and drawing from the University of South Dakota. Egan's prints, drawings and high-relief handmade paper casts have been exhibited in more than 200 regional, national and international juried and invitational exhibitions in North America, the Middle East, Asia and Europe. He has organized several portfolios, including *Fertile Crescent* and *Cultural Exchange,* and has participated in more than thirty-five national and international portfolios, now found in respected permanent collections.

MONA EL-BAYOUMI
Lucky Can't Find a Piece of Land to Sit and Eat his Falafel Peacefully (Page 71)

Mona El-Bayoumi was born in Alexandria, Egypt, and moved to the United States as a young child. Growing up in East Lansing, Michigan, in the 1970s, El-Bayoumi was exposed to many human rights struggles around the world. She believes that it is every world citizen's duty to be aware and try to fight injustices in their own unique ways. The brush has been her tool of choice. She has reflected mainly, but not exclusively, upon the Arab World. She studied Fine Arts at Michigan State University and has lived in Washington, D.C. for the past 23 years.

MICHAEL ELIZONDO
That Old Tune of "GARRYOWEN" & The Second Intifada (Pages 48 & 84)

Michael Elizondo, Jr., is a native of Oklahoma and received his BFA from Oklahoma Baptist University and his MFA at the University of Oklahoma, where he won first-place in the Native American Women & Others for Multicultural Preservation juried art show at the Jacobson House and the Fred Jones Jr. Museum of Art T.G. Mays Purchase Award in the 97th Annual OU Student Exhibition. In 2011, Elizondo won the Outstanding Young Artist Award state juried competition at the Red Cloud Indian School Heritage Center in Pine Ridge. He was an artist-in-residence at The Jacobson House Native Arts Center in Norman, Oklahoma, and served as an art instructor at Bacone College in Muskogee, Oklahoma, for the 2012-13 academic year. He is currently devoting himself as a full-time artist.

NAJAT EL-TAJI EL-KHAIRY
The Rock of Palestine in Basel (Page 58)

Najat El-Taji El Khairy is a porcelain artist of Palestinian origin. After attending French private schools in Cairo and completing a BA in English Literature at King Saud University in Riyadh, she became captivated with all forms of art expression and has studied music, ballet, painting, embroidery, stained glass, pottery and silk painting. In 1988, she moved with her family to Montreal, Canada, where she focuses on porcelain painting. Palestinian embroidery caught her attention early on and she began collecting traditional, vintage embroidered village dresses and other articles, often exhibiting them. This inspired a new medium: Palestinian art painted and preserved on porcelain tiles. This innovative merger of two art forms was El-Khairy's way of protecting and preserving, on a lasting surface, the rich heritage of Palestinian art for generations to come. Her artwork is displayed in various museums and galleries throughout North America.

PHOEBE FARRIS
Mohegan Wigwam (Page 73)

Phoebe Farris is a member of the Powhatan-Renape Nation and has six intertwined careers, stretching the concept of interdisciplinary and transnational research. She is the arts editor of *Cultural Survival Quarterly,* a licensed CCR/DUNS art curator/dealer, a registered art therapist, documentary photographer, professor and author. She also volunteers for the White House Office of Correspondence, the Washington, D.C. chapter of the American Association of University Women (AAUW), and the Fulbright Association. Farris explores issues involving race, gender, indigenous sovereignty, Native American studies, the environment, peace, and social justice from multiple perspectives. Her books, *Voices of Color: Art and Society in the Americas, Women Artists of Color: A Bio-Critical Sourcebook to 20th Century Artists in the Americas,* and *Art Therapy and Psychotherapy: Blending Two Therapeutic Approaches,* create a dialogue about the intersections of social activism and the arts. She earned a BFA in Fine Arts from City College of the City University in New York, an MA in Art Therapy from Pratt Institute in New York, and a Doctorate in Art Education-Curriculum and Instruction from the University of Maryland in College Park. She has received a Fulbright Grant to Mexico, a Rockefeller Humanities Fellowship, a National Endowment for the Humanities Grant, Purdue Research Foundation International Travel Grants, a Global Initiative Faculty Grant to Brazil, and had residencies at Harvard University's Institute on the Arts and Civic Dialogue and the Women's Leadership Institute at Mills College.

ELENA FARSAKH
Displaced (Page 78)

Elena Farsakh is the offspring of a United States diplomat and a Palestinian-American professor of Mathematics and Statistics, She has subsequently spent a large part of her life living and traveling in the Middle East. Her portfolio includes photographs of Tunisia,

(continued)

Egypt, Morocco and Palestine. Although she has lived in Los Angeles, Boston and New York, she is increasingly and uncontrollably drawn back to Palestine, where she spends as much time as the Occupation allows. Farsakh studied with Mark Osterman, a leading expert in 19th-century photographic processes at the George Eastman House, and with photojournalist Peter Turnley at the Maine Photographic Workshops. In addition to a BA in Visual Communications, she holds certificates from New York University in both Broadcast and Film Production. Her photographs are featured in the book, *Culture and Customs of the Palestinians*, by Dr. Samih Farsoun. Exhibits include works from Palestine, Egypt, Tunisia, Boston and Italy. Her latest work has been with a Palestinian legal aid and human rights NGO documenting the plight of Palestinians facing house demolitions, land separation and homes appropriated by settlers.

NAJIB JOE HAKIM
Passports to Exile & Fraternal Bonds (Pages 8 & 44)

Najib Joe Hakim works as a freelance photographer and photojournalist in San Francisco. His work has been published in numerous national and regional magazines and newspapers. He has had exhibitions in galleries on both coasts and internationally. His project – *Born Among Mirrors: Lebanon 50 Years After* – completed its third showing in November 2012. The project began as an exploration of war-ravaged Lebanon. Through a combination of coincidence and personal tragedy, it became a journey through Hakim's own family history from refugees out of Palestine to American citizenship. *Born Among Mirrors* provides insights into one immigrant family's successful survival through arguably the most intractable conflict of the last 100 years. Hakim's *Home Away from Home, Palestinians in America*. opened in California in 2014. Through audio interviews and photography, this project explores how Palestinians maintain ties to their homeland while living in a country whose political culture abhors their personal aspirations.

JOHN HALAKA
Hands of Time & Forgotten Survivors (Pages 34 & 65)

John Halaka is a visual artist, documentary filmmaker and professor of Visual Arts at the University of San Diego, where he has taught since 1991. An activist artist, Halaka's creative work serves as a vehicle for meditation on personal, cultural, and political concerns. His drawings, paintings and film projects are informed by the Palestinian experiences of displacement and the persistent desire of refugees to reclaim their homes and homeland. "Through my work," he says, "I attempt to initiate a dialogue with the viewer that might instigate transformation, one person at a time." Halaka received his MFA in the Visual Arts from the University of Houston and his BFA from the City University of New York Baccalaureate Program. He is of Palestinian descent and was born in El Mansoura, Egypt.

RULA HALAWANI
Palestinian I Am (Page 14)

Rula Halawani is one of Palestine's leading artists. In addition to being a practicing visual artist and freelance photojournalist, she founded and directs the Photography Program at Palestine's University of Birzeit. She has won many awards from, among others, the Open Society Institute, the Palestinian Journalist Union, the Arab Fund for Arts and Culture, the Kuwait International Photography Competition and the First International Photography Biennial in the Islamic World. Her work has been shown in numerous solo and group exhibitions throughout Europe, the United States and the Middle East, as well as Japan. She has been featured in myriad publications, has given presentations worldwide, and is herself the author of *Palestine*, published in 2008 by La Lettre Volee in Belgium. Her art is held in the permanent collections of Centre Georges Pompidou, The British Museum, Victoria & Albert Museum, Nadour Collection, The Khaled Shuman Foundation and the Museum of Fine Arts, Houston.

MICHELE HORRIGAN
Abandoned I, II, III (Pages 52 & 53)

Michele Horrigan is an artist and curator. She studied fine art at the Stadelschule Frankfurt and the University of Ulster. Since 2006, she is founder and curatorial director of Askeaton Contemporary Arts. The organization has commissioned more than fifty artists. As an artist, Horrigan has exhibited in the Gallery of Photography in Dublin, RIAA Buenos Aires, CENART (Centro Nacional de las Artes) in Mexico City, Frankfurter Kunstverein and the Royal Academy of Art in Copenhagen.

ANDREW ELLIS JOHNSON
Hex XX, Hex XXXIII, Hex XLIV and Hex IX (Page 63)

Andrew Ellis Johnson was born in Cortland, New York, to a jazz guitarist, civil-war historian father and science-major mother who, together, won many bowling tournaments. He made his first life-size faux bronze sculpture of Baron Manfred Von Richtoven at the age of 13, miniature marzipan figurines of Fats Waller at 11 and his first film cycle on the battle of Gettysburg at 9. Pursuing film and painting, he studied at SUNY Buffalo and completed his BFA at the School of the Art Institute of Chicago. After years in Europe and Asia, he earned an MFA in Art at Carnegie Mellon while serving as an artist-in-residence at the Pennsylvania Department of Corrections, curating an exhibition of inmate art at the City Theater. He attended Skowhegan School of Painting and Sculpture and a residency through Poznan Academy of Art in Poland. After teaching in Massachusetts, Nebraska and West Virginia, a five-month studio stint in Amsterdam, and five years at University at Buffalo, he joined the School of Art faculty at Carnegie Mellon in 2004. His work is included in numerous collections worldwide.

MICHAEL KEATING
Abu Dis – The Wall at Dusk (Page 18)

Michael Keating is the editor and primary photographer for *The VVA Veteran*, the bimonthly magazine of Vietnam Veterans of America. His photographs and articles also have been published in several other magazines, including *The Washington Report on Middle East Affairs*. His photographs have been exhibited at venues in Washington, D.C., New York and West Virginia, including one-man and group shows at The Palestine Center. Much of his work has concentrated on endangered landscapes in suburban Maryland and the people of Appalachia. His Middle East work has concentrated on Palestine and Tunisia.

TOM QUINN KUMPF
Burren Pony, Co. Clare; Child's Play, North Belfast; Killamery High Cross (Medb's Bowl), Co. Kilkenny & Moonstone, 3200 BC, East Chamber Knowth, Co. Meath (Pages 19, 80, 92 & 87)

Tom Quinn Kumpf grew up in a predominantly Irish, working-class neighborhood in Pittsburgh, Pennsylvania. He served with the U.S. Navy in Vietnam and has since been deeply involved in conflict resolution and international veterans' issues. He was one of the founding members of Vietnam Veterans of Montana, where he worked with Native American Veterans on the Northern Cheyenne and Flathead Indian Reservations. In 1990, he was part of a delegation of Vietnam Veterans to visit the former Soviet Union, working with Soviet veterans of the war in Afghanistan on PTSD and readjustment issues. Later, he helped organize similar programs in Belfast, Northern Ireland, working with former prisoners from both sides of the Peace Line. In response to his Irish roots, he documented the effects of the Troubles on youngsters in the award-winning *Children of Belfast,* a collection of essays and photographs. His second book, *Ireland: Standing Stones to Stormont* focuses on Irish identity as it relates to legend and landscape. Kumpf's photographs, essays and poetry have appeared in numerous publications and exhibitions throughout the U.S., Europe and the former USSR.

JANE MCMAHAN
Border Tunnels (Page 94)

Jane McMahan is a conceptual artist, painter, educator and social, environmental and political activist living and working in Boulder, Colorado. She was born in Wausau, Wisconsin, and received her BFA from the University of Colorado. She taught art in the public schools for fourteen years before returning full time to her own work in 1998. McMahan's art explores ways to visually capture the process of construction, deconstruction and reconstruction, sometimes with redemption, and the moments when they occur simultaneously. Current themes in her work include nature and environmental red flags, cultural and political interactions and human rights. Sense of place is often the foundation of her ideas. She has shown locally, nationally and internationally. She is part of Artnauts Collective and Ice Cube Gallery in Denver, Colorado. In 2013, she visited and made art in Palestine.

ALAN MONTGOMERY
Irish History Lessons #1 & Irish History Lessons #2 (Pages 85 & 86)

Alan Montgomery was born in Belfast, Northern Ireland, and is a tenured professor of Art at Dakota State University. His work was recently published in Henry Sayre's seventh edition of *A World of Art,* published by Pearson Higher Education. In a 1994 essay, "The Fragility of Connectedness," Akira Lippit writes about Montgomery's work as "exploring the connection between the physical reality of Northern Ireland's Troubles, and the metaphysical content of Montgomery's series *Irish History Lessons*, which continues to manifest itself in drawings and paintings." Montgomery's interests reside in topical issues ranging from environmental to socio-political and his formal application of materials reflects a contemporary approach to mixed media and traditional techniques. Place and time have been very important in the development of his work. "I would like viewers to see something they have not seen before," he says. "I want to provide an experience that can be recognized as authentic and real, that is, a thought that inscribes itself onto the psyche."

MALAQUIAS MONTOYA
Undocumented (Page 24)

Malaquias Montoya was born in Albuquerque, New Mexico, and grew up in the San Joaquin Valley, California, in a family of seven children by parents who could not read or write either Spanish or English. The three oldest children never went beyond 7th-grade education, as the entire family were farmworkers. Montoya's father and mother were divorced in 1952, and his mother worked in the fields to support the four children still at home, so they could pursue their educations. Since 1962, Montoya has lectured and taught at numerous universities and colleges in the San Francisco Bay Area. He was director of Oakland's Taller de Artes Graficas for five years, where he produced prints and conducted community art workshops. He is presently a professor in the Chicano Studies Program at the University of California at Davis. Montoya is primarily known for his silkscreen prints, which have been exhibited nationally and internationally. He has executed several murals, giving life to walls at Stanford University, California College of Arts and Crafts, the Centro Infantil de la Raza in Oakland and at seven schools in the Vacaville Unified School District. His art of protest depicts the struggle and strength of humanity and the necessity to unite behind that struggle.

MICK O'KELLY
Currency 1, 2, and 3 (Page 10)

Mick O'Kelly received his Ph.D. from the University of Ulster Northern Ireland in 2009. He studied for his BFA at the National College of Art and Design Dublin, and received his MFA from the California Institute of the Arts. He is a visiting artist to art schools in Ireland, UK, Germany, France, Finland, Brazil and the United States. He has exhibited nationally and internationally and engages in contextual art initiatives beyond the gallery and museum structure. Ongoing concerns in his work and research acknowledge the changing nature of contemporary art and issues of situated practice, location and context. His research and work explore art tactics as urban negotiations to produce social spaces of intervention. His projects operate within states of contingency and indeterminacy, where the dimensions of practice occupy an aesthetic-ethical, spatial-politics.

PARALLEL PATHS – THREE POEMS
William Butler Yeats, Second Coming, 1919; Gail Tremblay, Indian Singing in 20th-century America, 1988; Mahmoud Darwish, excerpt from Speech of the Red Indian, 1992; "Three Birds," artwork by Nora Collom (frontispiece)

William Butler Yeats was born in Dublin in 1865 and was among the foremost figures of 20th-century literature. He was a driving force behind the Irish Literary Revival and, along with Lady Gregory, Edward Martyn, and others, founded the Abbey Theatre. In 1923, he was awarded the Nobel Prize in Literature as the first Irishman so honored. In his later years, he served as an

(continued)

Irish Senator for two terms. He died in 1939.

Gail Tremblay is a Mi'kmaq and Onondaga writer and artist born in 1945 in Buffalo, New York. She currently teaches at Evergreen State College and is well known for her poetry, as well as her visual art, which mixes traditional techniques and materials with contemporary expression.

Mahmud Darwish, regarded as the Palestinian national poet and indisputably one of world's great poets, won numerous awards for his literary output, in which Palestine became a metaphor for the loss of Eden, and the anguish of dispossession and exile. He was born in the village of al-Birwa in the Western Galilee in 1941 and died in Houston, Texas, in 2008. This excerpt is from "Speech of the Red Indian" – a long and highly lauded poem, thought to be an inspiration for Jean-Luc Godard's 2004 film, *Notre Musique*.

VIVIEN SANSOUR
Don Alonso Lopez, Abu Nidal, Emilio & Candles for Water (Pages 49, 26, 42 & 74)

Vivien Sansour is a life style writer, producer, and photographer. Trained as an anthropologist, she has worked with farmers in Latin America and Palestine on issues relating to agriculture and independence. Her book, *Insisting on Life: A Community at Work*, emerged from her interactions with communities in Northern West Bank villages. She has produced several short films and one feature film, *The People and the Olive*, which received high acclaim from critics, including the Boston Globe's Loren King who called the film, "An inspirational thriller." It was the official selection for the Chicago International Social Change and the Unspoken Human Rights film festivals, among others. Terrain: Palestinian Agri-Resistance, a collection of landscape and portrait images, was exhibited in Washington D.C. Sansour has been a contributing writer and photographer for publications such as *Organic Processing Magazine*, *Specialty Food*, *Huffington Post*, BBC World Service, *Fair World Project*, *This Week in Palestine*, and *Danish Fair Trade Magazine*, and she won the Fair Trade photo contest for the Fair Trade Resource Network. She has been honored by several organizations for her community contributions, including her recent role in helping the farmers of the village of Nus Ijbail renovate and create a producers cooperative center. She currently works as Communications Specialist at the Institute for Middle East Understanding and designed and taught Agri-Cultural Palestine at Bard College-Al-Quds program Campus in Camps.

DONNA SCHINDLER
Hozhonahaslii: Stories of Healing the Soul Wound (Page 77)

Donna Schindler, M.D. is a psychiatrist who has spent many years living and working with indigenous people in New Zealand, the Navajo Nation and most recently in Northern California. She does tele-psychiatry with the community of Kayenta, Arizona, is also currently involved in trying to get more accurate information regarding historical trauma into the California Missions.

SUSANNE SLAVICK
Rend & Repercussion (Pages 40 & 41)

Susanne Slavick is Andrew W. Mellon Professor of Art at Carnegie Mellon University in Pittsburgh. She studied at Yale and Jagiellonian University in Krakow before earning an MFA at Tyler School of Art in Rome and Philadelphia. Her work has been exhibited internationally and recognized through National Endowment for the Arts and Pennsylvania Council on the Arts fellowships. She has held residencies at The MacDowell Colony, Mt. Desert Island/Four Seals Foundation, Skoki Castle/Academy of Fine Arts in Poznan, Blue Mountain Center and Fayoum International Art Center in Egypt. Works from her "R&R(...&R)" project premiered at Pittsburgh Center for the Arts and subsequently traveled to the Warhol Museum, Rutgers University, Bradley University and solo shows at the Chicago Cultural Center, McDonough Museum of Art and Accola Griefen in NYC. She is a co-founder of "10 Years + Counting," an online resource developed to commemorate a decade of senseless war and editor of *Out of Rubble*, an anthology of works by international artists who respond to the aftermath of war. Related curatorial projects are traveling across the country. Slavick has also published visual essays and articles for: *Cultural Heritage and Arts Review*, *Cultural Politics*, *Frontiers: A Journal of Women's Studies*, *Guernica: A Magazine of Art & Politics* and *AlterNet*.

JAUNE QUICK-TO-SEE SMITH
House and Home (Page 13)

Jaune Quick-to-See Smith calls herself a cultural art worker. She uses humor and satire to examine myths, stereotypes and the paradox of American Indian life in contrast to the consumerism of American society. Her work is philosophically centered by her strong traditional beliefs and political activism. Smith is internationally known as an artist, curator, lecturer, printmaker and professor. She was born at St. Ignatius Mission on her Reservation and is an enrolled Salish member of the Confederated Salish and Kootenai Nation of Montana. She holds four honorary doctorates from the Pennsylvania Academy of the Arts, the Minneapolis College of Art and Design, Mass College of Art and the University of New Mexico. Her work is in collections at the Whitney Museum, the Metropolitan Museum, the Brooklyn Museum, Smithsonian American Art Museum, the Walker, the Victoria and Albert Museum and the Museum of Modern Art, New York. Recent awards include a grant from the Joan Mitchell Foundation to archive her work; the 2011 Art Table Artist Award; Moore College Visionary Woman Award for 2011; induction into the National Academy of Art 2011; Living Artist of Distinction, Georgia O'Keeffe Museum, New Mexico 2012; the Switzer Award for 2012.

MARY TUMA
Lingering Presence (Page 39)

Mary Tuma was born in California in 1961 to a Californian mother of Irish descent and a Palestinian father. She began sewing and crocheting with her mother at an early age. Her love of these processes led her to begin her formal study of art as an apprentice at Beautiful Arts Hall in Kerdassa, Egypt, where she learned to weave tapestries. Later, she earned a Bachelor's degree in Costume and Textile Design from the University of California at Davis, and then went on to study women's fashion design at the Fashion Institute of Technology in New York. In 1994, she earned an MFA in Art from the University of Arizona. In 1997, she began teaching art at the University of North Carolina in Charlotte, where she now serves as an Associate Professor and the head of the Fibers Program. Tuma has shown her work in various venues in the United States, including the Crocker Art Museum, The Southeastern Center for Contemporary Art, Athens Institute for Contemporary Art, the Station Museum and the Urban Institute for Contemporary Art. Her work has also been shown in South Korea, Jerusalem, Rome, Tokyo, Kuwait, Hiroshima, Bethlehem and Turkey. Her art has appeared in, among others, *Contemporary Practices*, *Art in America*, *Dar Al-Hayat*, *The New York Times*, *The Christian Science Monitor*, *Counterpunch*, *NYArts*, *Mother Jones*, *The San Francisco Chronicle* and *The Jordan Star*.

KERRY VANDER MEER
Slab at Cill Rialaig & Untitled Potato Print (Pages 67 & 54)

Kerry Vander Meer received her MFA in sculpture from Mills College. Her talents extend into painting, printmaking, mixed media, installation and performance art. She has exhibited and taught extensively throughout Northern California, in New York, Seattle, Chicago, Santa Fe and numerous galleries and museums across the country, including the Yerba Buena Center and the Museum of Modern Art in San Francisco. Her works appear in collections in the United States, Germany, Spain, Ireland and Japan. She is the recipient of a number of prestigious awards including artist-in-residency awards, at the Cill Rialaig Project in Ireland, Millay Colony in New York, Villa Montalvo in California and Fondación Valparaiso in Spain. Vander Meer's content-rich art deals with such issues as the environment and the effect of the media on body image. Her work has been praised by the influential critic Lucy R. Lippard, and is featured in many books and publications, such as *Artweek*, *San Francisco Focus*, *The New York Times* and *The Oakland Tribune*.

SHERRY WIGGINS
Battles, Deeds, Fields, and Swords (Page 51)

Sherry Wiggins works from her home state of Colorado as a new-media artist, sculptor, public artist and cultural organizer. Wiggins received her MFA and BFA from the University of Colorado. She is a founding member of 6+: a women's art collective, a group that facilitates exhibitions, publications and workshops among women artists internationally. Wiggins has worked in the Middle East as an artist and arts organizer. Her work is reflective and often participatory and is centered on explorations of cultural difference, social justice and women's issues. Her practice is concerned with art as a transformative and relational process. Wiggins exhibits her work internationally including venues in China, Korea, Mexico, the Middle East and South America, as well as in Colorado and throughout the U.S. She has outdoor work at the Denver International Airport and in private collections in Colorado.

MELANIE YAZZIE
Seeing Each Other (Page 12)

Melanie Yazzie is a printmaker, painter and sculptor, whose work draws upon her rich Diné (Navajo) cultural heritage. Her work follows the Diné dictum "walk in beauty" literally to create beauty and harmony. As an artist, she works as an agent of change by encouraging others to learn about social, cultural and political phenomena shaping the contemporary lives of Native peoples in the United States and beyond. Her work incorporates personal experiences, as well as the events and symbols from Diné culture. Her early work brought Native issues to the forefront with depictions of the harsh realities of Native peoples (i.e., racism, identity conflict, poverty, abuse, etc.), but more recently she is making work focusing on quiet and balance. Her work is shaped by personal experiences and tries to tell many stories about things both real and imagined. She uses her world travels to connect with other indigenous peoples – in New Zealand, the Arctic, Russia and the Pueblos in the Southwest – the impetus for continued dialogue about cultural practices, language, song, storytelling and survival. She has exhibited nationally and internationally, from New Zealand to Finland and the Canary Islands. Her work is in the Phippen Art Museum, The Australian National Gallery and the Museum of Art, Rhode Island School of Design, Print Collection, Providence. She has been featured in numerous publications, including *The Los Angeles Times*, *Native American Art in the Twentieth Century* by W. Jackson Rushing III and *The Lure of the Local: Sense of Place in a Multi-Centered Society* by Lucy R. Lippard. Yazzie is an associate professor and head of printmaking in the Department of Art and Art History at University of Colorado, Boulder, Colorado. She strives to create safe, non-toxic methods of printmaking where toxic chemicals are commonly used.

HELEN ZUGHAIB
Woven in Exile & Beit/Salaam (Pages 57 & 12)

Helen Zughaib was born in Beirut, Lebanon, living mostly in the Middle East and Europe before coming to the United States to study art. She received her BFA from Syracuse University, College of Visual and Performing Arts. She paints using gouache and ink on board, transforming her subjects into a combination of colors and patterns, creating a nontraditional sense of space and perspective. Zughaib has exhibited widely in New York and the Washington D.C. area. Her paintings are included in more than eighty private and public collections, including the White House, World Bank, Library of Congress, United States Consulate General, Vancouver, Canada, American Embassy in Baghdad, Iraq, and the Arab American National Museum. Most recently, she served as United States Cultural Envoy to the West Bank, Palestine. Hopefulness, healing, and spirituality, are all themes that are woven into her work.

HANI ZUROB
Flying Lesson #3, #4 & #7 (Pages 36, 36 & 9)

Hani Zurob is a Palestinian exile working in Paris. He was born in the Rafah refugee camp, Gaza, and received his BFA at the University of Al-Najah, Naplouse-Palestine. He has exhibited his work throughout France and in the United Kingdom, Switzerland, Romania, Palestine, Egypt, Syria, Bahrain, Dubai, Qatar and Bahrain, among others. He is the subject of *Between Exits: Paintings by Hani Zurob*, written by Kamal Boullata and released by London's Black Dog Publishing in 2012.

CONTRIBUTORS' BIOGRAPHIES

RAWAN ARAR (see Artists' Biographies)

VALERIE BEHIERY is an art historian specializing in both historical and contemporary art from or relating to the Muslim world. After her Ph.D. in art history from McGill University, she completed a three-year postdoctoral fellowship at the University of Montreal examining the relationship between the cultural history of vision and Western media representations of the Middle East. She also worked for several years as the Islamic art consultant at the Montreal Museum of Fine Arts where she researched the collection and oversaw the installation of the new permanent Islamic art gallery. Presently, she is an assistant professor of Islamic Art History at Necmettin Erbakan University in Konya, Turkey. Her writing has been published in a number of reference works and academic journals, including *Social Identities: Journal for the Study of Race, Nation and Culture*, *Journal of Canadian Art History*, *Sociologie et sociétés* and *Comparative Studies of South Asia, Africa, and the Middle East*.

AISLING B. CORMACK is humanities research associate in English at the University of California, Irvine, and adjunct professor of English at Pasadena City College. Her research explores 20th- and 21st-century Anglo-Irish literature and film within the context of postcolonial criticism, cultural studies and psychoanalytic theory. She received an M.Phil. in Anglo-Irish literature from Trinity College Dublin in 2000 and a Ph.D. in English, with a certificate in critical theory, in 2012 from the University of California, Irvine. In her dissertation, *Specters of the Irish Borderlands: Writing Partition*, she examines literary representations of the partition of Ireland, focusing on the contemporary Irish writer Patrick McCabe and the filmmaker Neil Jordan. Her article, "Toward a 'Post-Troubles' Cinema? The Troubled Intersection of Political Violence and Gender in Neil Jordan's *The Crying Game* and *Breakfast on Pluto*" was published in the journal *Éire-Ireland* and her essay "On the Edge: The Legacy of Irish Partition in *The Butcher Boy*" is forthcoming in a volume of critical essays on the work of Patrick McCabe. She is currently working on a book-length study of McCabe's novels and Neil Jordan's film adaptations in the context of Irish partition and on a chapter, "A Garden Divided," about Samuel Beckett's representation of Irish partition in his novel *Watt* for the collection *An Art of the Impasse*.

NESSA CRONIN is Lecturer in Irish Studies and Director of the MA in Irish Studies Programme, Centre for Irish Studies, National University of Ireland, Galway. She read English and Philosophy at Trinity College, Dublin, and in 2000 received an MA in Continental Philosophy and Literature from Warwick University, before returning to Ireland to complete her Ph.D. in Irish Studies at NUI Galway in 2007. She has received an Irish Research Council Postgraduate Scholarship, an NUI Galway Arts Faculty Fellowship and a Notre Dame Summer School Fellowship, as well as awards from the Irish Research Council, European Science Foundation and Culture Ireland for her work in Irish Cartographic History and Place Studies. She developed the transdisciplinary group, *Ómós Áite: Space/Place Research Network* at NUI Galway, and is the Irish co-convener of the *Mapping Spectral Traces* international network. She has written extensively on Irish cartography history and cultural geography, in addition to essays on place-making and the Irish literary tradition. She is currently involved in collaborative work with artists and local groups in developing community mapping projects that combine socially engaged arts practice with interdisciplinary research in the west of Ireland.

PHOEBE FARRIS (see Artists' Biographies)

GERMÁN GIL-CURIEL is a research affiliate of the Department of Music at University College Cork, Ireland. He submitted his Ph.D. thesis in French and English Literature at the University of Sheffield in 2011. He holds an MA in Comparative Literature and a BA in Modern Languages (French). He has been an associate member of The Academy for Teaching and Learning in Higher Education, The Society of French Studies, the Institute of Romance Studies, and the Society of English Studies. He has taught in China and the United Kingdom and is a member of the research team Translating Cultures. His main research and teaching interests include comparative supernatural literature, the intersection between literature, film, music and fashion, adaptation across the media, the role of the arts in the contemporary development of cultural industries and identity and translation. His publications include *A Comparative Approach: The Early European Supernatural Tale, Five Variations on a Theme* and *Film Music in "Minor" National Cinemas*, "The Supernatural from Page to Screen: Ambrose Bierce's and Robert Enrico's *An Occurrence at Owl Creek Bridge*" in *Impure Cinema*, "Music, Literature and Cinema: A Comparative Approach to the Aesthetics of Death in *Tous les Matins du Monde*" in *China and Other Spaces* and "Dancing Tragedy: McQueen's *Deliverance* Collection" in *Fashion Semiotics Org*. He is also a certified literary translator and classical guitarist.

JOHN HALAKA (see Artists' Biographies)

VALENTIN LOPEZ is the Chairman of the Amah Mutsun Tribal Band, one of three historic tribes recognized as Ohlone. The Amah Mutsun comprise the documented descendants of Missions San Juan Bautista and Santa Cruz. Lopez is also President of the Amah Mutsun Land Trust. He is a Native American Advisor to the University of California, Office of the President, on issues related to repatriation and a Native American Advisor to the National Alliance on Mental Illness, as well as the Phoebe Hearst Museum of Anthropology. The Amah Mutsun are active in conservation and protection efforts within their traditional tribal territory. Lopez works to restore the Mutsun Language and is a traditional Mutsun singer and dancer.

FARAH MÉBARKI is a specialist in the histories of ancient Palestine history early Christian Ireland. She worked in Gaza, Nazareth and Ashqelon as an archaeologist. In Gaza, she was in charge of a Byzantine church whose robbed remains had been unexpectedly brought to light by a bulldozer near Jabaliyeh refugee camp and whose gorgeous mosaic floors bore several Greek inscriptions. She later worked as an epigrapher at the Hebrew University in Jerusalem helping French scholar Prof. Puech publish Aramaic fragments of the Dead Sea scrolls from Cave 4. She is an editor in charge of Middle Eastern files for the French review *Le Monde de la Bible* and has written many articles in reviews such as *Archeologia*, *Le Journal du CNRS* and *Etudes irlandaises*. Her doctoral thesis in Irish Studies dealt with the real and mythical contacts between Early Christian Ireland and the Levant. Some of her books about the Holy Land, all published in France, have been translated into Italian and Spanish. She has been interested in Palestinian cross-stitch embroidery and Bethlehem-style couching for years and practices this art herself. She has lectured on Palestinian embroidery at international conferences in Europe. She is French, but likes to say that her heart has been woven with Shawi-Berber and Palestinian threads. She paints in watercolors, creates oil pastel calligraphies and icons and enjoys singing sacred texts in Arabic.

CURATORS' BIOGRAPHIES

JENNIFER HEATH is an award-winning author, editor, curator, cultural journalist and activist. Selected traveling exhibitions include *Black Velvet: The Art We Love to Hate* (1990-1994) and catalogue; The Veil: Visible & Invisible Spaces (2008-2013) and catalogue, www.jenniferheath.com/theveil; and *Water, Water Everywhere: Paean to a Vanishing Resource* (2012-2017) and catalogue, waterwatereverywhere-artshow.com. Among Heath's twelve books – many translated internationally – are *SuperColón: Admiral of the Ocean Sea* (illustrated by Kristine Smock); *On the Edge of Dream: The Women of Celtic Myth and Legend* (Penguin, 1998), *The Scimitar and the Veil: Extraordinary Women of Islam* (Paulist Press, 2004), *The Veil: Women Writers on its History, Lore, and Politics* (University of California Press, 2008), *Land of the Unconquerable: The Contemporary Lives of Afghan Women* (with Ashraf Zahedi, University of California Press, 2011), *Children of Afghanistan: The Path to Peace* (with Ashraf Zahedi, University of Texas Press, 2014), and *El Repelente (Or the 2012 Antics of Anabela)*. She has written extensively for arts and other publications, such as *Art Forum, New Art Examiner, Performance, Ms.* and *Costs of War*, and contributed to many exhibition catalogues and anthologies. Baksun Books & Arts, which she founded in 1995, is dedicated to de-commodifying the word through small-press activities and to producing exhibitions and programs on behalf of social and environmental justice.

DAGMAR PAINTER is founder and curator of the Jerusalem Fund Gallery Al-Quds, Washington D.C.'s only full-time art gallery featuring the work of contemporary artists centering on issues of the Arab and Islamic worlds, with a special emphasis on Palestinian art. She has lived, worked and traveled extensively in the Arab and Islamic world for more than thirty years. In Washington, D.C., she established and ran the art gallery of the Embassy of Tunisia, directed Gallery Patina (featured on NBC's Today Show) for the National Council on Aging, and lectured at DC's Textile Museum and Meridian House International. She has been an advisory review panelist for the D.C. Commission on the Arts and Humanities, a nominator for the Smithsonian Institution SARF Awards, and a juror for the Torpedo Factory Arts Center in Alexandria, VA. In Cairo, Egypt, she curated exhibitions of Egyptian and American artists. For her work in Egypt she received the Meritorious Honor Award from the U.S. Department of State. She has written and lectured extensively in the United States and abroad on cross-cultural and arts issues. She also taught seminars on Middle Eastern textiles at the University of Tunis and the Centre D'Etudes Maghrebines, as well as classes at the National Museums of Lagos, Nigeria and Bangkok, Thailand. Selected publications include *Arts in the Islamic World, Ornament, Cairo Today, Focus on Pakistan, The Herald, India Today, Arts in Embassies, A Practical Guide to Cairo* and *Savior: Tunis*.

EXHIBITION CHECKLIST

"The Map is Not the Territory"
Parallel Paths – Palestinians, Native Americans, Irish

6+: a women's art collective
*Daughters of Palestine
Personal Narratives from the Young Women
of the Dheisheh Refugee Camp*
2008
Web-based project
http://6plus.org/deheisheh2.html

Nadema Agard
Tatanka Ska Oyate, White Buffalo Nation
2003
Watercolor/pastel/mixed media
20"x15" w/o ribbon; 20"x30" w ribbon

Norman Akers
Crowded
2013
Digital print
15 7/8" x 19 1/4"

Fatin Al-Tamimi & LisaMarie Johnson
Palestine Dublin, 2012
2012
Digital photo
16"x20"

Neal Ambrose-Smith
Baby Bird Brain
2012,
Digital print
15 3/4" x 20"

Neal Ambrose-Smith
Going Where No Man Has Gone Before
2008
Digital print
20"x15"

Neal Ambrose-Smith
Stealing a Ride on the White Man's Bus
2012
Digital print
20"x19 1/4"

Neal Ambrose-Smith
Weight of the Discussion
2012
Digital print
20"x19 1/2"

Rawan Arar
Free D
2010
Digital print
20"x16"

Scott Benesiinaabandan
Anishinabe Proclamation
2011
Digital print
16"x20"

Scott Benesiinaabandan
A Small Note from the North of Ireland
2011
Digital print
20"x20"

Scott Benesiinaabandan
Flags of Our Fathers
2010
Digital print.
20 1/4"x 13 5/8"

Scott Benesiinaabandan
God Save the Queen
2011
Digital print
20 1/2" x 10 1/2"

Scott Benesiinaabandan
Solidarity Flag Derry
2011
Digital print
15 3/4" x 20 1/2"

Claudia Borgna
Crumbs of Land: Khobz A Word for Freedom #4
2012
Digital print
23 3/4" x 18 1/2"

Rajie Cook
Birth of a Nation
2001
Digital pigment print
16"x22"

Rajie Cook
Epitaph for a Roadmap
2006
Digital pigment print
20"x16"

Wahsontiio Cross
Uncharted Territory
2012
Hand-stitched, hardcover book
7.25"x10.75"x1.625" closed
14.625"x10.75"x0.5" open

Manal Deeb
Diaspora
2013
Charcoal and photos on paper
19 5/8 " x25 1/2"

Manal Deeb
Passport.Palestine.
2013
32-page old passport with waxed photos
4"x6"

Rita Duffy
Police Station
2000
Digital print
18"x26"

Rita Duffy
Clearing
1999
Digital print
19"x19"

Rita Duffy
Territory
(excerpt from *Act of Union*, by Seamus Heaney)
1998
Digital print
14"x20"

Matthew Egan
Difference Machine, 1822
2011
Lithography
15"x20"

Matthew Egan
Divergence, Convergence, and Apparel
2008
4-plate color lithography
15"x20"

Mona El-Bayoumi
Lucky Can't Find a Piece of Land to Sit and Eat his Falafel Peacefully
2013
Acrylic and mixed media on paper
15"x20"

Michael Elizondo, Jr.
That Old Tune of "GARRYOWEN"
2013
Acrylic
16"x20"

Michael Elizondo, Jr.
The Second Intifada
2013
Acrylic
20"x16"

Najat El-Taji El-Khairy
The Rock of Palestine in Basel
2012
Giclée print
17"x22"

Phoebe Farris
Mohegan Wigwam
2012
Digital print
16"x20"

Elena Farsakh
Displaced
2010
Digital print
16 1/2" x22"

Najib Joe Hakim
Fraternal Bonds
2013
Digital collage
15"x15"

Najib Joe Hakim
Passports to Exile
2013
Digital collage
20"x16"

John Halaka
Hands of Time.
from the series: *Portraits of Denial & Desire.*
2013
Digital print
21"x5"

John Halaka
Forgotten Survivors
from the series: *Portraits of Denial & Desire.*
2013
Digital print
15"x 26 1/4"

Rula Halawani
Palestinian I Am
From the series: *Negative Incursions.*
2003
Digital prints
16"x 20" each

Michele Horrigan
Abandoned I, II, and III
2008
Digital prints
16"x20" each

Andrew Ellis Johnson
Hex XX, Hex XXXIII, Hex XLIV, and Hex IX
from *Pressed: When Words Were Earth*
2005
Archival digital prints
15 3/4" x 15 3/4" each

Michael Keating
Abu Dis – The Wall at Dusk
2005
Chromogenic print
30"x20"

Tom Quinn Kumpf
Burren Pony, Co. Clare
2001
Photograph
16"x20"

112

Tom Quinn Kumpf
Child's Play, North Belfast
1998
Photograph
16"x20"

Tom Quinn Kumpf
Killamery High Cross (Medb's Bowl), Co. Kilkenny
1998
Photograph
16"x20"

Tom Quinn Kumpf
Moonstone, 3200 BC, East Chamber Knowth, Co. Meath
2007
Photograph
16"x20"

Jane McMahan
Border Tunnels
2012
Graphite, ink, colored pastel
22"x17 ¾"

Alan Montgomery
Irish History Lessons #1
2010
Charcoal, graphite, printing ink, and gesso
30"x22 ½"

Alan Montgomery
Irish History Lessons #2
2010
Charcoal, graphite, printing ink, and gesso
30" x 22 ½"

Malaquias Montoya
Undocumented
2013
Archival inkjet print
Original silkscreen 1981
17" x 22"

Mick O'Kelly
Currency
1992
Digital Print
11 ¾ " x 16 ½"

Parallel Paths—Three Poems
"Second Coming," William Butler Yeats, 1919
"Indian Singing in 20th Century America," Gail Tremblay, 1988
Excerpt from "Speech of the Red Indian," Mahmoud Darwish, 1992
"Three Birds," collage by Nora Collom, 2013
Digital print
16"x20"

Vivien Sansour
Abu Nidal
2012
Digital photo
23-13/16" x 15-15/16 "

Vivien Sansour
Candles for Water
2013
Digital photo
15-15/16 "x 23-13/16"

Vivien Sansour
Don Alonso Lopez
2013
Digital photo
23-13/16" x 15-15/16 "

Vivien Sansour
Emilio
2013
Digital photo
15-15/16 " x 23-13/16"

Shaping the Enemy
Assembled by Grace Woodward
2013
Digital print
16"x20"

Donna Schindler
Hozhonahaslii: Stories of Healing the Soul Wound
2000
Looped DVD
Single-View DVD
Single-play running time: 45:28

Susanne Slavick
Rend
2013
Gouache on archival digital print
20"x16"
Photo source: Rosa Schiano
http://palsolidarity.org/wp-content/uploads/2012/12/41.jpg

Susanne Slavick
Repercussion
2013
Gouache on archival digital print
20x"16"
Photo source: Rosa Schiano
http://palsolidarity.org/wp-content/uploads/2012/12/6.jpg

Jaune Quick-to-See Smith
House and Home
2013
Archival pigment print
14-3/4"x20"

Mary Tuma
Lingering Presence
2013
Handmade abaca paper, maps, commercial sewing patterns, thread, mat medium.
14" x 15"

Kerry Vander Meer
Cross Slabs of Cill Rialaig
1997
Monotype
11"x15"

Kerry Vander Meer
Untitled Potato Print
1997
Giclée
12 ¼" x 31"

Sherry Wiggins
Battles, Deeds, Fields, and Swords
2013
Digital print
32"x 20 ¼"

Melanie Yazzie
Seeing Each Other
2007
Digital print
19 ¾" x16"

Helen Zughaib
Beit/Salaam
2013
Archival pigment print 1/20
20" x25"

Helen Zughaib
Woven in Exile
2013
Archival pigment print 1/20
18" x23"

Hani Zurob
Flying Lesson #03
2013
Archival pigment print
24 7/8" x29 ½"
Original painting, 2010, 200x160cm, acrylic & pigments on canvas

Hani Zurob
Flying Lesson #04
2013
Archival pigment print
24 7/8" x29 ½"
Original painting, 2010, 200x160cm, acrylic & pigments on canvas

Hani Zurob
Flying Lesson #07
2013
Archival pigment print
24 7/8" x29 ½"
Original painting, 2010, 200x160cm, acrylic & pigments on canvas

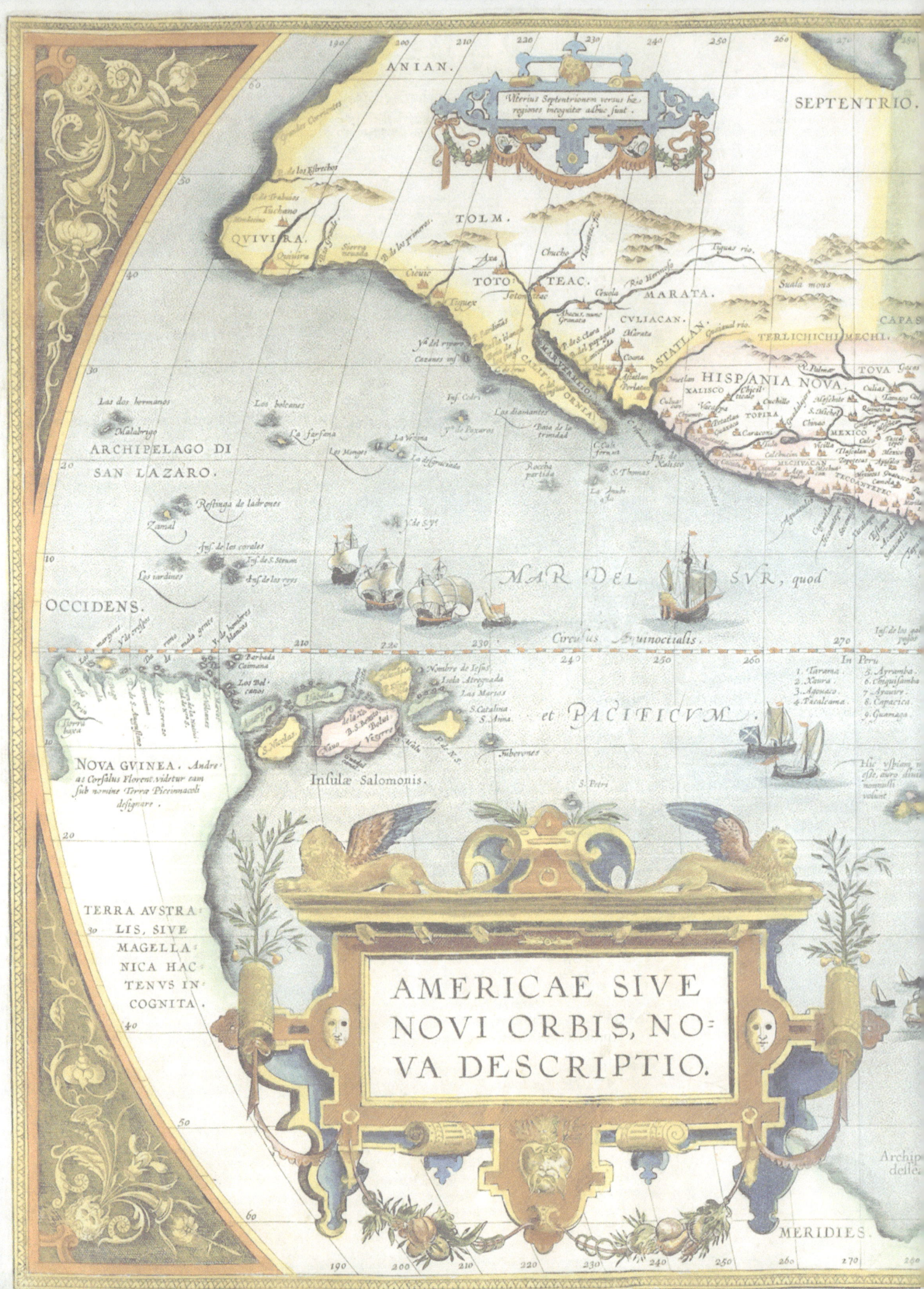

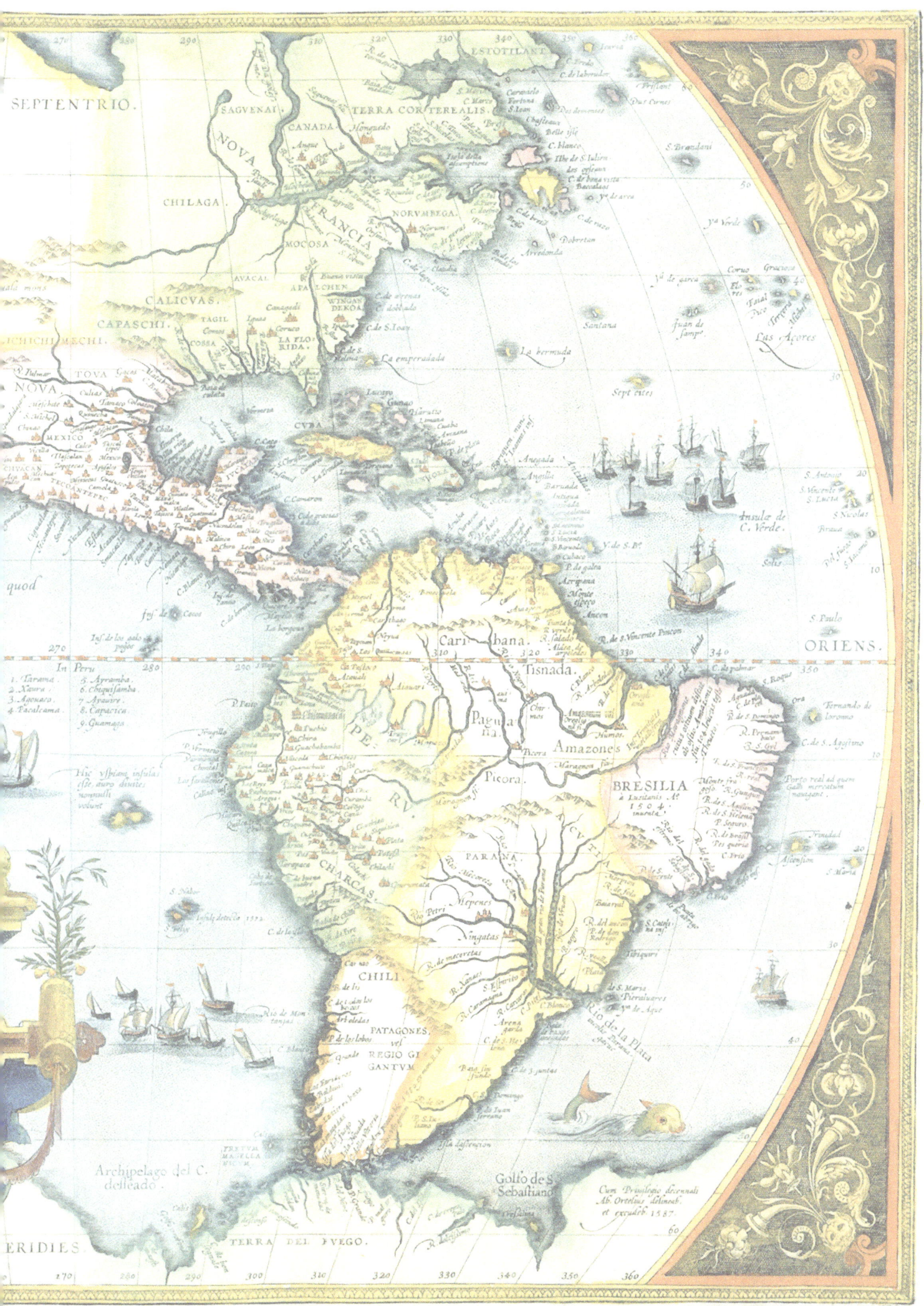

www.ingramcontent.com/pod-product-compliance
Lightning Source LLC
Chambersburg PA
CBHW051151220526

45473CB00003B/736